GOODNIGHT JIM BOB

**On the road
with Carter
The Unstoppable
Sex Machine**

JIM BOB

FOR MY BIG SISTER

AND MY LITTLE SISTER

This edition published in Great Britain in 2004 by
Cherry Red Books Ltd, 3a Long Island House
1-4 Warple Way
London W3 0RG

Copyright © 2004, J Morrison.

ISBN: 978-1-901447-23-1

ACKNOWLEDGEMENTS

Marc Ollington for his dedication to my many otherwise lost causes, Les, Wez, Simon, Salv, Steve, Ben and all the Crazy Carter Crew, Adrian Boss,
Ginny Keith, Mick Mercer, Mark Baker, Robert Newman, Andrew Collins,
Emma Moloney, Adam and everyone at Cherry Red, Tim Connery, Neil Witherow and The Monday Club. Lyrics for
The Music That Nobody Likes, Travis, Commercial Fucking Suicide Part 1 and *Sing Fat Lady Sing* printed courtesy of Island Music Ltd. Jacket photographs Jacqueline Ball, www.mickmercer.com and Ginny Keith (2). Jacket design by Carter USM assisted by Simon Joslin.

THIS IS NOT A DIRTY BOOK

t isn't a sex and drugs expose, it would make a pretty dull movie and is unlikely to be serialized in *The Daily Star*. I have no desire to stitch up or upset the status quo (I was always a big fan of the Quo). If you search for your name in this book and are relieved or disappointed to find it is or isn't there, it's nothing personal either way. Likewise if I try to describe your physical features by comparing them with those of somebody famous and it isn't either Brad Pitt, Johnny Depp or Michelle Pfeiffer, I'm sorry, I can't help it. I do it all the time. To me, everyone is a lookalike. It's a gift but it can also be a curse. I even do it to myself. When I look in the mirror I can see both Hugh and Richard E Grant, Tim Roth, Prince Charles and loveable *Neighbours* character Toadfish Rebecchi played by Ryan Moloney, an actor who started out performing on something called *The Bob Morrison Show* — that's Bob *Morrison*, now you can't argue with evidence like that. I've upset many of my friends during the course of my life by declaring excitedly how much they look like someone off the telly and I'm sure if you stood the so-called lookalike next to the lookalikee, there'd probably be no resemblance whatsoever. The obvious exception being my Carter partner Fruitbat and actor Tony Robinson, never seen together in the same room.

There may be parts of the book that you would prefer to skip through. For example there is an account of the *Smash Hits Awards* incident that you may have heard a hundred times before. Or this next bit because it's about trains: I wrote a lot of the stuff in this book on napkins, bus tickets and the back of my left hand in a coffee house just like JK Rowling did with Harry Potter. My coffee house was Croydon *Marks and Spencer's Cafe Revive*, where they serve a very nice almond croissant to go with your cappuccino when you need a break from buying underpants. I also wrote loads of stuff on the 10:03 from East Croydon to Goring-By-Sea when I was visiting my mum. The 10:03 was an old slam door train made up of various different coloured and aged carriages. It was not the Japanese Shinkansen, the French TGV, the Orient Express or the Blue Train that runs between Cape Town and Pretoria, South Africa with its leather seats, TVs and telephones. A ride on the three minutes past ten from East Croydon to Goring was a rickety ride, occasionally livened up by gangs of teenage train robbers after your mobile phone and eager to write on your face with felt tip pens if you nod off. Or some overseas tourists planning on alighting at Gatwick Airport and not realizing that the door handles are on the outside of the train. How I'd laugh to myself as they ran up and down the train in a panic, looking for a door that could be opened from the inside, eventually missing their stop and their flight home. I also wrote things down while I was on the station platform waiting for my train and I was perhaps unduly terrified that people might have thought I was a trainspotter.

Is this book a diary? No, I wish it was, it would have been a lot easier. Unlike Bridget Jones, Adrian Mole and Samuel Pepys I didn't keep much of a diary. I have always carried a small (about 3ins x 4ins) pocket diary with me so I know where and when I need to be. The kind that has a London Underground map at the back, useful facts and figures at the front and a thin pencil in a tube down the dairy's spine Luckily I didn't throw these little books of dates away, without them this would have all been impossible. And also, aside from knowing where and when I was between 1987 and 1997 I can now tell you how to get from Elephant And Castle to Neasden on the tube, what fish is in season, what wine goes with it and how to get the stain of the wine off your shirt. I can also say yes, no, please and thank you in eight different languages, convert inches into centimetres, gallons into litres and miles into kilometres. I know your birthstone, your Zodiac sign and the amount of calories in the apple you're eating and if you need to call your aunt in Trinidad and Tobago, the international direct dialing code is 1868.

I have tried to keep a basic chronological thread to the story although it will veer off at tangents now and then, anyone who knows me will tell you that I do this a lot in real life. So if I'm wittering on about being accused of murder while trying to get through passport control at JFK airport, this may well lead us sideways into a few tales of other amusing customs incidences that maybe happened a year later or a few weeks earlier.

Also, some of the facts may be a bit rickety and occasionally just plain wrong, there may be whole passages of time out of sequence or missing altogether. This will be either because, a) nothing happened, or, c) because I've forgotten what it was that did happen. When I look at the long list of gigs that we played (at least 757) I have no recollection of some of them at all, which is surely due to the passage of time and the way your brain forgets some things in order to remember others, but instead I've chosen to apportion the blame, equal parts; sunshine, good times, boogie. We all forget things. I was recently reminiscing with my daughter about how she used to get the words wrong to the *Club biscuit* advert and sing *Lippee la a lot of chocolate on your biscuit* instead of *if you like a lot of chocolate on your biscuit,* when it was of course not my daughter at all but my younger sister Becca. I've simply remembered two curly-haired females who were younger than myself and then mixed them up in my head over the course of time. I probably do the same in this book with say, Cardiff and Swansea or *After The Watershed* and *Sheriff Fatman.*

Perhaps a bit more research would have helped, but I didn't want to get too bogged down with a load of boring facts, figures and dates. And when I asked people about their memory of certain events they either, remembered them in exactly the same way as I did, were equally as confused as I was or, worst of all, their factually accurate memories spoilt my bloody story. I did flick through some old press interviews but all they did was remind me what a miserable, whingeing big head I used to be. However, here are a few titbits I found in the gossip pages of the *New Musical Express* and *Melody Maker.* I don't remember any of them.

At The Riverside venue in Newcastle I apparently slipped on a banana skin thrown onto the stage by a fan and fell on my backside receiving bruising that was described as, 'not particularly pretty'.

In the dressing room of a Glasgow college gig we were being interviewed by a French journalist, when 20 frogmen from the college sub-aqua club, dressed in flippers and snorkels burst in. The French journo walked out highly offended, get it? ... frogmen? ... French? ... no I don't remember that happening.

The next two I do remember: Somebody impersonating us hired a video camera from a shop and didn't bring it back. And the story about the Dutch sound engineer who had an epileptic fit at a gig in Holland because of our heavy use of strobe lighting seems familiar.

Finally. I found a nice answer to the question: 'What would I like played at my funeral?' Answer: 'Ice hockey.' I don't remember saying that but I'm glad I did.

For everyone who did help to jog my memory I'm very grateful - particularly to Les (Fruitbat) - even if I did then just go ahead and ignore everything you told me. Also, I have to say thank you to Paul Baran from the Rand Corporation, the American military think tank. Paul first came up with the idea for the Internet, which was intended as a communications network for the US authorities in the aftermath of a nuclear attack but would also be used by me to find out all the historical details and facts about *Semtex, The Magnificent Seven* and the Corby Trouser Press. Possibly the only accurate information in the whole book. Also computer-related but less helpful were some of the keys on the top row of my computer keyboard, I'll name them: numbers 1,2,4,5,7,8,9 and 0, the exclamation mark, the @ thing, the dollar sign, the percentage key, the asterisk and the closed bracket. All you bastard keys decided that you'd work sometimes - and other times not, thanks guys.

Finally, before and during the writing of this story, a number of its significant characters sadly passed away. If and when this is published as a book, I might take a copy outside and set fire to it and maybe the ashes and smoke will find their way to my absent friends, so they can read their part in the story and hopefully have a good laugh.

I've tried to keep the chapters short for the MTV generation but I've also chucked in a few long ones for fans of the *Old Grey Whistle Test*.

ON 4TH AUGUST 1997

as Billy Bob Thornton (an actor we had yet to become aware of) celebrated his 42nd birthday, a *Tinker Tailor Soldier Spy*-like meeting was taking place at a wooden garden table outside the cafe at the top of Streatham Common.

Traditionally, me and Fruitbat had always met there to begin and end our bands. Over a couple of coffees and a *Kit Kat* we'd make some great life-changing decision and then go for a walk around the Rookery gardens. The bigger the decision, the longer the walk. On this particular day we walked twice around the landscaped gardens, past the dead goldfish, through the tennis courts, up and over the big hill by the smashed up greenhouses and back round to the cafe again for a *Cornetto*. It was a pretty big decision. After ten years - almost to the day - as Carter The Unstoppable Sex Machine, we had agreed it was time to knock it on the head, to stop. Imagine the page going all wobbly and blurred and the hands of a large clock spinning backwards...

BABY BABY

I was born to boogie. I'm not going to tell you exactly when because I suffer from *gerascophobia*[1], as well as a touch of *mickandkeithaphobia*[2] and it upsets me to talk about it. If you don't know my date of birth and really need to know, you can download my birth certificate from a website that specializes in such nosy parker behaviour for thirty dollars including delivery. Before I was born, my mum sang in a close harmony act called The Four In A Chord and if you own an old Christmas compilation album with a wacky version of *Rudolph The Red Nosed Reindeer* on it, that's probably my mum. When not appearing on television in the early *Morecambe & Wise* and *Benny Hill* shows, the 'Chord toured. All over Europe, travelling on coaches and no-seater US air-force planes, they no doubt played the same dumb games as we would play years later, on their way to a lot of the same venues. I found a newspaper cutting of an article entitled ' *TWO SISTERS MET TWO BROTHERS AND NOW THEY'RE... FOUR IN A CHORD* ' and it packs in more drama, crazy antics and selfless acts of heroism in one review/interview than the whole of this book manages in all its many pages. The Four In A Chord were formed when my mum and her sister Gabby met Laurie and Louis Cleeton - the *Two In Accord* - at a party in 1951. Unlike S Club 7, who didn't have the wit or imagination to change their name to S Club 6 when Paul Cattermole left, or the boy band 5ive who threw in the towel when it appeared as though Sean Conlon was about to leave the band rather than carry on as *4our*. No - when the Muir sisters joined the Two In Accord, they became The *Four* In A Chord. I reckon my mum added the pun on the word *accord*. It's in the genes you know.

Here's what happened to the *'most televised vocal group in the country'* when they were on tour back in the fabulous fifties: At a live show in Edinburgh my mum's sister Gabby had tonsillitis and the Four had to sing as a Three, with Gabby mouthing the words and fooling the audience in what was an early example of Steps 'live'. After that they sang on a radio series in Belfast and on the flight home a wheel fell off their plane and the pilot had to make an emergency landing. Next, as they arrived in Ayr for what was to be their summer show, they saw the theatre where they were due to appear at was on fire. The show was cancelled. The sisters returned dejected to London on the train, while the fellas Laurie and Louis drove the car back with the luggage. Outside Kilmarnock after they'd been fined for

[1] The fear of growing old.
[2] The fear of turning into The Rolling Stones.

illegal parking, a small boy rushed up to their car and said that someone was drowning. Laurie ran to the river and saw two children struggling in the water; he dived in and managed to save one child but the current was strong and he couldn't find the other one. The eventual happy ending came when the group were offered a replacement show in Margate; they had to hurriedly rewrite the orchestrations for their songs which had been burnt in the Ayr Theatre fire, but the show went ahead. Hooray.

Perhaps inspired by such stories of on the road adventures I was always in some band or other when I was at school, whether in reality or just in my head. And as I rode around the streets of Streatham every Sunday evening on my ultra-violet *Raleigh Chopper* bicycle with my transistor radio sellotaped to the handlebars playing the new Top 40 chart, I imagined one day that mellow-voiced Radio One disc jockey Tom Browne might read my name out.

My first real live performance was unlikely to lead to *Top Of The Pops* though. It was on the stage of Dunraven Secondary School Hall at our end of year disco and the first song I ever performed to an audience was Buddy Holly's *Rave On* with Elvis's *All Shook Up* as the second. The audience loved us (perhaps because we weren't geography or double R.E.) But when we tried to encore with a third song - *Rock Around The Clock* - someone let off a firework and the show was stopped to avoid a riot just as the kids were about to build a bonfire and put the teachers on the top. The band was called Rock'N'Roll Revival 1975, the guitarist was our music teacher. He was still teaching at the same school a couple of years ago, I know because I saw him when I went to the school for my daughter's open evenings (yes, we went to the same school, we're like the Royal Family). I didn't speak to him, partially because I'm shy and cowardly but I suspect also because I would have hated him to either, a) not remember me or b) to have never heard of Carter. I prefer instead to think that he's been religiously following my every musical move since I left school, he's probably got framed pictures of me on his wall. After that one and only gig, R'n'R Revival went off the boil. Mr Daly had exams to mark and the bassist grew his hair and got into hippy music. I quit the group just before they changed their name to Cornfield.

Despite the setback I formed another - this time imaginary - band. I practiced in front of the mirror with a tennis racquet, I had a carpet sweeper for a mic stand and later when I left school and started working in the West End, I'd travel in on the tube, staring into the distance, trying to fix and dilate my pupils, look weird and pretend I had a drug problem. I was dedicated.

The two notable influences on me while I was at school were punk rock and David Essex's performance in the film *Stardust*. Punk was taken very seriously by the establishment in 1976; it was seen as a threat to the healthy development of the nation's youth. Our headmaster spent a whole morning assembly telling us that punk rock was just a phase and something that we - the pupils - should steer clear of; most did. At my school, punk wasn't something to boast about being a fan of and simply wearing straight-legged trousers could get you beaten up by the larger Lionel-wearing[3] populace. When I went into Cloake's record shop in Streatham High Road to buy my first punk single - a copy of *Baby Baby* by The Vibrators - I was treated with disgust and contempt by the bloke behind the counter, as though I was buying an actual vibrator.

Trying to be different has never been easy, as a thirteen year old teddy boy I was chased through many a council estate by irate 1970s squares with a complete misunderstanding of the fabulous fifties. And the same squares would no doubt later be chasing me in the opposite direction when the (rock'n') roles had been reversed with them now as the teds and me as a punk. I met my girlfriend when I was being beaten up by guests at her party for wearing a tie at a non-tie-wearing event, e.g. not a funeral, wedding, interview for job at NatWest etc. And when I hung around with mods, I liked to wear pink shoes and plastic binoculars, which confused the skinheads, who didn't know whether to beat me up for being a mod or a poof. Later on in life I would grow an enormous fringe and wear short trousers, subjecting myself to further abuse from narrow minded bullies at the *Melody Maker* and the *NME*.

Besides punk rock, the other big musical influence on me was David Essex. As Jim Maclaine in the film *Stardust*, he'd leave his wurlitzer-spinning day job at the fair to form a band. He'd go on the road in a shitty van, make a record, become famous, get chased by girls, get caught by girls, go a bit bonkers and buy an enormous castle in Spain, where he'd die of a drugs overdose live on television. I knew this was the life for me. I used to try and mimic the softly-spoken voice of David Essex that made girls' knees melt, but they could never hear what I was saying and just used to tell me to stop mumbling.

[3]Lionel (Blairs) - flares (cockney rhyming slang)

CHIN AND CHONG

My next proper band was after I'd left school and got myself a job in the dispatch department of a West End advertising firm. The band was called Jeepster, with me on vocals, Rik Serene (who lived in my loft) on guitar and a rhythm section that featured Derek Chong on Drums and Derek Chin on bass, which I've only just realized was an enormous coincidence. Derek Chin is my half-brother, he looked, dressed and acted something like a cross between Freddie Mercury and Howlin' Pelle Almqvist, the singer with The Hives and he liked to call himself Mister X. He once turned up for a fancy-dress party at my girlfriend's house a week late dressed as Tarzan and another time he came round when no-one was in and left a box of *Milk Tray* chocolates on the doorstep. Derek Chin was the *Milk Tray* man. On returning from a holiday in Germany he was held by the authorities at Heathrow Airport because in his luggage with his toy gun was a wallet containing his secret agent ID card and I suppose they thought, well maybe.

Me and Derek Chin used to attempt to chat up girls by pretending we were in a band together, long before we ever actually were. I was the singer and he was the bass player, we were a bit like The Monkees, we lived together. The first ever gig I ever went to was with Derek; it was Queen at Hyde Park. We were very young and nervous. When Derek decided to go and look for the toilet and then couldn't find his way back to the patch of grass where I was sitting, I had to spend the day alone but for about a hundred thousand long haired plastic bottle of piss throwing rock fans; it was terrifying. If I close my eyes and think about it, I can still smell the patchouli oil and see all those green glo-in-the-dark plastic tubed necklaces that liars will tell you can break open and give you cancer.

When we actually became a band, we were legendary. All of Jeepster's songs were about girls and how we couldn't get any. We had a song called *Nine Stone Weakling* which if we ever played it live, would feature my party trick of tearing a phone book in half. A party trick that has been sadly taken away from me by spoilsports at British Telecom who now make the spines of their directories out of indestructible plastic. We also had our own fan club at the City Of London Girls School, for whom we wrote the song *City Girls* (another vain attempt at making ourselves attractive to the opposite sex). After two years of dispatching and stealing a lot of stationery, Jeepster got their first gig at a youth club in Southgate and I resigned from the world of advertising immediately, to begin my brilliant new career. It was the only gig we did (I can see a pattern forming here).

WHEN JIM BOB MET FRUITBAT

Before Streatham Safeways' underground car park became Streatham Safeways underground car park it was a rehearsal studio called The Orchestra Pit. The Orchestra Pit was more like a yoof club and it was always a good place to hang around. Most of the bands who rehearsed there were on the dole and like some big daft workshy gang we'd all go drinking together, riding secondhand pushbikes, playing pinball and eating a hell of a lot of toast. The Orchestra Pit was run by an insane but lovely man named Cliff Cooper, who looked a bit like Mick Ronson. Cliff would often liven up a boring rehearsal by bursting in on you in the middle of a song to beat you up, kidnap your drummer, cut your guitar strings in half, throw urine at you, etc. I met Fruitbat at the Orchestra Pit in 1979, when he was bass player with Streatham punk rock group Dead Clergy and lead singer with a band called The End, although mostly he played Space Invaders. He looked like a cross between Woody Woodpecker and a young Russ Abbot. His name was Les Carter, later on we'd name a band after him. Back then I was the singer with an eclectic mod band called The Ballpoints whose bass player had just run away with the circus and Les took his place.

After a brief stint as the Ballpoints and a name change to Peter Pan's Playground we split the band and had a go at children's entertaining (we were awful), busking (too loud / people were too scared to give us money) and a couple of separate solo careers. As solo artists - me as Jamie Wednesday and Les as Cartoon Carter (yes) - we wrote and recorded a number of acoustic based songs that we'd later go on to rewrite and record as Carter songs. These included: *Chuckles And Smiles* which became *Sheriff Fatman*, *Khaki Dufflecoat = Lean On Me I Won't Fall Over*, *Swallows Forever = Turn On, Tune In And Switch Off*, *Love Mountain = After The Watershed* and a Cartoon Carter song, *Charlie The Bus Driver*, which over a decade later would become the non-animated Carter song, *Cheer Up It Might Never Happen*.

Incidentally, on the day that he joined The Ballpoints, there was a party at my house and Les snogged my sister's best mate. The rest is - as I would probably have put it in one of my fabulous puns around 1991 - geography.

ENGLAND
THE ASTORIA THEATRE
CHARING CROSS ROAD LONDON 6.8.87.

A BENEFIT GIG FOR SHELTER SUPPORTING
THE MEN THEY COULDN'T HANG

To say the first Carter set was cobbled together, is an insult to the shoemaking industry. It was supposed to be our previous band Jamie Wednesday's gig but we'd already had that particular meeting on Streatham Common and Jamie Wednesday were no more. With no band and no real time or desire to get one, me and Les decided to cheat our way to the top. We'd record some drums and bass and bits of keyboards, stick them on a cassette and play guitars and sing over the top of them, our tape deck and its contents would be our band, we'd sit them on a chair at the back of the stage. It couldn't fail. We thought we were Public Enemy or LL Cool J.

We wrote six songs in a week; *Everytime A Churchbell Rings, Good Grief Charlie Brown, An All American National Sport, GI Blues,The Taking Of Peckham 123,* something called Will *I Go To Hell If I Kiss You In Front Of Jesus* (later rewritten as *A Perfect Day To Drop The Bomb*) and we also did a cover of Wire's *Mannequin,* for our first gig we called ourselves Bob. There were a lot of confused faces in the audience that night, particularly among the Jamie Wednesday fans who would have been expecting a bit of indie cow punk Dexys and instead got a drum-machine duo chasing each other round the stage like Benny Hill on amphetamine sulphate. Unlike the Sex Pistols gig at St Martins College Of Art that half the country claims to have been at, I can't recall having ever met a single person who was at our first gig.

Two weeks later, after one more gig as Bob we changed our name to Carter The Unstoppable Sex Machine, this is why: There was another band called Bob. (Coincidence Number 1: Bob's drummer was Doctor Kildare lookalike Dean Leggett, the old Jamie Wednesday drummer). So via a mad moment as Cardboard City Cut Up (phew that was close) we did our next gig as Carter The Unstoppable Sex Machine. The gig was at The Sir George Robey in Finsbury Park, the main band was The Las with They Might Be Giants on before us (blimey).

DROP SOME MORE NAMES JIM

21.12.87. Heaven, London: *Buzz* magazine party with Vic Reeves as compere. We played last, it was late and I think Vic Reeves was keen to go home, so he introduced us as briefly as possible, while we were still tuning up at the side of the stage. We had to rush on and play the whole gig out of tune with Fruitbat repeatedly cursing the compere. *Like some freakish breed of fruit elephant he would not forget and years later would punish Vic at the* Top Of The Pops *studio by letting both him and Bob Mortimer drink us under a BBC table.*

12.9.88. City Hall, Newcastle supporting Siouxsie And The Banshees. We were originally booked for a couple of nights with The Banshees at The Royal Albert Hall as well but were chucked off the bill and replaced by a string quartet. At the time we were told there wasn't enough room for us on the stage but we naturally believed it was more likely because we were so brilliant and had blown them offstage in Newcastle. Self-belief was everything and we were the greatest band in the world.

We also supported Captain Sensible at The Cricketers in Kennington and on 14th October 1988 we played at Ealing College with an acoustic duo called Right Said Fred.

THE ROAD TO DOMESTOS

Travelling to and from these first gigs wasn't easy as neither of us could drive. Fruitbat had had about a million driving lessons and his instructor had eventually suggested that he should maybe give up, get a travelcard, get off the streets! aaarrrrgghhhh! The London gigs we did by bus, day bus there, night bus home. We wasted a good part of our lives waiting at Trafalgar Square for the night bus to come, so I could sit with the clubbers and pubbers with my guitar at my feet and a little practice amplifier on my lap. Trying to stay conscious and unsuccessfully stop myself vomiting down the front of the little practice amp. It wasn't until Adrian Boss started managing us that we had a designated driver and started hiring cars.

We didn't usually have enough money to hire them for long though and a lot of the time we'd drive from one end of the country to the other, to play for half an hour and then drive straight back home again so we only had to pay for one day's rental. We'd have to force ourselves to stay awake, because if we fell asleep, Adrian would have no one to talk to and fall asleep as well, crashing our *Fiat Tipo* and tragically cheating ourselves and the world of our impending fame and fortune. On a particularly long drive home through a thick blizzard one night, we tried to stay conscious by eating huge amounts of *Pro-Plus*, a legal but stupid overdose that not only gave us headaches and constipation but didn't keep us awake. At one point that night, Adrian slipped briefly into semi-slumber, only to be woken by what he believed to be an enormous white horse running across the M3 in front of us.

You know that car game for bored kids where you drive past pubs and count the number of legs in the pub names (eg. Dog & Trumpet = 4 legs for the dog, none for the trumpet) and at the end of the journey, the winner is the one with the highest number of legs? In our first year we played at The Cricketers in Kennington eight times. We would have won that game. A game, which coincidentally I've just found out 183 pages later from Robert Elms on Radio London is called *Pub Cricket*, with each leg counting as a run.

Later on when we were on a big posh sleeper bus, we'd play bus games. Stupid bus games. The one we played the most was probably 'Skinheads', which involved writing the name of somebody famous on a cigarette paper and sticking it on somebody else's forehead; they'd then have to ask questions about themselves to work out who they were. There were two great gags here: one was to always give our manager Adrian the name of some fascist dictator or other, eg Hitler, Napoleon, Thatcher, and the other side-splitter was giving our roadie Daz his own name. It helped pass the time and was a more interesting use for *Rizlas*.

And how stupid is this? Every once in a while we'd get so drunk/bored/drunk & bored, that we'd have a Freddie Mercury night. With black gaffa-tape moustaches and *Queen's Greatest Hits* in the CD player, tonight, Matthew, we'd be Freddie Mercury. And occasionally Brian May during guitar solos.

Music on the bus is an important and difficult affair; I'm a fan of the compilation tape, something for everyone. The choice of listening can be very political and the solitude of a Walkman a wonderful thing. At the point when things probably really started to go a bit-tits up with Carter, there was a lot of muso nonsense finding its way onto the tape-deck - long-playing records that played too long - and I knew the fun was finally over when I returned home after a long Carter tour, to find my *Queen's Greatest Hits* CD case contained the first album by The Police. It was the end of an era.

On the way home from a gig in Winchester, the first album by Mega City 4 was put on the car stereo one too many times for Fruitbat and he took it out of the machine and threw it out of the window. It was Jon Beast's copy and he retaliated by doing the same with the hat that Fruity was wearing, which turned out to be Adrian's favourite Greek fisherman's hat. They're both still probably somewhere out there on the M3.

Boredom is a common complaint with travelling musicians. We all love the 45 minutes on stage but can't stand the other 23 and a quarter. Bus trips are tedious, flying is either monotonous or terrifying, boats take too long, horseback isn't an option etc. It is of course sometimes the 45 minutes on stage that the audience find the most tiresome but no-one ever interviews the audience. They might love a seven hour flight to Los Angeles with movies and drinks and a stretch limo to meet them when they get there for six weeks of free food, booze and everyone telling them how marvellous they are.

And there are so many ways to pass your time at gigs.
Here are four.

1. **Count the penis drawings on the dressing room wall.**

2. **Taunt the security, by deliberately leaving your backstage pass backstage and taking a walk around the venue for ten minutes, then try to get back into the dressing room.**

3. **Open the bottled rider beer without a bottle opener, by banging the bottles on the edges of tables and shutting them betwixt door and door frame, bite the tops off, making the rest of the room squirm as though you're chewing the gold foil from a packet of Rolos or if there's somebody continental with you, why not get them to open your beer for you with their lighter?**
   I was told a story in New York about how one of Ned's Atomic Dustbin was opening a bottle by banging the top against the edge of a table with his hand when the bottle broke and went into his palm. Cass from The Senseless Things could get a cork out of a wine bottle by slapping its base repeatedly - you should try it, it really hurts.

4. **Wrestle.**

TWO GIGS IN A ROW

It's a lot easier to get gigs in the place where you live, where you can always depend on your friends and family to turn up and you can be the local support band promoters rely upon to bring in a bit of door money and help stimulate the ego of the main band who've left their friends and family at home in Hull or Devon watching *Stars In Their Eyes*. Out of our first twenty four gigs, eighteen were in London and we didn't manage two in a row until we went from Ealing College, back to Adrian's flat in Portobello Road and then straight onto The Africa Centre. And as the Africa Centre isn't in Africa (it's in Covent Garden) and - in spite of its Middlesex postal address - Ealing is still on the tube map, our new Holy Grail would be two gigs. In a row. Outside London.

And it was at those gigs outside London where we first really started to build up a loyal following. At venues like The Square in Harlow, Hull Adelphi, Oxford Jericho Tavern, Sheffield Take 2, Bradford 1 In 12, Liverpool Planet X, Gloucester Banana Club and also at regular gigs in Birmingham, Bristol and Bolton. We started to make friends, swapping gigs and contacts with other bands and sleeping on their floors. We toured with Pauline Murray and did gigs with Mega City 4, The Family Cat, Ill Logic and Ride. At a gig with Ride at The Electric Broom Cupboard above a pub in Sherborne, Dorset, Ride were in the middle of a song when half the audience suddenly left the room. We followed them downstairs into the street, where they were all gathered by the gates of a level crossing to watch a train go by. What's that all about?

I don't know if it was because audiences were spoilt for choice in London but we felt more welcome up the top end of the M1 or in a barn just outside Ipswich or in a community centre in Essex. Also, we didn't have to stand in Trafalgar Square in the rain waiting for the N2 to not come.

Sometimes the provinces were not so welcoming of course. After driving across the country for what felt like thirty hours, to Lampeter University in Wales in November 1989, we eventually arrived at the Uni entrance about four hours late and asked someone for directions to the gig. We were told that it was straight down the M4 to London, where we should fuck off back to. Or the time we played in Hastings and were booed by sailors, I'm not making this up. And at an early gig in a scampi in-the-basket disco in Lincoln, a video of the film *Alien* was showing on television at the back of the room and while we were playing everyone stood with their backs to us and watched the movie instead (which is a shame because they missed the moment when the extra-terrestrial burst out of Fruitbat's stomach midway through *Surfin' USM*).

A CHIP SHOP IN SHEFFIELD

I'm about to reveal a fiercely guarded secret, known previously only to the Carter freemasons. I apologize and resign my membership immediately.

As Carter became more popular, things began to snowball quite quickly and there were more and more people coming to the gigs. We were playing one of our many dates at The Sheffield Take Two Club, where we'd usually performed to one man and his dog Spot and now at last we'd managed to attract a small queue. As the queue grew, (Barney McGrew, Cuthbert Dibble and Grubb) somebody told Adrian that the landlord had put up the admission price to capitalize on it. Adrian wasn't happy. We went to get some chips over the road from the venue and, while we waited to be served, he came in and was ranting about how he thought the venue was ripping us off etc. Next thing, the man stood next to us leaned over and said, 'Yes, that's right.' He was of course the promoter.

Returning to the club to eat our chips, we were met by three angry men - one wielding an iron bar - demanding that we explain exactly what we were accusing them of. Being a creative coward, I apologized like an idiot, agreeing that we were southern shandy-drinking wankers and had made a terrible mistake. Not for the last time in our career we managed to escape a beating and the show - as it always must - went on. Although they did run out of booze at the bar very early on in the evening and we had to drink *Bols Advocat* (it's a lovely little drink).

AND SO, to this day - and no longer, now that I've let the cat out of the bag - whenever anybody entered a room when we were talking about them, somebody in the know would change the subject suddenly by talking about a chip shop in Sheffield. And there we have it - if you ever walked in on us and we appeared to go silent for a second and then start gibbering on about Northern fast-food establishments, you weren't being paranoid after all... we were talking about you.

CULTURE VULTURES

On these early tours we passed our pre-soundcheck daylight hours a lot more constructively than we'd do later on. In 1989 we followed the *Milk Race* cycling tour whenever it coincided with ours (which it seemed to be quite a bit, leading me to suspect that bicycle fanatic Fruitbat was in on the route plan). We'd park up with our packed lunches to cheer the competitors as they struggled up the Cheddar Gorge and had a sporting pint outside a pub while we watched them bomb round Liverpool City Centre on the final stage of the race.

We went to The National Museum of Photography, Film and Television in Bradford and to the Albert Dock in Liverpool to check out the Tate Gallery, where we were particularly keen to see *Twin Tub With Guitar*, a sculpture by Bill Woodrow we'd paid tribute to on the B-side of the *Sheriff Fatman* single. We didn't get to see it because that part of the gallery was shut, but at least we tried. We travelled on A roads and B roads instead of motorways, where we became experts on *Little Chef* restaurants and how to get round the restrictions of the set menu. We took scenic routes through the Lake District and Peak Districts, where Adrian almost crashed the car laughing at the place names Cockermouth and Penistone. We nipped into towns we had no business in, checking out Gretna Green for example (a crazy town full of lone bagpipers and wedding shops) and often visited my mum in the West Sussex village where she lived. We'd take the coastal route whenever possible, stopping to skim a few stones across the beautiful brown sea or to eat a bag of chips on the end of the pier if there was one. We also passed time by picking up local possibly true facts, like Stockton-Upon-Tees having the widest high street in Europe. And less constructively perhaps, on the way into Plymouth once, we happened upon a soft-porn shoot in the woods by a secluded B road. We had time to kill so we turned the car around and, like a cross between the SAS and a gang of giggling schoolgirls, zig-zagged our way through the trees for another look but both pornstar and pornographer had gone; maybe it was a dream.

ROLLING ROCK

There are two big showbusiness no nos. Number one is the old animals and children rule while the lesser–known no no number two is never do a gig to an audience made up entirely of music critics. When we played at the *NME* staff party at Subterrania in Ladbroke Grove prior to our brief stint as press darlings, Andrew Collins was the only journalist who actually watched us, while everyone else stood as far back from the stage and as close as possible to the free bar, talking very loudly and drinking the complimentary *Rolling Rock*.

On every bottle of *Rolling Rock* beer there's a number 33 and there are a number of urban legends and theories as to the significance of this number. Here are a few that I nicked off an American beer website:

> **'At a beer-drinking contest in Latrobe, the winner drank '33' Rolling Rocks...'**
> **Jon from Muskego, Wisconsin**

> **'The racing horse 'ROLLING ROCK' wore the number 33 with colors of green and white'...**
> **Joe from Centerville, MA**

> **'The States of Pa and Ohio picked the best 33 football players in each state and played an interstate football game between Pa and Ohio, that game is called the big 33'...**
> **Arnie from Lock Haven, Pa.**

> **'There are 33 mountain springs that flow into one pond. The water from these springs is the water used to brew the beer.'...**
> **Chuck Mick from Indian Head, MD**

> **'The beer is brewed at 33 degrees. It's ice cold, on the edge of the freezing point of water.' ...**
> **Russ from Fredericksburg, Va**

> **'The Rolling Rock distributors are huge fans of Larry Bird, and since Larry Bird wore a green jersey and the number '33' the Rolling Rock bottle is a tribute to the great Larry Bird.'...**
> **Justin from Pittsburgh, PA**

'33 planets are aligned to make a road map in the universe. Aliens use this to land their spacecraft in the Pa countryside at night to suck up batches of delicious Rolling Rock. The little fellas don't know it's for drinking but it does burn clean in their spacecraft and will not pollute the universe.' ...
Chuck from Hacienda Heights, CA

'33 is the number of bottles Carter The Unstoppable Sex Machine drank at The Subterania club in West London, England at a party for The *New Musical Express* before the singer Jim Bob tried to violently insert his guitar into the skull of his best friend Fruitbat.' ...
James Robert from Crystal Palace, London.

If me and Les ever fell out over anything it was invariably something stupid. He once decided that he wanted to take his racing bike on tour, so that everyday he could cycle eco-friendly-politician style triumphantly down the final hill of the journey and into the venue to the applause of Carter fans, the Green Party and Lance Armstrong[4]. We had to buy a special roof-rack so we could stand the bike upright on the roof of our car like we were in the *Tour De France*. Unfortunately, a lot of the hotels we were staying in had underground car parks with low ceilings and so every night we'd have to stop the car and remove the bike so that we could park; it was the only time it came off the roof on the whole tour. It led to some fierce arguments and sulking and almost split the band up.

Back at the *NME* party a similar trivial argument had begun between us about something that neither of us can remember. But because of all the free beer - a beer that Fruitbat claims makes him aggressive and that he calls 'fighting beer' - and sometime after one of my all-time idols Joe Strummer told me he thought Carter were great and me starting to believe him, the thick lenses of our free beer goggles magnified the trivial into the important and in the dressing room of the Subterania I attempted to kill Fruitbat. In a tribute to Sid Vicious, Paul Simonon and Keith Richards, I swung my guitar and tried to smash him round the head with it. Thank God I missed and hit the dressing room wall smashing my guitar. (Luckily I had a spare, which I also broke later that night back at Les' flat trying to murder

[4] Lance Armstrong is a Texan cyclist who battled against cancer and won the Tour De France five times in a row. He is known as 'The Boss'. Just like Bruce Springsteen.

our roadie and friend Angus (whose amp I had puked on earlier in my illustrious career as a twat). When I left Les' flat to go home, we had split the band. We would reform again in the morning. In much the same way as we did after a slightly more public incident on the night of the 1991 *Smash Hits Poll Winners Party*. Just in case you don't know about the Carter USM claim to fame, here it is...

...IT WASN'T ME IT WAS HIM

In October 1991 we were caught in the eye of a storm in a teacup on a saucer in a hurricane. We'd played all over the world, inciting riots, controversy and scandal wherever we went. We'd sold a shedload of records and we were on the way to our first Number 1 album, it was a dream come true and we should have been cock a hoop. But like a dog chasing its tail for half its life and then catching it, we didn't know what to do next. Our masterplan to follow a strict path of no compromise was unrealistic because no such path existed. So we'd gone with the flow and now we felt guilty about it. We'd left the independent record labels *Big Cat* and *Rough Trade* to sign a big fuck-off deal with *Chrysalis* and we seemed to be constantly defending ourselves for betraying our roots. When we released our first *Chrysalis* record we held a press conference for the fanzines and it was like the McCarthy witch-hunts. *'Are you, or have you ever been signed to a major record label?'*

Our first proper *Chrysalis* single *After The Watershed* was a fairly catchy pop song with a disco beat that also happened to be about child abuse, which bothered some people, who thought politics and pop didn't mix. And perhaps because we were aware of this attitude when we were asked to perform the song for our first *Top Of The Pops* appearance we were very conscious of not looking like we might be enjoying ourselves. We made a pact to not smile during the performance. A piece of piss for Fruitbat who was already on edge with what he thought were the phonier aspects of the programme. Even though we were miming we had to use guitar leads and the leads had to be plugged into amps. He didn't mind the miming but he wasn't comfortable with trying to fool the audience into thinking the whole thing was really live. To make him feel better we used the guitar leads but we left the mains plugs on top of the amps, ha–ha, tricked you *British Broadcasting Corporation.*

Also on the show was Kiwi (opera diva and friend of the Royal Family) Dame Kiri Te Kanawa, who was performing her rugby world cup song, which she did reading the lyrics from - I won't say 'idiot boards' - big cards, while standing on a tiny stage encircled by *TOTP* teenagers. She had the same look on her face that General Custer must have had at the Battle Of Little Big Horn. We were stood close by on the adjacent stage waiting to do our bit when we were asked if we wouldn't mind crouching down, so that DKTK didn't have to look at us as we were putting her off. Les didn't like her, and when she complained about Vic, Bob, The Wonderstuff, 2 Unlimited and Tin Machine smoking in the corridor, the usually fervent anti-smoker Fruitbat accused her of having some front seeing as how she was polluting the air with her awful song and how she should fuck off etc.

His patience was tested further back at the big new hotel where we were staying that night when we were asked to leave the bar as Fruitbat was wearing jeans in a 'no jeans' area. He probably would have accepted this if he hadn't seen David Bowie sitting at a nearby table, wearing jeans, so he kicked over a table and we went to the peasants' bar instead. When he got home, Fruitbat wrote a letter to the hotel to complain about the inconsistency in its fashion policing. The hotel manager replied to say they had reconsidered their dress policy and offered him a free room for the night by way of apology. Who says pop groups can't change things?

Shortly after we'd learn to love the *Top Of The Pops* experience, although I always found it unfair that I had to sing live while Fruitbat always got to mime his guitar, so he could spend the day casually boozing and getting matey with the casts of *Eastenders* and *Grange Hill* in the canteen (both shows were filmed at the same Elstree studios as *TOTP*) while I, meanwhile, sat in the pokey *BBC* dressing room, worrying about losing my voice and whether I'd be able to hear the backing music once the screaming started.

In that same week we were due to appear at the *Smash Hits Poll Winners Party* at London Docklands Arena. Once again we left the comfort of our tour to drive down to London, where we were picked up in the most uncomfortable, cramped and unstretched limo ever. There was no television, minibar or snob screen to stop the driver from challenging you to guess who he'd had in the back last week. There was only room for two of us on the comfy seat and, once our tour manager Terry had pulled down the bonus hinged chair (like you get in a black taxi) for himself, Adrian had to sit on the floor. You wouldn't have let your teenage daughter go to her school prom in it, it was basically a hearse.

All the acts appearing at the show, which included some big names at the time: New Kids On The Block, Marky Mark, Color Me Badd, Extreme, Dannii Minogue, The Farm and us were put in the same one big dressing room. It seemed a bit cheap. And while all the dancers went through their routines and Marky Mark monopolized the use of the toilets by sticking his security guards outside the door to keep people out while he was having a pooh (what's wrong with whistling Marky?), Jim Bob, Fruitbat and The Farm went to the off licence.

Inside industry secret Number 1:
Earlier at a rehearsal for the show, representatives from the record labels would stand in for the stars who were not there or were too big to rehearse, miming for the TV cameras and generally taking the piss out of their absent artists.

The Smash Hits Poll Winners Party likes to have a theme and in 1991 the theme was Halloween. The stage was done out like a haunted castle, with spiders' webs and huge pumpkins along the back wall. The show's host, children's TV presenter Phillip Schofield, was going to make his big entrance flying down onto the stage on a broomstick from the back of the hall like the wicked witch of the East (end). The bloke who was responsible for operating the harness used to be the singer with 1980s indie band Stump (You don't tend to see ex-pop people when they've had to find alternative jobs later in life, at least I haven't. Although the singer with punk band 999 did help carry my dad's coffin into the crematorium (well, I've always presumed it was him)). Anyway, the bloke from Stump jokingly asked us at rehearsals how much we'd pay him to drop the airborne Schofield. We laughed and went back to watch Dannii Minogue work out in front of a mirror and got drunk on an empty stomach with The Farm and swapped gags with white-soul legend and *Chrysalis* labelmate Kenny Thomas.

Later, live on TV to thirteen million people on a Sunday afternoon we were very very drunk. We stormed around the big stage, confusing the 10 thousand kids in the audience who carried on screaming regardless (isn't that two separate *Carry On* films in one?) and then the tape of the song was faded down with embarrassing haste leaving us miming to silence like a couple of idiots.

Overcome with embarrassment and too many lagers, Les started kicking over amplifiers and microphone stands, then threw his guitar at the pumpkins and stormed offstage. Phillip Schofield walked on, and back announced us with *'Blimey, that was original! After The Watershed from Jim Bob and "the" Fruitbat pushing back the frontiers of music'*. It was just one more bitchy, sarcastic and snide comment in what had been a whole show full of 'em, although at least he wrote this one himself. Sadly 'the Fruitbat' wasn't interested and ran straight back on and rugby-tackled the startled presenter to the floor.

The TV cameramen looked desperately for something else to film during the scuffle until security guards finally removed Les from the stage. They focused briefly on the stunned audience - it was the only time they stopped screaming all day - before returning to show a dazed and confused Schofield looking like he'd been dragged backwards and then, once again, forwards, through a long row of hedges.

I hadn't see any of this, I too had stormed off, as unimpressed by the amp trashing as Phil, or perhaps wishing I'd done it myself first. I was accosted at the side of the stage by a clipboard-wielding researcher from the *BBC* shouting in my face about **g**rievous **b**odily **h**arm and microphone stands hitting children and I was told to get out of the venue or else I would be arrested.

I walked the deserted Sunday streets of East London, lost and alone, not knowing what had happened but believing I was now not only a solo artist but also a child murderer. As I punched street furniture and looked for a bus to throw myself under, Les was having a great time. He first tried to get back onstage again for the Live Aid- style all-star wave and sway at the end of the show, unable to understand why he wasn't going to be allowed to do so. He then took the hearse back to a plush hotel by Tower Bridge where he tried to give away copies of Carter CDs to Japanese businessmen, demanding that they take them as they had invented them. He then went home where he woke up the next morning convinced that he was in his hotel bed. Later on that day, I went round to his house where I was shown a video of the programme and laughed my head off.

As a crisis meeting was taking place at *Chrysalis Records*, where they were deciding whether or not to throw us off the label, we drove to Nottingham to get on with our tour. On the way I had to pick up my bag that I'd left at The Docklands Arena that had been taken back to The Farm's hotel in the West End. And while we sat in our car outside the hotel waiting for our tour manager to return with the bag, a crowd of New Kids On The Block fans - who were there waiting for their heroes to leave - came over and told us that if we ever hurt the New Kids they would kill us.

On the journey up the M1 to Nottingham Rock City, people in service stations stared at us and whispered. There were pictures of Les wrestling with Phillip Schofield on the front cover of all the tabloids. So feeling that it was getting a bit out of hand our crew had been told to not mention the whole thing and not talk to any press etc. There was a strange atmosphere when we arrived for the soundcheck with everyone looking at their shoes unsure of what to say, so nobody said much at all and the plan was to try and forget about the whole thing and put it all behind us. Of course, later that evening as we walked onstage, we were greeted by the entire audience singing, *'Phillip Schofield, what a wanker, what a wanker!'* This would go on all night for the rest of the tour and off and on for the next six years. Taxi drivers would know who we were and ask to shake our hands and suggest who our next victim should be. And like Mahatma Ghandi, JFK, James Dean and Eddie The Eagle Edwards, we would be remembered forever. It's probably on the television now.

NOTE: Since the historic event and while Phillip Schofield was appearing on stage as Joseph in his *Amazing Technicolor Dreamcoat*, the show's lighting operator, who was a Carter fan, would come backstage at our gigs to say hello from Phil. It's all water under the show business bridge now, Fruitbat gets to re-tell the tale on television documentaries about badly-behaved celebrities every now and again, he doesn't get all itchy about the subject anymore and even quite enjoys it. He sometimes gets paid as much as one hundred pounds for his time.

HOW TO GET THROWN OUT OF FESTIVALS

The first festival that Carter played was The Treeworgey Tree Faire in Cornwall in the summer of 1989. Forget the *Mastercard Route Of Kings* in Hyde Park or V Two Thousand and Something, this was more of a West Country Altamont held in a big field where I think they must have been growing dust. We pitched our tent close to the stage to ensure that we couldn't get any sleep and near a big fire so that a pyromaniac friend of ours could set light to it when we finally did. (The same friend would later try to leave the festival in a hurry by stealing our car and attempting to drive it over about half a mile of unhappy campers: this was a man who was later arrested on holiday for biting a dog.)

On the night after we played, as we strolled to the bar(n) for a drink, a baseball-batted gang passed us by, on their way not to a baseball match but to the promoter's office to take the takings, which was when we realized this wasn't going to be summer camp with the Brownies. For the next three days there were pitched battles between opposing groups of the great unwashed who wanted control of the festival. They drove around in converted fire engines, ice-cream vans and aboard horse-drawn chariots of fire and brimstone (I made that last bit up). One afternoon we were standing by a huge ditch full of shit having a wazz into some bushes, when a man ran past in front of us pursued by another who was wielding an axe. Perhaps thinking he had escaped, the man in front looked back to check and tripped and fell into the shit ditch with momentum bringing the axeman in after him. Man number one, now covered in number twos, picked up an empty whisky bottle and started to hit the other bloke over the head. The bottle didn't break spectacularly like in a western and it wasn't made of sugar.

The beer ran out, the shit ditch got fuller and the bands didn't get paid because the money was gone and it was 72 sleepless hours of funky rock and just saying no to drug dealers until people started to leave and a path finally cleared between our car and the exit so we could escape. We were covered in dust for about a week afterwards and it put me off camping for life. I understand that some of the audience still haven't gone home yet.

A month later we'd play our second festival which was more like a private party, I suppose. This time it was in a field somewhere near

Oxford. They put on a good spread, slaughtering a pig especially and spit-roasting it in front of the stage (we're vegetarians). Our manager Adrian Boss fell asleep by the bonfire, setting fire to his leg and we were blown offstage by a didgeridoo player.

BUT

In spite of these early nightmarish experiences, I learned to love playing festivals. I liked the whole going onstage early, hanging around in a field with all the other bands and getting drunk aspect of it. It gave us time to spread rumours. A good festival rumour needs a nice three-day gestation period to really get going. Tell someone a fib in the beer tent on a Friday afternoon and by Sunday it could have reached 40 thousand people and be in the *NME* the following Tuesday. In 1992 when Nirvana's Reading headline experience was in doubt because of Kurt's health, we managed to spread the rumour that Morrissey was standing by backstage to step in if they didn't show. Morrissey had been cancelling shows himself and was unpopular in the press for refusing to answer accusations that he was a racist and the idea of him playing instead of Nirvana wasn't a popular one. The truth according to the *NME* that it was in fact us who were the Seattle grunge kings' understudies may or may not be true. I have found a letter from the promoter implying it might have been but I suspect it was just our little joke.

We were offered money to be stand-ins the following year for Public Enemy, who might also have been about to pull out. We turned that one down very quickly. I think, 'Ladies and gentlemen, unfortunately the most dangerous and controversial hip hop act on the planet can't make it tonight but here's Carter USM!' would have started a piss and mud-throwing onslaught of the like not seen before.

My favourite - if a bit sick and I hope he doesn't really die in the meantime - rumour we started at Reading one year, was that Cliff Richard was dead. Not particularly hilarious, but strangely quite satisfying to hear somebody asking you if you've heard the tragic news about Cliff that you yourself made up a couple of days earlier.

While on tour in the States, somebody from the *NME* was with us on the tour bus and we told him that we'd been asked to tour with U2; we were only joking but it made a whole page in the paper that week and U2 were asked on Radio 1 whether or not it was true. Bono said that he wouldn't have anyone in short trousers on stage before him. Which reminds me of a time me and Fruitbat were on a radio show in Texas, we were playing that night in town and so were U2, so the DJ decided to interview us as though we were Bono and The Edge. We didn't bother with comic Oirish accents or anything but listeners believed we really were U2. We took phone calls from screaming girls and everything.

GLASTONBURY
- BIZARRE - ROSKILDE WEEKEND
JUNE 1992

At a certain point (somewhere near the top) in your career it's possible to get paid absurd amounts of money for arseing around on a big stage in a field for an hour or so. This happened to us once or twice in the early nineties and we liked to spend most of our footballer-sized fees on making ourselves look good. We built a wall of TV sets at Reading and hired a ton of lights, including a square of lights that spelt things out, which we set up upside down by mistake in the rush to get it onstage.

At Glastonbury it was balls. Five thousand of them, with the name of our new single *Do Re Me So Far So Good* printed on, that we planned to distribute amongst the audience in an exciting and stupid way. The original idea was to drop them from helicopters but it was pooh-poohed by air traffic control and bands on the other stages, so we hired these two big AC/DC-style cannons to fire the balls at - sorry, *into* - the audience. This stunt got right up the bugle of someone at a monthly music magazine, who had discovered the balls were made from a material that was bad for the environment and decided - what with it being a Greenpeace benefit gig and all - Carter The Unstoppable Sex Machine were fools.

Fruitbat spent most of his day at Glastonbury, playing his favourite game of, sneaking off into the crowd alone when our security man 'Handsome Dave' (more later) - who was supposed to stay with Les to stop him getting mobbed - wasn't looking. Dave would have to go and look for him and bring him back to the safety of the backstage area like a mischievous toddler (which is of course exactly what he was). We had a great day lazing around in the sunshine, filming bits for our new video until then we had to go onstage. Where, unfortunately, over the course of the day, things had been running late and, as we were the last band on, all the lost minutes that had mounted up had to come out of our set so as to keep to the strict curfew and not get slapped with a huge fine by the council time police (I think it was a £2,000 fine per minute past curfew). We had to finish prematurely without an encore and it was very frustrating, imagine being lifted up by a huge crane with a giant magnet that's attached itself to the keys in the back pocket of your jeans that were down around your ankles as you approached a glorious climax on top of your lover - it was a little bit like that.

After a heated debate with the stage manager and Glasto promoter Michael Eavis, Fruity was foolishly allowed back onstage to apologize (hadn't they *seen* the *Smash Hits* Awards?) for running out of time and not playing an encore, to thank the audience, say goodnight, wave cheerio etc. Of course, he walked up to the microphone and proceeded to accuse Michael Eavis of everything from provincial sloppiness and not letting the travellers into the festival to eating babies and starting the Second World War. Throwing the microphone to the floor, he stormed off stage (another pattern here), to more heated debate and we were asked to leave the site.

We had to go anyway. To Germany to play The Bizarre Festival in Alsdorf. We flew there on a small private plane via Holland. I was expecting a terrifying flight full of turbulence and bird strike followed by a spectacular crash into the side of a mountain. But I was wrong; it was my first ever enjoyable flying experience and as smooth as a baby's bum. Even the airplane food was edible, a simple flask of coffee and some biscuits to pass around and the pilot even let Fruity navigate (hadn't he seen the *Smash Hits* Awards?) When we landed in Maastricht we walked through the small hut that was customs, shook hands with the pilot, hopped in the back of a BM Dub and drove across the border to the festival site in Germany.

A bizarre thing happened at The Bizarre Festival when The Ramones were on. Their bass player - the late Dee Dee - had injured his arm and had to be given an injection before he went onstage so that - as long as he kept his arm moving - he'd be able to play. Unfortunately, halfway through their set (about three hundred songs in), the stage barrier collapsed and the gig was temporarily stopped. While the barrier was being fixed, Dee Dee's arm froze stiff and The Ramones had to give up and leave the stage.

Apart from us and the Ramones there was a great line-up on that sunny Saturday in Freizeitpark. EMF, Blur, The Pogues, Ned's Atomic Dustbin, Kirsty McColl, Slowdive and many more. We spent the day doing interviews, sunburning and hanging out with our showbiz mates. And then, to cut this story short, after we played we had a row with some security guards and their German shepherd friends about backstage passes. Big Nige and Handsome Dave (even more later), our 'minders', got involved in the argument and, in spite of being outnumbered, Big Nige's size and Handsome Dave's good looks put the fear of God into the uniformed festival security and stopped us getting a slap. And then the incredibly itchy promoter - who we'd been arguing with all day about various things - came over and asked us to leave and so we did. We had to go anyway. To Denmark. So, managing to talk Fruity out of tipping the promoter's Portakabin office into the lake as we left we knobbed off. Two out of three: we just had to get ejected from the legendarily nicest and bestest festival in the world and we'd have the complete set.

The people at Roskilde were lovely, their reputation is justified. We used all our best moves: stealing the other bands' beer, shouting, falling over, hanging around with Cass from The Senseless Things but we just couldn't seem to get thrown out; those people were just too bloody nice.

We'd been using a lot of pyrotechnics and coloured smoke at these festivals and I don't know if it was because of this or the hectic gig schedule, the late nights, the intensive drinking, smoking 180 passive cigarettes a day, the endless Freddie Mercury impersonations or a combination of all six but the next day I woke up and couldn't speak. I'd lost my bloody voice. We went ahead with the gig that night at the Hamburg Markthalle with Fruitbat and the audience on lead vocals and the following morning we flew home to film *Top Of The Pops*.

A throat specialist was brought down to the TV studio to have a look down my neck and he gave me his diagnosis. Now, when a top Harley Street doctor tells you that you have acute laryngitis, it is your absolute comic duty to flutter your eyelashes and reply, 'Why, thank you doctor, yours isn't so bad either.' Well I would've if I could've. I was given a steroid injection in the jacksie and instructed to not speak a single word for 48 hours or I would permanently damage my voice and never sing again. As much as such an outcome might have pleased a number of music journalists, I chose to follow doctor's orders and keep my big fat trap shut.

The steroid jab in the *Daily Mail* didn't loosen up my larynx and I couldn't make it through my live vocal take for *Do Re Me So Far So Good*, they showed the video instead and we went home. Where I was even less talkative than I usually was when I returned from a tour and I had to communicate with my family with a series of written notes. Incidentally, at the *TOTP* studios in Elstree the day before, I managed to upset Geordie brick shithouse Jimmy Nail by passing him a piece of paper with the word 'Hello' written on it. He presumed I was trying to be clever and told me to fuck off. 48 hours later, when Terry picked me up to re-start our tour of Germany, I hadn't uttered a single word for the whole two days. I wanted to choose my first one carefully. I chose 'Bollocks'. Don't know why.

Voice tips for new singers. If you lose your voice don't whisper as this is as bad for you as shouting. Instead, speak in a measured normal tone, or if possible don't talk at all. Honey is not as great as old wives in the music industry may have you believe, as it coats the throat and eventually causes more damage. Gargling soluble aspirin is good, as is inhaling *Karvol* in boiling water. Vocal warm-ups and exercises are obviously good but you will sound like a tosser to everyone in the dressing room next door. Although, both Fred from The Family Cat and Niall from The Frank And Walters used vocal warm-ups when they were on tour with Carter and neither of them were tossers. Fred also used to drink about four different types of tea on stage to help keep his vocal chords happy.

THE THREE TENNERS

On 1st September 1991, we played at an indoor festival in Rotterdam called *Abent in Wien* or *An Evening In Vienna*. Everybody who worked there was dressed as a doctor, there were hospital beds everywhere and live pigs in pens. We played in a room along with Nine Inch Nails - drop another name Jim - who I think I watched with DJ Norman (ski) Cook, who was there with his band Beats International, while in another hall Les swears blind he watched Nirvana.

Earlier that day we'd attempted to check into our hotel up the road but weren't allowed into our rooms because fat opera prima donna Pavarotti and his enormous entourage (ooer) - who'd been staying there the night before - had left all their stuff in their rooms and gone sightseeing. They had however left one of their room doors open, so we sneaked in and emptied their mini bar. Oh ha ha ha, how that mysterious extra £30 on the bill for the *Toblerone* must have pissed the old tenor tub of lard off when he finally checked out.

ZWANZIG VIER MINUTEN VON BERLIN

Up until I joined Carter, my foreign travel consisted of: one school day trip to Bologne and two holidays in the South Of France. Peter Ustinov I was not. My tiny, emaciated mind needed broadening.

On 22nd February 1990, Carter began their first European tour. We played three gigs in Holland and I can remember arriving back in England four day's later for a gig in a pub in Norwich where I'd accidently try and pay the barmaid for a drink with Dutch guilders. She must have thought I was so exotic and Palinesque. Our second European excursion included a gig in Aarhus, Denmark's Isle of Wight. I have an exaggerated, warped and selective memory of a lot of the places we visited and the people that lived there, so when I say that Aarhus was entirely populated by bald women, punk rockers and rockabilly-haired gay guys, you'll know that it very likely wasn't at all. The same inaccurate racial stereotyping goes for the following gig two days later in East Germany, which was above a disused diamond mine in Halle where everybody walked with a limp.

RACIAL STEREOTYPES

Some German Carter crowds had a real problem with the whole drum-machine thing. Someone would always shout, 'Where's the drummer?' and a few thought the whole show was mimed, heckle put-downs, topical ad-libs, flat singing and all. At one gig we honestly found someone trying to get behind the stage to see if that was where the drummer was hiding.

Japanese people are incredibly methodical and polite. In Japan we'd play in clubs on the third floors of shopping centres, the audience would arrive at 6pm in the lift, we'd play at 7 and the venue would be closed, emptied and swept clean by 8.30. We'd travel on the bullet train, which would arrive and leave exactly on time and where you stood on the platform corresponded exactly to the number on your ticket and where your carriage would stop. Food would be a problem for us pernickety western vegetarians on the move and at Tokyo train station we'd eat strawberry sandwiches with the crusts removed and perfectly cut into tiny bleached white triangles.

The fine folk of Finland are fabulous boozers. At the Ilosaarirock festival there, we arrived the day before we played so we went out on the town that evening and the whole place seemed to be drunk. The next day we played to a crowd of people fast asleep on the grass, it was dark by 8pm and light again at two.

Some Scandinavians never get the chance to seasonally adjust their disorder.

The ex-pat Englishman abroad knows more about the country that he's settled in than anyone who was born and lived there for a hundred years could ever possibly know. There's nothing like flying to the other side of the world to be sat in a dressing room in a club in Tokyo and have somebody from Croydon in a Union Jack shirt pop his head around the door to say hi. Particularly if he's still with you six hours later at three in the morning, telling you how sexy Chinese girls are.

Belgians are not boring.

Canadians can be a touch kooky and strange and French Canadians moody.

Australians are all great and the Irish really are very friendly.

Regions: A Carter fan in Dundee once offered to show me a great trick. He rested a beer bottle against my forehead and headbutted it as a show of affection - awwww, how sweet.

Our first tour of Eastern Europe was a magical mystery one. We never really knew where we were going, what venue we were playing in and where we'd be sleeping that night. We weren't too sure who was responsible for booking some of the dates either, I think various arts councils were involved, as I believe were MI5, MI6, the KGB, the FBI, the CIA, the German secret police, Cilla Black and someone called George. In East Germany we'd turn up for soundcheck and the club owners would have no idea who we were, but they always seemed to let us play anyway.

It was 1990, the Soviet Empire had collapsed, the Berlin Wall had just come down (I've got a piece of it at home) and most people seemed to be in a pretty welcoming mood. For some reason, a charming couple called Tomas and Waltraud let us stay in their Berlin flat for about a week; we didn't know them and they didn't know us but they let us stay in their house. When we said goodbye to them, we bought them a coffee machine with all the East German marks that we'd been paid for the gigs and weren't allowed to leave the country with.

One terrible moment of western capitalist guilt and embarrassment led to another when we went shopping for our farewell party at Tomas and Waltraud's flat. At the local supermarket while we queued up to pay for our four bottles of wine and the last box of chocolates on the shelf, we realized that we were supposed to have queued up for a shopping basket first. We also noticed that everyone else in the queue who already hated us for the lack of basket etiquette and effectively pushing in was buying the same pack of bland meat and bread while we stood there with armfuls of booze, fags and soft centres. And then when we dropped one of the bottles of wine which smashed, spilling wine all over the supermarket floor, the earth really could have swallowed us up right there and then.

On 20th April 1990 we passed through Checkpoint Charlie from East to West Berlin, paying the Checkpoint Charlie soldiers a few quid for yet another stamp in our passports. They'd probably soon be out of a job and were trying to build up some redundancy money by scamming the tourists. 20th April 1990 would have been Adolf Hitler's 101st birthday and hundreds of Nazi skinheads from the east and west, with no wall in the way anymore, had united to honour the occasion with a march, ending at a well-known left-wing Berlin rock venue called The Kob Club with a big scrap with the crusties.

So what? you say. The Kob was plastered with posters for our new album *101 Damnations,* we say. That's *101* Damnations. And we were playing there that night.

Bizarrely, Berlin feminists were also planning a protest at The Kob. They objected to the name of our band, which they thought was sexist. They'd been in earlier on in the week and cut out the word 'sex' from the posters on the walls inside the club (next to other posters for bands with far more PC names such as Anal Cunt). With the prospect of attack from both left and far right, Carter The Unstoppable   Machine were a touch apprehensive and hid in a cupboard.

But hooray, neither threat materialised, the gig was brilliant and afterwards we piled into a taxi with our pockets full of empty beer bottles and headed down to the riots to throw them at the Nazis. Luckily the cab ride took a while and by the time we reached the police water cannons, sobriety got the better of us and we took the cabbie's advice and turned back to The Kob, where we ate a hummus kebab and slept upstairs in the club flat (another Euro custom that hasn't yet caught on at The Bull And Gate or The Brixton Academy).

ICH BIN EIN WICHSER

On a night off in Berlin at one of the many Jugenclubhaus venues of which there seemed to be as many as there were Nelson Mandela Student Union Buildings in the UK at the time, we were drinking ourselves stupid with whisky colas. Adrian was trying to impress a German girl he was talking to by demonstrating the German he'd learned and was attempting to explain that he was the manager. When he thought he'd said, 'I am the manager', the girl fell off her chair laughing. 'Ich bin ein Wichser' in fact actually meant, 'I am a wanker.'

For many years after, when we were struggling with a tough audience in Munich, or needed to win over a festival crowd in Frankfurt, I would resort to the nifty trick of repeating Adrian's immortal confession. 'Ich bin ein Wichser!' I'd proudly declare and the crowd would roar with laughter before carrying me shoulder-high through the centre of the town, declaring me to be the funniest man in all the world.

We finally met George, the tour's 'promoter', at our last German gig in Dresden. We had sworn that when he did finally appear we would kick the shit out of him for his bad organisation and elusiveness, for booking us a gig at an East German holiday camp for OAPs and because we hated him. But the sun was shining on Dresden that day and after two weeks of cabbage and boiled eggs we were given deep-fried French cheese for dinner, so by the end of the evening we were lying on the floor of the bar (where we slept that night) looking up at the ceiling and repeatedly demonstrating the new German beer trick we'd just been taught (banging the base of our beer bottles on the top of somebody else's so that the contents froth up and overflow all over the floor). Next to us was George, the greatest man that ever lived.

Our next gigs were in Czechoslovakia, where - like Berlin - the times they were 'a-changing. The new president was people's playwright Vaclav Havel, a groovy moustachioed Ken Livingstone character, and people were getting on down with their bad selves all over the city.

The first gig was in a big old theatre near Wenceslas Square called Lucerna supporting legendary beat poet Allen Ginsberg along with a bunch of Czech punk bands (who all sounded like Dire Straits). According to tour manager Terry, Czechoslovakia was not only famous for brewing *Budweiser Budvar* beer (not the US version) but also for making monkey boots. I was and still am a fan of both and was looking forward to getting drunk in some new footwear. But it turned out that the plastic explosive Semtex was the new chief Czech export and consequently there was no Bud anywhere in the city and no boots. We had to drink champagne in our plimsolls (no, not *from our plimsolls,* we weren't cabinet ministers) and we once again found ourselves feeling guilty for gate-crashing someone else's party. Unlike all the English architecture students falling over each other and dropping their trousers on the birthday cake building'd streets of Prague, who really didn't seem to give a shit.

I had a great view of the famously stunning architecture from the window of my hotel room, which didn't last long as, after one night in the hotel, the money ran out and we had to leave to spend the next night in the back of our van until our guide Peter found us a flat where we would stay for the rest of our visit. Unlike Tomas and Waltraud's in Berlin there was nobody home, although it did look as though they'd only just left. Or rather, just been temporarily evicted to make way for us. There were half-finished cups of coffee on the table, still warm fag-ends in the ashtray and a child's bike upturned with its rear wheel still spinning in the hall (well, nearly). It was a bit weird. Terry cooked us a lovely pasta and Adrian blocked the toilet and the bath with his magic pants, which I might tell you about later.

While we were in Prague, aside from the Ginsberg gig, we played a festival at a huge student halls of residence and a gig in an art gallery. After packing our gear away at the end of the art gallery gig and as we sat in the bar getting drunk, we were asked if we'd set up again to play some songs for the new President who was on his way over. We were probably too pissed to be any good but this was the leader of the country and a hero of the people so we unpacked the gear again and tuned up ready for our date with the big Czech cheese. The dull part of this story is that he didn't turn up - bloody politicians.

This might be an urban Czech myth but, in the days of communism there always used to be secret policemen in among the audience at rock gigs checking for any anti-government lyrics. And when heavy metal bands played they had to employ a lip reader.

THE LONELINESS OF THE LONG DISTANCE PUNNER

The life of a long distance pop star is like that of an oil rigger or a soldier (drilling for oil on an 18 to 30s holiday, or fighting a war in Ayia Napa maybe). But it ain't normal.

In the busy year of 1991 I was gigging on 129 days and of the other 236, I was travelling on 39, doing interviews and having my photo taken for 51, recording or rehearsing for 16, while a further 6 days were spent looking at sleeve designs, meeting accountants and lawyers etc. For the 124 days when I was at home, I wasn't really there at all; the flesh was willing but the body was still on the tour bus. I'd come home feeling tired and listless, unable to make my own cup of coffee; I'd go to bed at night and lay awake for hours, unable to get to sleep so early, so sober and so not rattling around in a bunk bed on a motorway with a gaffa-tape moustache.

After the initial few days feeling inexplicably depressed, waiting for soundcheck and for someone to bring me my dinner, I'd start to relax a bit and feel good about being at home. With no desire to ever leave the house again I was ready to finally finish painting the bathroom and do my own cooking. And then I'd get bored and want to get back out on the road again. It must be the gipsy in me. Or the David Essex.

I hate certain roads. The South Circular as it hits gridlock around East Putney. There's a hotel there which I've driven by so many times on my way home that it always fills me with horrendous *déja vu*. Returning from a long journey, dog tired and feeling equal parts: eager to get home out of this traffic jam, into my own bed. And: wishing we were doing just one more week of pubs, clubs, toilets, Nelson Mandela buildings or leisure centres (depending on the stage of our career).

I hate the A4 (the paper road) as it flies over the flyover, either west towards Heathrow and Reading or back on home past the Lucozade bottle time and temperature on the left. That road really bores the pants off me. The A40, where they forced everybody to move out of their houses so they could widen the road and then changed their minds after they were all empty and boarded up and covered in graffiti, that road annoys me. And of course, Gary Rhodes the spiky-haired TV chef.

For those early years of saying goodbye to my family, it was a painful process. My girlfriend didn't want me to go and my daughter would soon feel the same, it was horrible. Later of course, when I was away from home a lot less, on the rare occasions when I did finally get out of the house, Jakki would virtually kick me out the door, offering to post my clothes onto me having already chosen the women's movies she planned to rent from Blockbuster Video before she went upstairs for a good night's diagonal sleep in a less smelly bed.

When I was away Jakki also liked to redecorate the house to surprise and confuse me upon my arrival home again. I loved this. I hated coming home to see that nothing had changed, no new buildings had shot up in less than a month and a sandwich shop where there were was once an estate agents next door to a shoe shop that now sells Chinese medicine and a barber shop that's gone all unisex. Maybe that was why I went away, just to see things change. Maybe God only moves stuff around when I'm not looking.

I HAVE BAD GIG DREAMS

I'm standing on a stage that's angled downwards at the front so I'm almost falling off into the audience. My microphone keeps dropping down on its stand, making me look like an idiot. My guitar is out of tune and I can't remember the words to the songs. Before I go onstage I'll be struggling to get my trousers on while the intro tape is already playing out front. And it's said that you can't die in your own dreams. But in mine I died on my arse every single night.

Fruitbat is meanwhile having his usual dream about aliens flying through the bedroom window of his Walnut Whip chocolate palace at the top of the candyfloss mountain where he lives with Kylie Minogue and Bananarama.

YOU MAY GET WHAT YOU WISH FOR
AND IF IT HITS YOU ON THE HEAD IT'LL HURT

On the first Carter album *101 Damnations*, the song *Midnight On The Murder Mile* features the lyrics, 'It was 3 O'clock on the murder mile when I came to my senses / And my only death wish was that I had a sockful of fifty pences.' Now once upon a time, when we were playing this particular number at The Harlow Square, at the precise moment I sang the above line some hilarious Essex wag threw - yes you guessed it - a sockful of fifty pences at my head. In fact it was probably a couple of fifties and about 60p worth of twos and ones but the joke was the same. How do you think of such a thing and at which point do you decide to do it and exactly when do you not talk yourself out of it at the last minute?

Note 23B: In the same song, the opening line is, 'It was midnight on the murder mile, Wilson Pickett's finest hour / I was walking towards the flashing smile of the Crystal Palace Tower'. This related to my walk from where the number 2 bus stops in West Norwood to my home in Crystal Palace, a stretch of road that used to be known as *The Murder Mile* because so many murders had taken place there (and – I'm guessing here - it was a mile long). In the distance I'd be able to see the warning light for aircraft that flashed on and off at the top of The Crystal Palace TV transmitter, or 'the flashing smile of the Crystal Palace Tower'. These days the tower neither flashes nor smiles; instead, a series of red lights from top to bottom come on when night falls, which - although I realize rhyming isn't everything - doesn't scan too well. It's also fucked up my *London Tour Of The Lyrics of Carter USM* retirement plan.

OTHER THINGS THAT HAVE BEEN THROWN AT US ON STAGE THAT I SUPPOSE WE ASKED FOR:

CADBURY'S TWIRLS... I said in a magazine that my favourite chocolate bar was the *Cadbury's Twirl*.

TOMATO SAUCE FLAVOUR CRISPS... I said in a magazine that my favourite flavour crisps were tomato sauce flavour.

(Paul Conroy from our record label *Chrysalis* once brought a large box of *Twirls* and tommy sauce crisps over from England to a Carter gig in Vienna, we'd been away from home for a long time and it was like a Red Cross parcel).

PEANUTS... When *Shopper's Paradise* was used in a *KP Nuts* TV ad. (I ruined any chances of a follow-up ad and accompanying wad of cash by wearing a t-shirt with the words 'I HATE PEANUTS' across the front for a whole tour).

A TOILET SEAT IN DUNFERMLINE: No comment.

AND FINALLY, in a less amusing version of the fifty pence tale, I had my head cut open by a pound coin that was lobbed at me when we supported Madness at Wembley Arena.

THE CRAZY CARTER CREW

We played thirty gigs as part of the *Rubbish* tour to celebrate and promote the release of our new single. We started off by playing a short set at the single's launch party at The Bull And Gate in Kentish Town, to an audience of fan club hardcore and invited celebrities. If I remember this right, Bob Mortimer and Sean Hughes were both there. Carter were always popular with comedians, I don't know why exactly but I'm sure someone at *IPC Magazines*[5] could explain it to you hilariously. It might have been a South London thing. All comedians live in South London. Just like all indie musicians live in Camden and that's *all* indie musicians, I'm not exaggerating, it's a geographical fact, look in the *Yellow Pages* under 'I'.

Carter have made guest appearances on the television or radio shows of Sean Hughes, Newman and Baddiel and John Shuttleworth. Written the theme tune for a Sean Hughes TV series and had *Bloodsport For All* used as the intro music for Newman and Baddiel's live show. I've met Vic and Bob, Eddie Izzard and Keith Allen and I've been to the pub with Arthur Smith, Mark Steel and Mark Lamarr.

Carter were the punchline to a gag in the TV series *Drop The Dead Donkey* and John Shuttleworth took the piss out of my haircut in one of his live shows.

Shuttleworthy note: Years ago I was an enormous fan of Jilted John - a previous Graham Fellows (John Shuttleworth) incarnation - and when I met him at The Subterania club (again) in Portobello Road - when I was drunk (again) - I kissed his shoes and told him that he was God. Apart from being terrified of this inebriated knobhead kissing his feet, Graham was also confused at such a display of hero-worship as he was, at the time, working as a milkman.

For the launch party at The Bull and Gate Andy Mair recreated his sleeve design for *Rubbish* on the Bull And Gate stage with old junk he got out of a skip while, at the back of the venue above the audience in his lighting and heckling cupboard, Jon Fat Beast was imagining a far more elaborate and expensive stage show for the future. Jon ran his Hype Club at The Bull And Gate, had done the lights for us a few times and was trying to convince us that we needed a proper lightshow to make up for the lack of band members. We weren't convinced, thinking that

[5] Publishing home of *NME, Melody Maker* etc.

our music and personalities were all we needed for a good show but agreed that if he paid his own way Jon could come on tour with us. Three days later he turned up in Bradford for the first date of the tour and would be with us until the middle of 1992.

Jon Fat Beast was the fat bastard, THE fat bastard. He'd come onstage before us to abuse the audience, abuse the band, get his knob out, wobble his enormous belly, cover himself in squirty cream, have beer thrown at him and eventually introduce us before running (yes, I know) to the back of the hall to operate the lighting desk. I loved watching the Beast from the stage, banging away on the lighting desk like he was a mad classical pianist playing the concert of his life and raising his arms aloft like he'd just won the FA Cup.

On that first tour with us, apart from the lights and the MC-ing Jon also sold the T-shirts. He took a percentage of the money so he could buy food (it's funny but in spite of his Rubens-esque stature I can't remember ever seeing Jon eat anything) and drink (the opposite applies here). He also videoed the gigs and sold copies on tour and as a sideline he wrote 'Carter The Unstoppable Sex Machine' in felt pen onto toilet paper and tried to sell it as official bog paper, or maybe very thin monogrammed scarves.

I don't know if it's the same for all bands, I'm sure they'll tell you it is. How they have all these colourful characters working with them who are way more interesting than they - the band - will ever be.

I tried making a list of everyone who ever went on tour with Carter but it's too long to print, it's like the telephone directory of a small European country and I'd forget somebody and feel bad. As it grew in size, the Crazy Carter Crew turning up at a gig could be overpowering, it was like an invasion. We annexed the venues. We were the Spartans and the Ghurkas. It was always us and the crew against the world, we didn't trust people. Perhaps, after years of being treated like a karaoke act by a lot of sound engineers because we used tapes and weren't a proper band. They thought we were 'just a duo' and so they'd put our microphones really close together and give us two square feet of stage space and five minutes to soundcheck. They thought we were The Proclaimers when we were really The Clash. We weren't a duo, we were a band with two members (yes, I know the dictionary may tell you that *is* a duo, but what did Doctor Johnson know about punk rock?). All this tended to put us on the defensive; as soon as we turned up at the venue, we expected the worst. Actually it was more offensive than defensive.

In 1990 we were travelling in the back of a van and were a still a fairly small army - say the Pope's Swiss Guard Vatican City army or a troop of sappers from Liechtenstein (both Swiss connected, so we'd have the right tools) (the bottle opener attachment chiefly) - but we'd expand in time and then, look out rock'n'roll, here come the Romans!

If you look at the centre-spread picture of the *30 Something* album sleeve you can see who was working with us around that time. If you haven't got a copy, firstly, why? And secondly, the photo can be found somewhere in this book, it was taken by Mark Baker at the Paddington Recreation Grounds on 7th January 1991 and it was bloody freezing.

So, starting at the back and working clockwise from left to right is Terry Coyle. Terry first tuned our guitars for us when we played with Right Said Fred in Ealing and when he left his job at a children's playgroup (pretty good qualifications for working with us) he became our permanent guitar tech and tour manager. Terry very likely saved our lives when he steered the shitty white van that we'd bought off The Claytown Troupe onto the safety of the hard shoulder of the M4 when the rear wheel fell off at 70 miles an hour in 1989, he tour managed us for almost five hundred of our gigs. Sixty thousand words into the writing of this book, Terry suddenly and tragically died.

It was less than a year and a half after the equally sudden and tragic death of his younger brother Johnny and it was devastating. Like most funerals, Terry's brought a lot of people together who hadn't seen each other for years and so many turned up to pay their respects that somebody booked a coach to ferry everyone from Glasgow Airport to the church in Maryhill, on to the cemetery, and then to a bar afterwards for a drink. As Terry's family and friends waited to lower his coffin into it's final resting place, the coachload of musicians - including Death In Vegas who Terry had been working with most recently - and various roadies, sound engineers, lampies and production people (about forty of us) had driven to the wrong part of the cemetery and were lost. After about half an hour of walking around like headless chickens, we found a gravedigger who drove his truck with its orange lights flashing as we followed him to the other end of the vast Glasgow cemetery and finally to the graveside where Terry and his family were waiting for us.

I think the ironic sight of a coachload of musicians and roadies, lost in a cemetery, in severe need of tour management would have - and, I'd like to think, did - make Terry piss himself with laughter.

Back in that cold London park in 1990. Next to Terry and past Carter producer Simon Painter, manager Adrian Boss and what appears to be a young Tony Robinson in a cycle hat is Daz (*The BFG*, *The Wookie* etc), a 17 year-old Blackpudlian friend of Jon Beast who used to follow us around on tour. As a Carter fan, Daz was nearly always drunk at the gigs and very rarely made it to the end of our set – on at least one occasion he passed out before the doors opened. Daz is big; he once punched a test-your-strength punch-ball completely off the machine at Blackpool Pleasure Beach, where incidentally there's a rollercoaster that's named after him[6]. As a member of the audience Daz liked to taunt the pit security by shouting abuse at them and the band and repeatedly trying to get onstage. One night, at Canterbury University, Daz stagedived and landed on his head, ending up in hospital. For both his safety and ours, we gave him a job. He became our chief of security and *über* roadie. One more thing about Daz is that he used to speak in his own language based almost entirely on the scripts of *The Fast Show, The Young Ones* and *The Comic Strip Presents*. Every morning Daz would ask, 'And how are you this morning sir?' and I'd reply with a pre-coffee mumble, 'mmrrgnnh alright.'

'Oh dear,' Daz would say, 'Sir being a trifle rude?' To which I would have to reply, 'And yourself?' so that he could say, 'Radiant sir, radiant' and then we could get on with the rest of the day.

Continuing on past Daz is Jon Beast who, typically, has refused to wear a *30 Something* shirt like everybody else. In terms of lookalikes I think we're talking Timmy Mallett and Christopher Biggins. Then next to what really is a bad, bad picture of me is Pip, a hyperactive Bonsai Yorkshireman who worked with Jon on the lightshow. Pip once condemned the electricity of an entire country (Denmark) and sawed a hotel bed in half because he couldn't find any chocolate. On a tour of Europe his hyperactivity used to rile the sound crew so much that to keep him out of the way while they set up the PA we used to send him to the shops to buy everyone cigarettes. Pip sometimes looked like Lester Piggott and at other times you'd swear he was the actor Paul Whitehouse playing one of the *Old Gits* from *The Harry Enfield Show*.

Freezing his nads off next to Pip is Angus Batey, pictured here shortly after his Frank Spencer cycle accident - across the road, up the pavement, over a hedge and down the steps of someone's groundfloor flat - and before the reconstructive dentistry. It was Angus' amp I threw up over on a night bus and Angus' head I tried to stove in after the *NME* party. He was our first ever roadie, before 17 year-old Essex boy Marlon, who we tried to get onto the Youth Training Scheme so the government would pay him twenty five quid a week to go on tour with us. Predictably the government said no.

Skipping on past Sarah from *Rough Trade*, Adrian Boss' assistant Tim Webster, Andrew from *Rough Trade*, our press officer Ginny and our agent Lisa, is Scotty, who sold

[6] 'The Big One'

our T-shirts and according to the Carter website has slept with someone from *EastEnders*. On the end is our sound engineer Helen who - having neither mullet haircut nor penis - was treated with about as much respect by in house venue soundmen as we were for being a duo with a tape machine. They were often surprised to see a woman walk over to the sound desk and introduce herself as Carter's sound engineer. It was a bit like in the old comedies when the female doctor walks into the surgery and the patient says, 'Oh... er... it's just that I was expecting... someone *older*.'

Crouching down on the front row are Michaela and Eileen from *Rough Trade* and Kate, who also worked there when the photo was taken but later joined Adrian Boss Promotions to be driven round the bend by us. Next to Kate is Les' girlfriend Crissi, Terry's girlfriend – and early Jamie Wednesday manager - Jo, press officer Anton and his dogs Herman and Wilf (Wilf has three legs, domestic pet fact fans and appears with his Pal (or perhaps chum) Herman in the video for *The Only Living Boy In New Cross*).

Finally, my family: Holly, Ernie (more on him later) and Jakki Ball.

Carter roadies were not stereotypical roadies. They kept their arsecracks covered and their keys on the inside of the pockets of their trousers. We didn't put a classified ad in *The Roadie* or go to a roadie employment agency. They just turned up. Aside from those I've already mentioned, there was Big Al and Nick Ely who both used to follow Carter around Europe as fans and ended up working for us. Big Al was a softly-spoken man who sold shirts for a while and eventually tour–managed us. Nick was in the RAF where he did something that he couldn't tell us about or - as he often told us - he would have to kill us. He claimed to be afraid of flying. Nick did lights and introduced pyrotechnics to the Carter live show, nearly killing me on a number of explosive occasions and bringing a whole new meaning to the phrase being blown off stage. Neither Big Al or Nick were qualified or experienced in tour managing or lighting when they joined us but Big Al went on to be a permanent employee of Radiohead, while Nick did lights for Therapy? and a number of well-known metal acts. We were a school for roadies.

And sometimes if there wasn't a job for someone to do, we'd make one up. Like social Chameleon 'Mole' who used to dance onstage with Wez's band International Resque and would later work on the Carter T-shirt stall with Terry's brother Mad Dog and his glove puppets. Mad Dog is a great storyteller and I poached a lot of his conversation for song titles and lyrics. The writing credits on *1992 The Love Album* should really read 'Morrison/Carter/Bottomley.' Mad Dog's surname is actually Coyle but he claimed to be the love child of Virginia Bottomley and so that was the name he used. When Dog and Mole were on the T-shirt stall they invariably pulled a bigger crowd than the support band.

In 1992 Mole went to America with us. On the itinerary next to his name it says 'production assistant'. There's no such job.

CRAZY CREW STORY 369786

Beast, Mad Dog, Pip and Daz used to visit the football grounds of the towns and cities that we were playing in. They'd somehow manage to blag their way inside where they'd point dramatically at the pitch, shout, 'You're shit aaarrhhhh!' and leave.

CRAZY CREW STORY 369786B

Daz and Mad Dog wore red headbands for a whole week in Europe because they believed they were Vietnamese soldiers. They'd hide behind trees and in undergrowth waiting for American GIs to ambush. All over Holland and Germany.

CRAZY CREW STORY 369786C

I've just had this flashback to 1991 and I can picture quite vividly the crew walking down the high street in Gloucester and they looked like a Tom Waits song.

Picture this: Beast, who as you know was big and weighty, he's probably wearing a football kit. Then Pip, the pint-sized silver-haired fox who - like Prince - only dressed in purple. Then there's Helen, who at the time was a bit of a new-age hippy and Daz a big friendly teenage giant. Add to this, Andy the seven-foot-tall monitor man, long haired, middle-aged and tattooed Gloucester lighting man 'Bob from Gloucester', Glaswegian tough guy Terry, Fruitbat dressed in a cycling cap and a gorgeous looking man with a short back and sides and a foot-long fringe. I might have forgotten somebody, the bloke who looked after the elephants and the bearded lady.

A VALUABLE ROCK 'N' ROLL LESSON

On the Thursday following Jon Beast's arrival I learned a valuable rock'n'roll lesson. We were playing the Barrel Organ (the pub not the instrument) in Birmingham, when I stormed offstage because of persistent PA and technical difficulties. Unfortunately, there was no dressing room at The Barrel Organ and so I ended up in the toilet at the side of the stage where three or four members of the audience were calmly taking a piss. I felt pretty stupid with everybody looking at me, wondering what I was doing there and why was I so irate. I had no choice but to swallow my pride, leave the gents and go back onstage.

A similar thing happened at another venue when I'd stormed offstage (once again for PA / technical trouble) this time I left the room and sat on the stairs sulking with no intention of going back on. Adrian Boss and various other people came out and cajoled and badgered me until I eventually came back on, feeling once again, stupid. I also walked off and back on again in a small theatre in France, this time because the mayor and various specially invited local grands boutons[7] were sat down the front, in the good seats ignoring us. The real audience meanwhile were shoved at the back of the theatre half a mile away, upstairs in the circle. After dramatically (some might say melo-dramatically) throwing my guitar across the stage on the first song, I exited stage left to inevitably re-enter stage right shortly after.

Basically, what I'm trying to say is, if you ever walk offstage, make sure you've got somewhere to go and won't have to walk back on again as you will look stupid. If you're not in a band the same applies to storming out of your house after an argument with your boyfriend/girlfriend/husband/wife without your door keys. Eventually you'll probably want to come back home again and it's less embarrassing if you don't have to ring the doorbell. Oh, and take a coat and make sure you're wearing shoes.

Incidentally, the absolute worst thing that can happen when you lose your temper onstage is for the whole audience to go, 'Woooo!' and hold imaginary handbags up in front of their faces.

Anyway, I managed to stay on stage for the rest of the tour and the gigs continued for the next couple of weeks without memorable incident. We nipped home briefly to visit *London Records* looking for a new record deal and the A&R ▮ [7] Big knobs man told us he loved us, he loved the songs, we were great, we were amazing... now had we ever considered getting a drummer? We kicked his desk over, dangled him by his legs out of his office window until he said sorry and then we went to Hamleys and bought a *Subbuteo* table football set. We needed to practice because the *NME* and radio station *Q102* (later became *XFM*) had organised a *Subbuteo* competition for popular indie groups and we were going to win. We bought a team with white shirts, Fulham or England maybe and my girlfriend meticulously painted tiny little black dots on the shirts, so that they could play in the Carter *101 Damnations* home strip. The tournament took place at popular Carter trouble spot The Subterania, where once again there was too much free booze. We were eventually barred from the competition for cheating, stealing the other teams' players and finally because Jon Fat Beast, dropped his shorts, sat on the pitch and mooned at the TV cameras. I don't know who won because we were also eventually ejected from the venue for arguing with the bouncers but I suspect it was someone who, like Feargal Sharkey's perfect cousin, flicked to kick (and we didn't know).

A week and a half later on Friday the 13th of July the *Rubbish* tour ended at the London Astoria. I remember the gig's promoter coming into the dressing room before the show with a bottle of *Jack Daniels* to tell us that the gig was sold out and how good that felt. After the gig we signed a publishing deal with *Island Music* in the Astoria dressing room I thought I'd have to sign on Les' behalf as he'd drunk half the Jack Daniels and was in a strop and decided he wasn't signing anything. We had a huge girly row in the corridor until eventually he put pen to paper. A week later we went into *Island's* in-house studio for a week to record some new demos but our recording methods were a tad unorthodox for the studio engineer; I think he thought we were half-wits. Being cowards, we said goodbye to the engineer at the end of the first day's session and told him we looked forward to seeing him tomorrow and then rang our manager Adrian, got him to tell *Island* we wouldn't be back (I can't remember our excuse, we weren't ready or something) and we went back to our little garage studio in Simon Painter's garden. Simon understood the way we worked and he *knew* we were half-wits.

SO, TO RECAP.
AFTER YEARS OF HARD SLOG AND DAYDREAMING,
WE'D FINALLY GOT WHAT WE WANTED...

PERPETUAL MOTION...

n. The hypothetical continuous operation of an isolated mechanical device or other closed system without a sustaining energy source.

OK, strictly speaking it might have been inertia but we were on a roll anyway.

And then everybody started picking fights with us and trying to sue us. Didn't they realize we were invincible, we could not be vinced? Yet still nevertheless, in the latter half of 1990, some people seemed determined to get us into a courtroom, a hospital bed or both. It was a great time for our lawyer Alexis.

We played a gig at a polytechnic (remember them?) that I won't name. The local muscle they'd hired to do the security for the night were among the most frightening people I've ever come across in my entire life and while we were on the stage, they stood in front of it looking hard. Jon Beast was asked to make a request for people not to stage dive when he introduced us but Jon would always do the exact opposite of what he was asked to do. I think his introduction that night was, 'Please put your hands together for the best kick arse rock'n'roll band in the whole world... Carter The Unstoppable Sex Machine!...*STAGEDIVE NOW!*'

When the first wave of crowd surfers floated over towards us the bouncers pushed them back, the next wave were manhandled roughly over and dropped onto the floor and then eventually they grew bored with both these crowd-control tactics and started punching people in the face. We had to keep stopping the gig to ask them to take it easy and be a bit more gentle but they ignored us and when they punched a girl square in the face - I'm all for equality but - we stopped the gig again and I questioned their parents' marital status. They then turned their backs on the audience, facing us instead to give us dirty looks and the international cut throat sign. Just in case there was any doubt, they told me they were going to kill me. I was really looking forward to leaving the stage.

Back in the dressing room we wedged a chair against the door to stop the bouncers getting in and I prepared myself for an untimely and ugly death. When they eventually burst their way in, after a bit of close-up swearing and shouting they informed us that they'd be waiting for us outside and they left. About ten minutes later the president of the students union - if you looked in a dictionary next to the word speccy you'd find a picture of him - came into the dressing room to chastise us for provoking the crowd, attempting to cause a riot, blah de blah and – finally faced with someone who I might possibly have beaten in a fight - I had to be restrained from pulling off his glasses and shoving them up his spotty presidential arse. We had to eventually leave the venue through the fire escape.

A short while after the gig, somebody sent us a copy of the polytechnic's student union newspaper which had an editorial piece in it that accused us of incitement to riot and intimidating the security who had only been trying to do their job, protecting the audience and the band. Stupid fucking me.

The night after this narrow escape and another bunch of beefy bouncers. They'd been hired in from a local nightclub - called something like, *Legends, Tramps, Mr B's, Scandale, Chantels* or something ending in 'ers' like *Sparklers* or *Spanglers* - where they were used to standing by a door all night, checking people's shoes and trousers and dealing with the kind of drunks who only went home satisfied on a Saturday night if they were covered in someone else's blood. The dickie-bowed doormen were neither trained nor prepared for a hall full of indie fans throwing each other at them and fearing they might get DOCTOR MARTEN - AIR CUSHIONED SOLE printed all over their lovely white shirts every time a scud student was launched in their direction, they made sure that they got out of the way. After a couple landed badly we decided to get involved and we suggested the security could maybe try catching a few people every now and again, which they had a go at for a bit, but their hearts weren't in it. They soon started being all butterfingered, letting people fall head-first over the stage barrier and onto the pit floor.

After this gig we used to insist that the blokes in the pit between the stage and the audience weren't wearing black bow ties and white shirts because it intimidated the audience and spoiled everybody's fun. Eventually we'd take our own security with us. They became a part of the show and they used to dress up, sing along and give out water when it was hot, at one point using high-powered water pistols - until someone slipped over in a puddle at a Carter gig and decided to sue us and we had to let everyone die from heat exhaustion instead - at the risk of sounding like former police chief John Stalker, I genuinely believe that the Carter security team helped change the way rock audiences are treated at gigs today. Three cheers for us, hip hip...

A couple of days later, as a minor stage invasion at a venue in the South of England started to get out of hand, the in-house lighting man - fearing for the safety of his equipment - panicked and pushed one of the invading audience off the unusually high stage onto the hard venue floor where he cracked his head open, knocking himself unconscious. As the house lights came up and an ambulance was called, the lighting man did a runner and (this is true) was chased down the road - and possibly out of town - by enraged members of the audience. (If you imagine the lighting bloke as Frankenstein's monster, the enraged audience as the flaming torch-bearing villagers and the unconscious teenager as the small innocent child who befriends the monster, it was just like the end scene of Frankenstein... no hang on a minute, the small innocent child befriends the monster doesn't he, as opposed to getting pushed offstage? Oh forget it.)

The tour ended at another polytechnic that again I won't name. All day long the fire alarm kept going off; the manager of the venue said it was broken and he might fix it or he might not. He was a pain in the arse, telling everybody how the building was his and he could chuck us all out for no reason if the fancy so took him and basically acting like a head of a dick. Midway through the sold out gig the alarm went off again and the building had to be evacuated. We stood outside for a while until the audience - expecting to be allowed back in again as there was obviously no fire - started to get a bit uptight. Firstly, some of them blamed us and then turned on the venue and eventually the poor sod who was sent outside to tell everybody, 'terribly sorry but please go home.' The audience drowned him out with abusive songs and refused to leave the grounds. When we were allowed back inside and everyone finally gave up and buggered off home, I went looking for the venue manager (I was allegedly carrying a chair).

I didn't find him.

But when we returned to the same unnamed city for a gig at a different venue, I dedicated a song to him and I referred to him as the 'biggest cunt in *********' Unfortunately, he or one of his mates was in the audience that night and, not appreciating either the namecheck or the dedication, he sued us. The case never made it as far as the courts, as our lawyer argued that it couldn't be proved that being 'the biggest cunt in ********* ' was necessarily a bad thing, it was hilarious to read it all typed out in legal jiggery-pokery though.

We didn't go out of our way to incite or invite trouble but we cared about the audience and didn't want anyone getting hurt just because they went to one of our gigs. And maybe sometimes when we were up onstage, we got a bit carried away. If the venue was empty I'd be retching with nerves but when it was packed, with the crowd not only in front of us but also behind us and on our side, I couldn't help but get mesmerized by the power. There were times when it was as if we could have stopped the gig and led the audience out of the building and on into the centre of London, where we would march on the Houses of Parliament, burst through the doors and bring down the government. Hooray! If you saw us before a gig, sitting backstage not really talking much, quietly drinking a beer and looking tired and bored, you wouldn't think it was the same people who, five minutes later, could be completely out of control in front of a large crowd. Pete Townshend once said something about losing control when he was onstage and how it could be dangerous for anyone who got in The Who's way when they were off on one. And this is what Keef said:

In Hampton, Virginia, during the song *Satisfaction* when a fan ran onstage towards Mick Jagger, Keith Richards thinks they're under attack, took off his guitar and swung it toward the fan's head who ducked out of the way just in time. Keith put his guitar back on and continued with the song. When he was asked about the incident later, Keith said the fan was on his turf and 'could have been a nutter...I'm going to chop the mother down! '

It was like that onstage with Carter sometimes.

ABBASFIELD

On a lighter note, on the same tour after a great gig at Huddersfield Poly there was an aftershow party in the students' union bar. *Abba - The Movie* was playing on a big screen on the wall and seeing as how it was the bar manager's birthday he decided to celebrate by giving the entire contents of his bar away in perhaps the worst example of bar management in the profession's history. Eventually, unable to physically drink anymore we started to throw it around. And all to the great songs of Abba. We were quite simply 'having the time of our lives.' 'Oo woo oo, see that girl, watch that scene Carter The Unstoppable Sex Machine.'

We stayed till morning when some keen early risen studes turned up for breakfast to find us scattered around the bar still asleep, the entire place covered in sticky booze, it must have stunk.

We returned to Huddersfield Poly on the day that *30 Something* went to Nnumber 8 in the album charts and we attempted to repeat the party to celebrate. The Abba film was put on again and everybody tried their best, but it was futile.

I understand both the wonderful ents officer and bar manager were later sacked. Some people are just bloody killjoys.

TALKING OF KILLJOYS

On 22nd November 1990 which was my birthday, two things happened that were intrinsically linked. We finished the recording part of the *30 Something* sessions and Margaret Thatcher, without whom most of the songs on it would have been instrumentals, resigned. My muse had gone.

This is what I wrote about her in my rantzine *Art Wank And 6th Form Poetry* round about 1995.

THATCHER

It was my thirtieth birthday, we were halfway through recording our second great pop album, when The Antichrist decided to hand in her notice. I should have done a cartwheel, put another candle on the cake and got fantastically drunk. But I put the candles and the cartwheel on hold. I wanted to see the stake through the heart, the smoking pistol with the missing silver bullet or, at least, get a look at Peter Cushing's Polaroids.

Margaret Thatcher - Milk Snatcher, Iron Lady, the girl next door who lived above a grocer's shop and had to eat Spam for Christmas.

I definitely got a lot of inspiration from her, as far as songwriting was concerned. Two whole bands' worth of hatred and bile, set to music, recorded and sold - we were a small business, she would have been proud of us. But we couldn't go to the dentist, get a decent education or ever get to perform at one of those free GLC concerts or enjoy one of their over-the-top Bonfire Night fireworks displays. She was basically a spoilsport who turned selfishness and single-bloody-mindedness into an Olympic sport, she set the standards that helped to lower ours. I don't know for sure but I have my suspicions that if it wasn't for Margaret Thatcher Wet Wet Wet would never have made it past the fourth week at Number 1.

My mum really didn't like her. Whenever Thatcher was on the TV it was almost too much for my mother. She'd bang the arm of the settee ranting about, 'That bloody woman!', which was the only thing my mum ever referred to that bloody woman as. I don't know what it was that made Margaret Thatcher so aggravating. The clothes? The smile? That hairstyle? The patronising manner that would have made Cilla cringe? A voice more irritating than Whitney Houston's? All this and politics too.

CHRISTMAS 1987

I remember cycling down to the DHSS in Norwood Junction, it was nearly Christmas, the padlock for my bike was frozen and I didn't have any WD40 (only a UB40, ha ha ha!). Anyway, I left my unsecured bike outside Kwiksave hoping that all the Kwiksavers would keep an eye on it for me. It was still there seven hours later when I left the dole office, fed-up and empty-handed, having spent the whole day sat on an orange plastic bucket seat , fighting off bored children, growing a fantastic beard, waiting for my number to come up, and wishing I'd brought a good book with me (maybe *War And Peace*).

I was finally seen by the clerk and told to come back tomorrow. I think I managed to get a Giro the day before Christmas Eve, so I could cash it just in time to nip down the shops and get some Spam.

I held Margaret Thatcher personally responsible for my long hours at the dole office and, quite frankly, for just about everything else that depressed or frustrated me at the time.

Before she left office she made herself a Baroness, I would have made her walk the plank.

My muse had gone.

SMART BOMBS
AND STUPID PEOPLE

In a dimly lit underground room deep beneath a tobacconists in the centre of Baghdad, Saddam Hussein is plotting the downfall of the indie pop band Carter The Unstoppable Sex Machine. He begins by invading Kuwait, provoking the United Nations to issue a deadline for him to get the fuck out and go home. The deadline was 14 January 1991, the release date for the Carter USM single *Bloodsport For All*.

THIS IS MY WAR DIARY:
Day 1: Wednesday, Jan 16
As the first laser-guided smart bomb of the Desert Storm campaign heads towards the Iraqi forces in Kuwait, the BBC bans the Bloodsport For All single from the radio. It also bans any songs that could be in any way war-related - in fact it made a list:

> Jose Feliciano & The Doors - *Light My Fire*
> Something Happens - *Parachute*
> The Cure - *Killing an Arab*
> Little Angels - *Bone Yard*

And the following were among those included on a much longer list that were deemed 'unsuitable' to play during the Gulf Crisis:

> Abba - *Waterloo*
> Alarm - *68 Guns*
> Bangles - *Walk Like An Egyptian*
> Pat Benetar - *Love Is A Battlefield*
> Blondie - *Atomic*
> Cher - *Bang Bang (My Baby Shot Me Down)*
> Eric Clapton - *I Shot The Sheriff*
> Phill Collins - *In The Air Tonight*
> Cutting Crew - *I Just Died In Your Arms Tonight*
> Desmond Dekker - *Israelites*
> Frankie Goes To Hollywood - *Two Tribes*
> Elton John - *Saturday Night's Alright For Fighting*
> John Lennon - *Give Peace A Chance* and *Imagine*
> Jona Lewie - *Stop The Cavalry*
> Lulu - *Boom Bang A Bang*
> Rick Nelson - *Fools Rush In*

Nicole - *A Little Peace*
Queen - *Killer Queen* and *Flash*
B.A. Robertson - *Bang Bang*
Kenny Rogers - *Ruby (Don't Take Your Love To Town)* ???!!!
Specials - *Ghost Town*
Edwin Starr - *War*
Status Quo - *In The Army Now* and *Burning Bridges*
Rod Stewart - *Sailing*
Tears For Fears - *Everybody Wants To Rule The World*
10 CC - *Rubber Bullets*

Also Massive Attack dropped the word 'Attack' from their name during the gulf war and became simply 'Massive', while Bomb the Bass didn't get a whole heck of airplay either.

Now I agree with less Clapton and Collins on the radio at the best of times but some of this was a bit of an over-reaction. We were also asked to not talk about the war when we were interviewed on the radio; DJs had already been sacked for doing so. The whole country was stuck in an episode of *Fawlty Towers*. Conversely, when we went to do press in Germany and Holland, the radio's reaction there was the exact opposite. *Because* there was a war on they *were* playing *Give Peace A Chance* and while we were Sellotaping the front cover of *The Sun* newspaper to our windows the Germans were hanging out white flags and peace symbols.

Day 2: Thursday, Jan 17
Saddam Hussein declares: 'The mother of all battles is under way.'
Carter play a 20-minute live set at the *HMV* megastore in Oxford Street which ends in chaos with people crowd surfing and climbing up onto the record racks to dive off from A-ha to Cher to Devo to Genesis. Piles of CD cases are knocked over and trashed and eventually somebody from *HMV* cuts the electricity and stops the gig. Everyone starts hissing and booing and Jon Beast is asked to go onstage to calm things down. He does so by announcing, 'FEEL FREE TO SHOPLIFT NOW!' and they had to close the shop. The store's manager told me that it was worse than when Bros had played there.

Day 4: Saturday, Jan 19
US troops raid oil platforms off Kuwait, capturing first Iraqi prisoners of war.
Carter appear at *The Great British Music Weekend* at Wembley Arena

with The Cure, Jesus Jones, Ride, The Wedding Present, New Model Army and Billy Bragg. We spent most of the day hiding in a wardrobe in the dressing room from Billy Bragg - who wanted to talk to us about the war - and also from the show's organizer and Carter fanatic Jonathan King who had been raving about us in his music column in *The Sun* newspaper called *Jonathan King's Bizarre* (nobody could argue with that). Back in 1991 King was only a hate figure because of the way he talked, for releasing *Una Paloma Blanca* and discovering Genesis.

After we played that day I got in an argument with a member of the Wembley Arena security who wouldn't let me into the seats to watch The Cure. I'd had too much to drink and when my waving my pass in front of his face and shouting, 'It says Access *ALL* Areas!' argument failed, I tore my pass in half and threw it on the floor in front of him. Later I'd have to go back and pick it up and stick it back together to avoid spending the rest of the night sat in the dressing room on my own. When I die I expect to be greeted at the Pearly Gates by Saint Peter in a black bomber jacket: 'It says Access *ALL* Areas!' I'll remonstrate as he refuses to let me backstage to meet God.

Day 13: Monday, Jan 28
Iraq says captured Allied pilots have been injured in Allied bombing raids.
Me and Fruitbat go to Brussels for a week of interviews and radio shows, glad to get away from the TV.

Day 14: Tuesday, Jan 29
US and Soviet Union issue communiqué offering Iraq cease-fire if it makes 'unequivocal commitment' to withdraw.
Carter in Amsterdam.

Day 16: Thursday, Jan 31
Saudi and Qatari troops, backed by US artillery, retake Khafji, Saudi Arabia.
Cologne.

Day 21: Tuesday, Feb 5
Syrian troops, in first combat action, repulse Iraqi probe at Saudi-Kuwait border.
We play a gig for CND at The New Cross Venue with Billy Bragg (he found us in the Wembley wardrobe).

Day 30: Thursday, Feb 14
United Nations Security Council meets in closed session to discuss war.
We headline a rammed cancer relief benefit gig at the University of London Union along with The Family Cat, Bleach, Th' Faith Healers and secret surprise guests EMF. The secret is out and an unsympathetic Carter crowd see EMF as a pop threat and as we sit in the dressing room before the doors are open we can hear the queue singing 'We're gonna get EMF!' Nothing prepares us for what follows however as they take the stage to a hail of plastic glasses, beer and at least one plank of wood. The Mef play on bravely in spite of the barrage, occasionally jumping into the crowd to hit back. Backstage after and EMF seemed to have enjoyed the experience, saying it was their best ever gig. I was embarrassed by what had happened and, looking for someone to blame, end up in a scuffle with EMF's *EMI* A&R man. The papers called the gig 'The Saint Valentine's Day Massacre'; it's the beginning of a long friendship between Carter and EMF.

Day 34: Monday, Feb 18
Air Force helicopter rescues US pilot who parachuted 40 miles north of Saudi border.
30 SOMETHING released to rave reviews.

Day 36: Wednesday, Feb 20
Baghdad Radio says Foreign Minister Tariq Aziz will travel to Moscow with Saddam Hussein's reply to Soviet peace proposal.
Jim Bob receives 'Dundee kiss'.

Day 40: Sunday, Feb 24
The Queen, in first wartime broadcast of 39-year reign, tells country she has prayed for victory.
We try to repeat Abba party at Huddersfield Poly to celebrate *30 Something* entering the charts at Number 8. We fail.

Day 43: Wednesday, Feb 27
President Bush declares suspension of offensive combat and lays out conditions for permanent cease-fire.
We play an uneventful gig at Keele University.

1991 WAS A PALINDROMIC YEAR

In the 1991 *Melody Maker* End of Year Readers' Poll we were voted Number 1 Best Live Act. We also came equal tenth with Paul Gasgoigne as Prat of The Year. I hope the following chapter helps to explain why.

'And they say it in Mexico, London and Jericho, Berlin and Birmingham, Belfast and Tokyo, Amsterdam, Vietnam, Iran, Afghanistan, Disneyland, Narnia, former Yugoslavia.'
The Music That Nobody Likes - Carter USM

I don't know what the gig scene is like in either Jericho, Vietnam, Iran or Afghanistan and we didn't quite make it to Mexico, although San Diego is bloody close. Our trip to Disneyland did actually only entail us driving past it on the motorway into Tokyo and Jon Beast going there on his day off to buy some Minnie Mouse ears to go with the big spotted dress he'd wear at Reading Festival later that year. And even if we could have got the tourbus up my stairs we'd never have got it through the doors of my wardrobe, so Narnia was out of the question.

But in 1991 we had a fair crack at the rest.

FORMER YUGOSLAVIA

When we arrived in the Bosnian town of Banja Luka it was still in Yugoslavia. Mega City 4 had been caught up in rioting a week earlier in the Serb capital Belgrade and tensions right across the Balkans were high. We were told how people still kept guns under their pillows at night in case of attack from neighbouring Serbs, Croats, Slovenes, Macedonians, Montenegrins, Turks, Communists, Nazis, Martians etc. If you look in an encyclopaedia under Yugoslavia you'll probably find the words *'turbulent history'*. Yugoslavia had had a turbulent history. The Banja Lukan gig was in an old converted bomb shelter and before we played we ate pizza in the dressing room which was also an indoor rifle range.

And on the subject of guns. The previous night we'd been in Zagreb on a stage in the courtyard of The Jabuka Club (The Apple Club), just up the road from the presidential palace where a crucial meeting about the current Serb/Croat troubles was taking place. The noise from the soundcheck was disrupting the meeting and a small troop of soldiers was sent down to the venue to check out what was happening.

Seeing that we were no great threat to national security, just two soldiers were left behind to guard the stage and check we didn't stop the gig to lead the audience out of the club and on into the centre of Zagreb, where we would march on the Presidential Palace, burst through the doors and bring down the government. But if they were looking for trouble, they'd come to the wrong place. I'm terrified of guns and - in particular - bullets, and not really understanding the political situation and how volatile things might be we thought we'd better show the army a bit of respect and not do anything dumb that might be somehow misconstrued and get us shot. So Jon Fat and Cantankerous Beast introduced us completely naked but for a *Pepsi Cola* cup over his not so private parts. The soldiers looked on poker-faced and remained so for the rest of the gig, standing guard at the side of the stage, their rifles over their shoulders, desperately trying not to tap their feet. Or shoot us.

Our last Yugo date was in Maribor which today is in Slovenia. The club was in the middle of a rough-looking housing estate, there wasn't a proper PA and we didn't think it would be possible to play. The promoter fell to his knees and pleaded with us to go ahead with the gig because if we didn't, he would lose those knees. So to save his leg elbows we improvised. We plugged the tape machine into a small guitar amp for sound onstage and, with a couple of speakers borrowed from another Maribor club, the packed gig went ahead. When we went to the other club after the gig we could see the two rectangular patches of new paint on the wall, previously protected from the harsh fading properties of the light by a pair of hi-fi speakers. There was no music.

Our time in what would later be the former Yugoslavia was a humbling experience. We made a lot of friends (we dedicated our *1992 The Love Album* to them) including our guide Ante who would soon have to flee his home and family in Croatia to escape the war. We'd meet him again every time we played in Amsterdam where he was living, still unable to return home. We'd go back to Croatia twice later. I'll tell you all about it in a while.

BERLIN

Every time we went to Berlin after our 1990 trip we'd usually play at a club called The Loft and after the show we'd walk round the corner to The Irish Bar. There was a great atmosphere there and they did cheese toasties in little baskets. We went there on 14th April with John Williams from *Chrysalis* to celebrate the new record deal we'd just signed back at The Loft. Apart from the truckload of advance cash we were going to get, *Chrysalis* also bought us a photocopier. It's still photocopying to this day and I probably used it to make duplicates of this book so I could give it to publishers.

AND BIRMINGHAM

At the Birmingham Hummingbird, while I was stood at the side of the stage watching Pop Will Eat Itself play their secret support slot, I noticed a broken light switch on the wall and a lot of exposed wiring. Throughout the Poppies' set I had to fight against the powerful urge to touch the open wires. I've had this kind of compulsion before when I was a small boy and I put my hand on a very hot iron (100% cotton setting), severely burning myself. And if I'm on the big wheel or a rollercoaster when it stops and I'm stranded a hundred feet off the ground, I really have to stop myself from climbing out of my seat and falling to my stupid death. I don't know where this all comes from, I'm not a fan of danger, I'm no bungee-jumper or free-faller. Although after the iron incident I was treated like Ralph Fiennes in *The English Patient* and my mum rewarded my daredevil dumbness with penny sweets, cherryade, colouring books and a *Dinky Toy Tonibell ice cream van*. I've still got the ice cream van today although I've lost the Dinky ice cream man. My older sister Vicky never really got over this spoilt younger brother incident.

BELFAST...

By the end of 1991 the rapidly expanding Crazy Carter crew were travelling and sleeping in a big Cliff Richard double-decker tour bus. The band travelled with tour manager Terry in their new *Renault Espace* and stayed in posh hotels. The bus and crew had to be at the venue earlier and earlier in the day to set up the ever more elaborate stage and me, Les and Terry usually had to be on the other side of town to do interviews and so the poncey car and hotels were merely practical. And we didn't like getting up in the morning. On the way to Dublin McGonagles in the winter of '91, the car in front of us pulled up sharply at a red traffic light and we drove our lovely new people carrier into the back of it. We had to hire a car to get us to Belfast the next day and Terry was convinced that three men driving across Ireland in a jet black Rover with foreign number plates looked too much like three members of Special Branch driving across Ireland in a jet black.... So when we returned to the car on the night after the Belfast gig, he checked underneath it for explosives.

This was 1991 and we'd seen a lot of television news and armed soldiers patrolling the streets of Britain made me uncomfortable. I'm sure if you lived in Belfast you'd tell me I was an idiot and it's really safe, etc etc. But it's the same as when we talk about living in Brixton and people think we're talking about downtown Beirut or the Bronx. What you don't know may not hurt you, but the little bits you do know can scare the shit out of you.

The most dangerous thing that happened in Belfast was at the gig, where I fell off the stage. Les tells me that this was the first of many times that I did so.

...AND TOKYO

After our first US tour with EMF which I'll get to eventually, I flew back to London to stand in for my father and give my sister Vicky away at her first wedding in Thornton Heath. Before the ink was dry on the register I was off up the M4 to Heathrow again to catch a flight to Japan. I was a jetsetter. A member of the jet set - which according to my dictionary of new words is 'a set of smart rich people who travel the world by jet, seeking a succession of expensive pleasures' - which sounds about right. Tokyo for the first time is an experience, it really was like nowhere else I'd ever been. It was the first time we'd been met at an airport by fans, who gave us chocolates and sweets and hats and teddy bears. They followed us around if we went shopping and would be waiting for us in the lobby of our hotel where they too had booked rooms. I found it a bit claustrophobic sometimes, in spite of my chosen job I'm not that good with crowds.

While we were in Tokyo we did a lot of magazine, radio and TV interviews and the jetlag from my Boston to Tokyo via Thornton Heath round trip began to get the better of me. But any kind of early night was bang out of the question.

The gigs may have been over by 8 pm but we always went out afterwards and usually ended up in a club or a bar on the seventh floor of an office block. This disoriented us and we were always surprised when we finally paid the bill and left, the lift doors opening on the ground floor in the bright morning sun. The three gigs we did on our first Japanese tour - in Tokyo, Nagoya and Osaka at each city's branch of Club Quattro, a few floors up in a shopping centre - were also reached by lift. And the buildings moved. The Osaka Quattro was like the QE2 on a very calm sea, and I felt slightly seasick. It was all to do with anti-seismic control. The high buildings swayed in the wind to protect them from earthquakes.

I don't want to harp on about it but it's an amazing place. Looking out over Osaka at night from the hotel room, Pip our hyperactive lighting man said it was like being on the set of the sci-fi film *Bladerunner*. For the week we were there I don't think I ever had to carry my own bags as we were shuttled across the country in little vans and on the bullet train. And speaking as someone who frequently has to travel from South London to my mum's in West Sussex on a dirty old slam-door *Connex* train, the bullet train is something else.

And walking the streets in the middle of the night looking for a bar, although a lot of people were falling down puking in the gutter drunk, there was no violence. I felt safe there. Despite being the most densely populated nation in the world, Japan is a pretty peaceful place and the only time we experienced any real threat of trouble was from a group of US Marines on shore leave. I'd later get the same feeling of inner-city non-violence and good nature in Australia. I remember seeing a homeless old bloke collapse in a shopping centre in Perth and about four people stopped to help him up! They didn't step over him or set him on fire. I thought I was on the Moon.

One more brilliant thing about Japan was the way they translated our album titles. Japanese students have to learn three different kinds of alphabet, Hiragana, Katakana and Kanji. Hiragana is used only for writing and is based on phonetic symbols with your basic vowels and consonants, while Katakana is used for the names of animals and plants to write foreign words that don't translate into Japanese. It has the same vowels and consonants as Hiragana but it's written differently. And then there's Kanji which is the Chinese characters. And stuff like, for example: 'Ii desu' can mean 'yes please' and also 'no thank you', depending on the gesture or facial expression of the person saying it. I, on the other hand used the same 26 letters to write all the lyrics and titles of everything we ever recorded. Consequently, the title of *101 Damnations* in Japan is apparently *Exploding London Diary*, while *30 Something* is called something like *The Struggle of The Working Classes*. I may have got these the wrong way round but you get the picture.

GILBERT AND JIM

When we played in Osaka we stayed at the Osaka Grand Hotel, where it was against hotel rules to take aspirin in the corridor and where they had spelt out 'OSAKA GRAND WELCOMES GILBERT O'SULLIVAN AND CARTER USM' in plastic letters on a board in the foyer. At least that's what it said until the Carter crew changed it to 'OSAKA GRAND WELCOMES GILBERT O'SULLIVAN AND RATS CUM'.

I was a member of Rats Cum and I'm a Gilbert O'Sullivan fan. Not in an ironic way. I think he's written some fantastic songs. *Alone Again Naturally* and *Nothing Rhymed* are two of the saddest songs ever written. Gilbert O'Sullivan is genuinely big in Japan. So when I was sitting in a Tokyo bar talking to Kaoru from the international division of *Toshiba-EMI* and she told me that Gilbert O'Sullivan was also on the label and how he had a copy of our *1992 The Love Album* and he liked it, I nearly fell off my stool. She suggested that I drive across town to the studio where he was recording to meet him the next day. I was probably fairly drunk and so I said I'd love to; had I been sober I would have been too chicken and would have made up an excuse why I couldn't have made it. The next morning, there was a package and a note from Kaoru waiting for me in the hotel reception. The note told me that Gilbert had left the studio for Narita airport and the package was a boxed set of all his albums from 1971-1977. On the inside lid of the box he'd written, 'To Jim - all the best - Gilbert O'Sullivan'.

So when I left Japan I left a happy man. With my Sake hangover, my signed Gilbert O'Sullivan box set and more chocolates, sweets, hats and teddybears from the fans who'd come back to the airport, this time to say goodbye as we walked through the departure gate to take a flight about three weeks back in time. Back when my sister was still single and we were 20 thousand feet above the Atlantic on the way to the place that was so good they'd named it twice.

USM. USA. EMF.

JFK Airport in New York was named after President John Fitzgerald Kennedy who was assassinated in Dallas, Texas on my third birthday. They say that everyone knows where they were on that day. Well, at the point that the governor of Texas John B Connally's wife Nellie, who was sat on a jump seat in the front of the open top presidential limousine turned round to say, 'You can't say Dallas doesn't love you Mr. President' and three shots rang out, hitting her husband in the back, chest, wrist and thigh and fatally wounding the President, I was tucked up in bed, having the first of many bad gig dreams brought on by all the jelly, ice cream and cake that was digesting in my birthday belly.

We landed at JFK Airport on 9 July 1991 at the start of our first US tour supporting EMF. I'd filled in my customs and immigrations forms on the plane, I'd ticked 'NO' next to the questions about drug convictions and political extremism and in my passport I had my visa ready to be stamped. I was ready to be welcomed into the Big Apple and waved on my way with instructions for my day to be nice. But as I made my way to the front of the queue for immigration and passport control nothing prepared me for the lunatic behind the counter. I told him how long I was planning on staying in the country and where I'd be going and what my business would be while I was there. He looked at his list of stolen passports, wanted criminals, bail-jumpers and undesirables and asked me if I had a criminal record in Canada and I said no. 'You're wanted for some pretty bad shit in Canada.' 'No, not me.' I replied, grinning slightly to emphasize what an obviously insane question this was.

'It says here you murdered someone in Canada.' I continued in the negative, now I was starting to get a bit nervous, who was I being mistaken for? Was a Jim Bob impersonator terrorizing North America? Was I about to be arrested for Murder One? Did they have the death penalty in New York?

'I don't like your hairstyle, boy!' he said and stamped my passport and I walked on into America. On my next visit I'd make sure I wore a hat.

I hate going through customs. I'm not a drug smuggler, I love rare reptiles and would never fold one into the lining of my suitcase. I hate guns. I'm harmless.

So why did I have to put up with the above half-wit because of my hair? Was he a disillusioned amateur barber? Did he write for

NY Hairstyle Monthly? No, he was a customs officer and it's his job. About a year previously as we crossed a remote border into France at 6.30 in the morning we were led one by one into a small room by armed border guards and strip-searched. When I tell people this story they always say, 'What, *finger up the bum !!?'* And then I have to say, 'Well no, not finger up the bum' and then they suddenly look unimpressed. As if standing stark bollock naked in a foreign police station with two armed men who'll only communicate in grunts and gestures of the head, with one of these gestures meaning 'lift up your stark naked bollocks so we can get a better look.' As if that was somehow a walk in the park, something that happens to them everyday. Anyway, as luck would have it, none of us kept things stored up our bums and we were released. But the most sad and pathetic thing of all was that, when they let us go, I was so relieved that I said thank you.

ADRIAN BOSS'S CUSTOMS TIP

Fill your trouser pockets with snotty tissues, sweet wrappers, condom packets and bus tickets. When the rozzers ask you to empty your pockets they'll be so disgusted by all the snotrags, johnnies and poor pocket hygiene that they'll only do a tentative fingertip search before sending you as quick as possible on your merry way.

And the best way back then to smuggle stuff into a country I discovered, was on *Concorde*. Me and Fruitbat flew to the States on one in 1992, because we'd been doing interviews every day for about a year and *Chrysalis* wanted us to do some more in America. We didn't want to go but said we would if we could go on *Concorde*. Record labels don't like spending money but they love wasting it so they said yes. When you flew on *Concorde* you got a hologrammed strip of sellotape stuck on the back of your passport and it was like being in the Masons for the day. We breezed through customs and through the special *Concorde*-only check-in and made our way to the free whisky and sandwiches lounge. Sitting there with all the businessmen and pensioners on their lifetime's ambition trip, we looked like gatecrashers. I think they thought we must have won a *Corn Flakes* competition. And the butler-like air steward, who served us drinks on the surprisingly cramped plane certainly did. At least I didn't see him ask any of the other passengers if they'd like to come into the cockpit to meet the pilot. Still, it was a great flight, ridiculously quick - quicker than sound, actually - we were welcomed with open arms at JFK customs (posh section) and we were given a certificate to prove it had all happened.

Not so in 1991. Still shaken from my near-arrest and deportation before I'd even got into the country, I stepped out into the blazing humidity of New York hustle and bustle. It was my first trip to the States and I found it overwhelming. I felt a bit like I did back at the Queen gig in Hyde Park in the 1970s when Derek Chin had gone to look for a toilet and left me marooned alone in a world of weird.

We were picked up from the airport by a guy called Ray (do you notice the way I've been in America for less than a thousand words and already I'm calling people 'guys'?) who loaded us into an eight-seater *Dodge van* with a *U-Haul* trailer for the gear and drove us to the Mayflower Hotel on Central Park West. After checking in, we shared the lift up to our rooms with Mr Sulu (actor George Takei) from *Star Trek* and when we came down to the hotel bar later, we had a beer with Kirsty MacColl and some dancers from *The Royal Ballet*. Charlie Watts from The Stones was sitting behind us and when we checked out a few days later, various exotic animals from the New York Zoo were checking in for the night before their appearance the next day on a TV chatshow. True story.

We were playing six shows on the East Coast, opening for EMF from Chicago to Boston. Their single *Unbelievable* was at Number 1 in the US pop charts and there really couldn't have been a better time for us to be here with them. Every night there'd be an aftershow party at a club somewhere. The club owners would have roped off a VIP area for the Mef, us and any friends and freeloaders. A lot of the freeloaders didn't really know what EMF looked like, they just knew their song and that it was at the top of the charts. We were frequently mistaken for them and didn't always put people right, I'd pretend I was James from EMF and he'd be Jim Bob from Carter. Andrew Collins from the *NME* put on a cycling hat one night and passed himself off as Fruitbat to confuse people even further. It seemed to those who wanted to believe that they were meeting them, that all British progressive/alternative pop stars and journalists all looked the same. These were the same people who had asked me whether I lived in Downing Street, if I knew Lady Di, whether or not we spoke English in England and did we have a president or a king.

KICKING ARTIE FUFKIN'S ASS

These days, when boy bands, girl bands or boy/girl bands play a gig, they have something called a meet and greet. This is where they get to meet (and greet) and sign autographs for various competition winners, nieces and nephews of the promoter and local sick and orphaned children backstage before the show. In our day, a meet and greet was strictly an American phenomenon. All the employees from the record label, along with various journalists, DJs and the manager of the local Virgin Megastore would come into our dressing room after the gig to shake our hands and tell us how we rocked. This happened every night with varying degrees of sincerity. I'm sure the same sales rep who high-fived us in Cleveland on Friday and told us we were the greatest kick-ass rock'n'roll band he'd seen in his entire life, would be doing the exact same thing on Saturday night backstage with Mike And The Mechanics. Because we were British this kind of thing made us feel uncomfortable. We didn't have to do it anywhere else and hadn't had the practice so we weren't particularly good at it. In fact we were probably the worst PR people in the country. I don't know if this lack of transatlantic brown-nosing stopped us being a huge success over there or if was because our music was - as everyone kept telling us - too English.

Every time we toured the States it was with a different record label. We'd sit in a big office with a loud man, who'd inform us that we were the next Jesus Jones and his number one priority, destined for very big things. A special breakfast celebration would be held in the boardroom and we'd be introduced to the record company staff. A few months later we'd be back. We would have been moved sideways to another subsidiary of the label because we were 'too English' and we'd have a whole new boardroom full of new people to meet for croissants and coffee. It was like starting over. Over and over again. Incidentally, I'm not even English. I'm Scottish. I was born and raised in London but my Dad was from Edinburgh and since I was a boy, in spite of my birthplace I've always considered myself to be Scots. I'm the indie Rod Stewart. Or as Fruitbat would put it, a 'Scotch git.'

TORTOISE HEAD

We returned to the States with EMF in November for a tour of American Universities. The gigs were usually in huge basketball courts and we got there on a bus. American tour buses are single-deckers. It's because of all the low bridges. To make up for their lack of height they go to town on length, width and... *Jesus! ... look at the air-brushed and busty blonde astride the Harley Davidson following a flaming (literally) red guitar down the immaculate paintwork on the side and just check out the Gerry Anderson's Space 1999 interior!* Climb aboard and meet the driver, what a character, Reg Varney would have been proud. He says he was a Vietnam vet, even though he's only 22. He drives a bus because he loves it, he doesn't need the money. He's practically a millionaire. And he takes no shit.

We used to go to *Taco Bell* in the middle of the night for aftershow 59 cent bean burritos to keep us going (ooer) as we made our way to the next town. At a *Taco Bell* drive-thru on such a night, we had to all pile out of the bus to jump up and down on the button in the middle of the road that lets the bloke with the microphone taking the orders know there's a car full of hungry people waiting to be served. We weren't heavy enough to trick him into believing we were a car and as it was a drive-thru and not a walk-thru, they wouldn't serve us. But when our driver came over and told them that if they didn't take our order, he was going to 'drive his fucking bus right through their fucking restaurant' they changed their minds. Most tour bus drivers - American or otherwise - are like this. They are fearless. As a passenger you should never upset them. They are in control of your house, which is actually their house, that you're hiring. You should treat it with a bit of respect. More so than a hotel or dressing room which decades of rock'n'roll tradition allow you to mess up. Above all, you should never do a number two in the bus toilet, because it won't flush and the driver will have to put on the Marigolds and remove it by hand.

I won't dwell on this, but I can't think of many more unpleasant feelings than waking up in the morning in a bunk bed on a no-solids-in-the-toilet bus that's heading down a motorway with absolutely no chance of stopping for the next fifty miles, when you've got the threepennies.

AND WHILE WE'RE ON THE SUBJECT...

One of my worst travel experiences was on a ferry across the North Sea which was so rough that I got stuck on the stairs on the way back from the bar to the place where we were sitting while I struggled to stay upright whilst holding onto two pints of beer, the handrail of the stairs and the contents of my stomach. Pretty much everyone on the ferry had either thrown up, was throwing up or thinking about it. Either in the toilets or the sinks, which were all blocked up with puke. Or into paper sick-bags, duty-free carriers or just wherever they happened to be at the time, the whole place stunk. It was disgusting, it's making me feel nauseous just writing about it. I think I'll go up on deck and wait for a seagull to fly alongside so that it looks like it isn't moving at all. I love that.

And one more ferry tale before we get back to the EMF tour: On a boat home from Dublin at 7 in the morning there was not only breakfast bingo in the bar but also a disco, where the DJ badgered a famous Irish singing priest to come up and do a couple of numbers. The picture is so vivid in my mind that I hope I'm not just telling you about an episode of *Father Ted* that I saw.

Back on tour with EMF, every night we had to battle with the booze and fags police. There were strict no alcohol or cigarettes rules on the Uni campuses and this would sometimes extend as far as the bands' dressing rooms. These were strict rules that we were going to be flouting. We had to be clever. As the security patrolled the venue with their torches looking for drink and smoke offenders, we'd hide our beer bottles behind our backs and in our pockets like naughty schoolboys. And somewhere along the way I even bought myself a plastic LA Raiders sports drinks bottle and seeing as my sport was ROCK, I filled it up with whisky that I sucked up through the special sports straw attachment right in front of those unsuspecting campus cops. My God, we must have been desperate for a drink.

And on one of these campuses we were invited to a party after the gig. Up until that night I'd always believed that *National Lampoon's Animal House* and all other movies in the crazy 'frat-house' genre were highly exaggerated works of fiction.

Aside from all the University basketball shows there were other gigs in less sports/educational venues, like the Roseland Ballroom in New York. After the gig there we stayed the night at The Paramount Hotel. It was designed by someone called Phillipe Starck for someone else called Ian Schraeger, it was a minimalist's dream. It was designed so that when you're booked into the smallest room (which is really bloody small) you won't notice because you'll pay more attention to the designer lamp or the screen printed canvas above the bed. Why didn't they just make the rooms bigger instead? If it's possible for a building to be up its own arse, then that's exactly where The Paramount Hotel was. And we made the place look untidy. They told us so. Every time we put a drink down on a table we were asked by the concierge to remove it because it messed with the interior decorating. If we wanted to put *Coca Cola* cans on the table we should go stay at the Ho Jo.

Next door to the hotel there was a bar that was owned by a brat-pack actors' collective including Rob Lowe. The waitresses took the New York reputation for bad service and manners very seriously indeed. The one who served us drinks all night was rude, sarcastic, tactless and offensive. We really liked her. Her party trick was to spill a drink all over me and then tell me off for it. I presume it was a party trick, as she did it three times.

That night I couldn't sleep for all the noise from the police sirens outside and also because the minimalist room design with all its chrome bathroom fittings and harsh lighting made me feel like I was banged up in a cell at Wandsworth Prison. I stayed up all night and wrote the lyrics to Watching *The Big Apple Turn Over* for the B-side of *The Only Living Boy In New Cross,* all about how I felt that night in the New York Paramount Hotel. Have a listen, it's cheaper than booking a room.

The tour finished at the Universal Amphitheatre at the Universal Studios theme park in LA. We weren't allowed to use our wireless packs for our guitars that night as the radio signals might have interfered with the explosive special effects of the *Miami Vice Stunt Spectacular* show next door, setting them off and killing the doppelganger Crockett and Tubbs who we saw flying through the air in a speedboat on our way in. I haven't played many gigs that can boast a *Conan The Barbarian Indoor Stage Spectacular with Special Effects,* an *Old Wild West Town Outdoor Comedy Stunt Show,* the *Animal Outdoor Show with Performing Trained Show Animals doing Tricks and Stunts* as well as other attractions including *Battlestar Galactica* and *King Kong.* For some reason it never occurred to us to get there a bit earlier in the day so we could go on the rides but I did go back a few years later on a day off. It was fantastic.

SOME OTHER HIGHLIGHTS AND LOWLIGHTS OF 1991

1. To celebrate the success of *30 Something*, *Rough Trade Records* threw a small party in their office and seeing as how everyone was gathered together they took the opportunity to make half their staff redundant - including new employee and original Carter roadie Angus Batey, who had resigned from his previous job less than one week earlier and was probably beginning to wish that he had never met Carter for they had surely put the hex upon his life – sacking half the guests wasn't good for party atmospherics. Neither was the *Rough Trade* hi-fi which only had one speaker. When you're in a band and you've spent weeks trying to make your new record sound amazing and you're finally satisfied that you're somewhere near to achieving this, you take it in to play to your label to blow their minds. At *Rough Trade* they only got to hear the left side of *30 Something*. At *Chrysalis*, we had to re-master *After The Watershed* three times before we realized their record player's needle was broken and our manager Adrian Boss used to listen to new CDs through the little speaker on the front of his computer monitor.

2. In August we made our legendary Reading Festival appearance. It was probably our most perfect ever gig. We went on second top of the bill before James, who had chosen to follow our crowd-pleasing set with some mellow new songs and experimental jazz versions of their hits. Music should never be a competition but at Reading in 1991 we won. Even the journalists who hated us had to concede that we were the festival favourites. We got paid a lot of money to play and we spent most of it on the lightshow which God was in on. Jon Beast spoke to God and God had a word with the Sun and got it to set behind the crowd at exactly the right moment during *GI Blues*. Winston Churchill, who was stood at the back in between the signing tent and the crepe stall, said it was 'our finest hour.'

And 3. We were sued by The Rolling Stones' publisher for using the words 'Goodbye Ruby Tuesday' in the chorus of our single *After The Watershed*. Some people have got no sense of humour.

HOTEL. MOTEL. HOLIDAY INN. MRS MIGGINS'

Before the high art-high rise-accommodation of The New York Paramount we got to stay awake all night in a lot of different places. On a long drive back from Cornwall one night we parked the car in a field and tried to get some sleep. Adrian was incredibly dedicated to the Carter cause: without him none of the events in this book would have been given the opportunity to happen. And that night in the field as me and Fruitbat slept in the car, Adrian slept underneath it. This was a man who must have taken *Roy Castle's Record Breakers* theme song very seriously.[8]

When we weren't parked in a field, most of our first nights away from home were spent in sleeping bags on the living room floors of the audience. We couldn't afford hotels, so if we couldn't kip at the promoter's flat or at a friend's house we'd have to put out a request for floor space during the gig and just hope that there were no serial killing students in the audience who'd be delighted to 'have us' stay the night. Most of the time our hosts were not just good but *lovely* samaritans who'd make us feel very welcome and let us stay up half the night watching Pete Waterman on *The Hitman And Her.*[9] However, occasionally we'd be invited to spend the night with the most obnoxious person in town who merely wanted to show off to their more permanent flatmates by going to a gig and bringing the band back home with them afterwards. When this happened we'd invariably spend a few hours cruelly taking the piss out of them until they went to bed, leaving us to sneak into their kitchen to look for the *Marmite* and *Jaffa Cakes*.

There was never any *Marmite* or *Jaffa Cakes*. Or coffee or tea. Or milk or sugar. I'm generalising here, but a lot of flat-sharing students do live like they're in an episode of

[8] *Dedication*
[9] *The Hitman And Her* was a late night TV programme, presented by pop producer/expert Pete Waterman and bubbly Children's TV dish Michaela Strachan from real discotheques all over Britain. The show featured drunk geezers and their scantily-clad-girlfriends dancing badly and gurning at the camera, and also dance competitions ('Showing Out'), bad karaoke ('Pass The Mic') and games like 'Kiss, Cuddle and Feel' , where a blindfolded bloke had to touch up a line of women and identify which one was his girlfriend (who would leave him after the show for touching up other women.) Pete Waterman is one of those people for whom it's difficult to look back at all his old television appearances and laugh at how funny he looked back in those crazy, bad-taste 1980s. He looked like a dickhead then and he looks like a dickhead now.

The Young Ones. The only time the washing up was in danger of being washed up was when Carter came to stay and Fruitbat did it. He always liked to get up to his elbows in hot soapy water before we left, perhaps destroying the cure for the common cold that had been growing in the cracked mugs blocking up the kitchen sink for the past six months. Then if we could find any coffee we could all have a cup. And if there was any milk in the fridge that wasn't too far past its use-by date, we could have it white. 'Cheese and two sugars?'

THE DOOBIE BROTHERS

We once spent a night with a bunch of Cambridge University toff Carter fans who smuggled us into their student residence through a window. They kept us up until we left at nine in the morning, smoking their way through a lorryload of hashish, marijuana, Lebanese gold, Mexican green, Turkish pollen, ganja, mootah, mooter, mother nature's own, sinsimilla, homegrown bad-shit, wacky backie and weed. They smoked it in spliffs and pipes and bongs and various Coke cans, skoofers and doobies, never once falling asleep or climbing back out the window to walk down to the all night garage for a *Mars* bar. They used to go to a lot of our gigs and they were a great bunch of blokes. I wonder where they are now. Probably the Houses of Parliament.

Or the church. We stayed in a vicar's house once. He was away on holiday and his son had invited us back after a gig. He had too much to drink and started melting his dad's record collection in the microwave. When the vicar returned from his holiday there must have been hell to pay (or at least a harsh version of Heaven).

Another Carter accommodation story that actually made it into the newspapers was when we stayed the night round someone's house in Stockton Upon Tees. We were woken up at five in the morning by the vice squad. They'd heard that snuff videos were being copied and sold from the house and were confiscating all the tapes as evidence. The bloke whose house it was did copy and sell videos but they were music videos. And in amongst them were a number featuring the ska-punk band 'Snuff'. It was all a hilarious forehead-slapping mix-up and was soon explained to the police and they left. We later sued the bloke for selling bootleg Carter videos. It was time to move up the accommodation chain.

MRS MIGGINS' (NO-STAR BED AND BREAKFASTS)

Mrs Miggins is the B&B everywoman. She runs all the bed and breakfasts and guesthouses in Great Britain. We named her after a character in *Blackadder.* Mrs Miggins is the stern Yorkshirewoman who wouldn't let us back in after the gig because it was later than 11 o'clock and the couple in Liverpool who've been up since the crack of dawn cooking sausages and bacon only to be told when we finally crawl out of bed long after morning has broken, that we're all vegetarians. Mrs Miggins is also the posh widow with the huge house in Cambridgeshire who's fallen on hard times and has had to let out her bedrooms to dirty rock bands. She's laid out the breakfast table with all her best silver cutlery and bone china teacups and saucers because they're the only cutlery and teacups and saucers that she owns.

We once got snowed in at a B&B in Birmingham. We were there for two days, we had to cancel a gig in Bolton and the only way we could pass the time was to play *Monopoly* with an old set we found under the bed until it was late enough to trudge through the thick snow to the nearest pub for a couple of pints and a snowball fight with local students, before returning to the guest house to continue - but never finish - our game of *Monopoly*. Our vehicle was incapacitated and we were trapped in a snowbound old house run by a large landlady with a short temper with no telephone or means of escape, it was like the film *Misery* (without Kathy Bates, the hobbling or the iron pig). (the typewriter, the tranquilisers, James Caan, Richard Farnsworth lying dead in the cellar, she wasn't our number one fan etc) (It was nothing like the film *Misery*.)

MENEER MIGGINS[10]

In Nijmegen, Holland the promoter always used to put us in the same hotel, it was the worst one in the country. It was run by a Norman Bates character whose best friend was his talking parrot - I don't know what it said, it was Dutch. Everything Norman did for his guests he did reluctantly, whether it was handing over door keys or boiling you an egg for your breakfast. After our gig at the club up the road I came back to the hotel and found a fat dutch businessman fast asleep in my bed. When we managed to talk Basil Fawlty into reluctantly coming upstairs to have a look he just told the bloke to get out of the bed and went back downstairs to his parrot. It took a lot of complaining to get him to eventually give me another room as he couldn't understand why I didn't want to get into my already-slept-in-by-overweight-smelly-Dutch-businessman bed. Eight months later, we'd be back in Nijmegen and lo and behold, same hotel. If you ever visit the charming Dutch town and find yourself booked into a hotel that's run by an old misery guts and his parrot, please say hello (the parrot might even reply).

[10] Dutch for Mister Miggins

MOTEL

After the sticky living room-floors of student towns and in between the bed and breakfasts and the Dorchester are the motorway Travelodges and Travel Inns, the Crossroads motels. For a very reasonable amount of money - if you keep moving around when you're checking in at two in the morning so the night receptionist can't count you - you can squeeze about five people in a room for the price of two. I've noticed recently that the management of these places has got wise to this practice and have done their best to make things as unwelcoming and uncomfortable as possible for anymore than one lonely travelling salesman/indie pop star per room. Just two sachets of decaffeinated *Nescafe* (enough for nearly one cup) and a kettle that, although it is so small, takes almost half an hour to boil. The wheelie mattress that rolls out from under the sofa is now a lot shorter than it used to be and would only really suit a small child or Kylie Minogue. But having said all this, you can get a good night's sleep and wake up in the morning feeling refreshed, pick up your stinking gig trousers from the *Corby Trouser Press*,[11] collect your complimentary copy of the day's Tory propaganda broadsheet from outside your room and walk the fifty yards across the car park through the pouring rain to the *Little Chef* to order your *American Style Breakfast* (without the bacon and with beans instead).

FRED MAUS AND JOHNNY LAW

In 1991 when the stage collapsed during the soundcheck at a gig in Newcastle we had to pull the gig. We went back to our hotel which was about a hundred yards up the road. Later in the evening as the audience were turned away from the venue some of them decided to take a stroll up to the hotel to see if we were staying there

[11] Although the Corby Trouser Press was invented by John Corby way back in 1930, unless you've ever spent a night in an English hotel, it's likely that you've never seen one. Usually wall-mounted or hidden away in the wardrobe with the theftproof clothes hangers and spare blanket, the mock teak trouser press does pretty much what its name suggests. You just shut your sweat-soaked trousers - that you've drunkenly screwed up in a ball and hurriedly stuffed into your bag as the venue security are telling you they've got homes to go to and need to lock up - in-between the hinged doors of the trouser press. Set the timer knob to 30 minutes or an hour or so, then sit back and relax while your trousers slowly get ironed. My relationship with the Corby Trouser Press first began when I was working as a messenger for advertising firm Castle Chappell, Pearce & Partners in 1977, when they were working on the campaign for the revolutionary sales-rep strides-care product and I'd like to think that I was in some small way instrumental in helping a touring Paul Weller or Simonon keep his Sta-prest sta-prest.

CELEBRITY CORBY FACT: In a fantastic episode of BBC2's *I'm Alan Partridge*, a bored Alan dismantles his Corby Trouser Press and can't put it back together again.

and maybe have a go at us for not playing. The hotel reception staff were ever so helpful and they gave anybody who turned up and asked for it my hotel room number. After a dozen irate phone calls from angry audience members downstairs in reception and a couple of personal visits to my room, I started to get a tad nervous and had visions of being the victim of the first Geordie lynching of the 20th Century. Largely due to this and our rapidly rising popularity we decided it was time to get some funny aliases for booking hotel rooms. When we were with EMF in America I'd heard Derry checking in as Mr Torpedo and the idea had appealed to me ever since.

It was like choosing a new band name - it had to be right and it took ages. We wanted names that were believable even though we'd know that they were ridiculous. For the next few years I checked into hotels all over the world as Johnny Law (Glaswegian for policeman), while Les became Fred Maus - a rough translation of Fruitbat into German and then back into English via some Chinese whispers - and pronounced Mouse, as in Mickey. This was particularly amusing. We'd often turn up at a hotel reception to check in and the receptionist - terrified of getting it wrong and embarrassing the guests - would say, 'Mister... er... Mister *Morse?* ' to which Fruitbat would reply, 'No it's Mouse actually'. It was like Hyacinth Bucket in reverse.

By now the hotels were getting nobbier. We were getting fussier. We wanted more channels on the TV and a telephone *in* the room. We wanted 24-hour room service and we wanted those 24 hours to be in a row. When we staggered upstairs from the hotel bar - which had to be open later than 11pm - we wanted to be able to have a nightcap from the mini bar. We wanted *Toblerones* and late checkouts. Unfortunately, the price you pay and the number of stars in the window of your hotel don't always relate to the quality of the place. Here's a few tips: Hotels bang in the city centre will be more expensive than those on the outskirts. If they are the same price then they probably won't be as good. Those in the middle of nowhere are invariably a lot nicer but it'll take you hours to find them at two in the morning in the dark, especially if you've got two drunk indie pop stars in the car with you asking you if they're there yet every five minutes. And most importantly of all: You should never judge a book by its cover, or... Nice reception = shit rooms.

In just such a hotel in Sydney Australia, I checked into the plush reception and took the lift up to my sixth-floor slum bedsit where I switched on the hotel TV info-mation channel. It gave me a list of the hotel's services and told me where to go in Sydney, what to do if there's a fire and how, when you're in bed asleep, sometimes cockroaches climb into your open mouth. I was left with two options. Finding some gaffa tape and sealing my mouth shut or staying awake all night staring at the ceiling and walls checking for insects. I didn't have any gaffa tape.

At the Hyatt Hotel on Sunset Boulevard in LA I met Little Richard. He was living there. He had a whole floor all to himself. I was really chuffed that he acknowledged me and said hi as he walked past. He was dressed in purple with a lot of make-up on and - in spite of the fact it was 10 o'clock at night - he was wearing shades. With him were a couple of burly minders who accompanied him outside into the street where they climbed into a king-size stretch limo, both minders and motor directly at odds with his name. Then with a quick honk of the horn *'A wop bop a loo bop a lop bam boom!'* he drove off into the sunset (well, the evening smog) and I never saw him again. I was so excited that I had to go up to my room and ring my mum to tell her that I'd just met Little Richard, *Little bloody Richaaarrddd!* I forgot that it was probably half past four in the morning in England.

Also at The Hyatt, I think - it doesn't matter as it's irrelevant to the story - we were on our way down to the ground floor in the hotel lift when it stopped at the fourth or fifth floor. The doors opened to a completely naked man, standing there with his hands cupped between his legs attempting to hide his embarrassment. He told us that he'd got out of bed in the dark to go to the bathroom and - half asleep - had instead walked out of his hotel room door, locking himself out. He asked us if we could get reception to send somebody up with a master key to let him back in. After two or three minutes of 'Really, Sir?', 'I see', 'A naked guest locked out of his room, you say?' and even a couple of 'Yeah, rights', they sent a porter up to let him in. It's true. It isn't a scene from a Peter Sellers film. It bloody well happened, okay!

ERNIE AND BERT

Before we were in a position to afford single rooms and later double rooms with single occupancy, we used to share. Me and Fruitbat in the same hotel room was something like Ernie and Bert at home on *Sesame Street*. I was Bert and he was Ernie. I could never get to sleep without him wanting to say just one more thing to keep me awake. I suspect nowadays if we shared a room I would be the Ernie character - in fact no, we'd both be Bert. Bert and Bert.

Note 7B: To the best of my knowledge Fruitbat never had a rubber duckie like Ernie had, but he did have a collection of rubbers which he'd accumulated from various vending machines in the toilets of gigs around Europe. You can see part of his collection on the sleeve of *The Only Living Boy In New Cross* single. (Sadly, shortly after the photographs for the sleeve were taken, Fruity's collection of prophylactics was stolen from his hotel room).

I shared rooms with a number of other people from our touring party. I have very vague memories of our nights together but remember these few examples: Me and Jon Fat Beast - with Jon keeping me awake the entire night puking up and then apologizing. Me with Pip, him keeping me awake all night talking, much like Ernie had done. Mad Dog Bottomley at a chalet by a lake in Maribor - in an interesting twist on talking in his sleep - threatened to kill everyone in the room, in his sleep. Early Carter roadie Angus Batey and his dad, who, getting ready for bed, removed his trousers and pants next to me, his bare Cumbrian buttocks a nanometre from my face ruining my chances of sweet dreams and a good night's sleep. And Adrian Boss, who'd stop us from sleeping by grinding his teeth all night and throwing his arms and legs around, gradually freeing himself from his sleeping bag. By the morning he would have escaped completely, lying on his back, legs akimbo, revealing his magic pants (which I might tell you about later) to all the world. Mainly though I remember my worst room mate of all, the one who kept me awake at night the most, the one who almost drove me completely insane... myself.

GOODNIGHT JIM BOB

I've been sleeping with Jim Bob from Carter for a number of years now. I've slept with him in single beds, double beds, kingsize twin beds, bunk beds, camp beds and flower beds. We've slept together in hotels and motels and in the back of cars, vans and buses. We've spent the night together under tables, in fields and in gardens and in at least twenty six different countries in four out of the seven continents of the world. He is crap in bed.

If he's got a day off in a hotel he'd lie awake all night, hoping to make the most of his time away from the confined space of his bus bed and the cheesy honk of the twenty seven socks (someone's only wearing one) of the other fourteen passengers. He's a got a double room all to himself and he wants to relax in the lavender and jasmine *pot pourri* of his Holiday Inn accomodation. He craves some solitary confinement. And he's paying for it. So he might as well get his money's worth by staying awake all night watching CNN rolling news reports and bizarre Spanish gameshows that made no sense back in the days before *Big Brother* and *I'm A Celebrity Get Me Out Of Here!* In the afternoon he may drop off for a couple of hours, only to wake up in the early evening, shivering and confused not knowing what time it is and convinced he's coming down with the flu that's been floating around the bus. So he runs himself a big deep bathfull of bubbles, washes his hair twice and has a really close shave. All the time he'll be having a conversation with his reflection in the mirror which, even primary-school kids will tell you, is the first sign of madness. He washes his socks in the sink and hangs them over the hotel table lampshades to dry. He then nods off again, this time in the bath, which makes him feel awful again when he awakes in two feet of lukewarm water looking like a prune.

After the bath he might call room service and order a cheese sandwich. *A cheese sandwich!!* Even on his day off it's the only thing on the menu. Then it's either down to the hotel bar for a drink with the others or locking himself in his hotel room to channel-hop until the battery in his remote control is flat. When he finally does fall asleep at about 4 am he has these bad-gig dreams until, what seems like about five minutes later, he's woken up by the chambermaid who doesn't understand either *Do Not Disturb, Ne Pas Déranger,* or *Stören Sie Nicht* as she attempts to get through his locked and chained door to Hoover the carpet, change the sheets and put a fresh square of chocolate on the pillow. So he gets up. He's missed breakfast, which he always does because he can't face food first thing in the morning and he'll feel sick for the rest of the day as a result. And then finally, after checking that he's removed his still damp socks from the lamp shades, he'll place a Bible in the bedside table drawer on behalf of *The Gideons* and leave.

BRUSSEL SPROUTS

In the *NME* End of 1991 Readers' Poll we were voted Number 2 Best Band just behind REM. *30 Something* was fifth best album. *After The Watershed* was the sixth best single. The year's Number 6 event was *'Fruitbat vs Phillip Schofield'* with Phillip Schofield as Number 7 bastard of the year. Meanwhile, *'You Fat Bastard"* came in at Number 1 in the word/phrase poll and Carter USM T-shirts were the third most popular fashion items just behind *Doctor Marten's boots* and *Levi 501s.* No wonder we were called a 'T-shirt band'. Everyone thought we'd sold more shirts than records. This wasn't true of course, but for a while it did seem like we were shifting more clothing than some small branches of Marks And Spencers. We even had our own shop *Bizniz Ad* in Kensington Market. It was run by our future drummer Wez, tour-manager Terry's brothers Mad Dog and Johnny, and Big Al - the softly spoken John Candy lookalike who sold shirts with Mad Dog on tour. The shop was opened partly to compete with all the T-shirt bootleggers and also because we didn't sell shirts at London gigs due to the venue merchandise concession charges. The bootleggers were selling a lot of inferior stuff outside the gigs with no refund offered if not completely satisfied. While inside, some of the bigger venues wanted 25% commission on whatever we sold and we didn't want to pass that on to the audience. Consequently we didn't sell shirts at The Brixton Academy when we played there and more famously, at the London Town & Country Club. This led to so much publicity that we received a letter of support from Sting.

OTHER FASHION NEWS

Our 'Mad As Fuck' pastiche of the Inspiral Carpets *Cool As Fuck* shirt led to legal threats and a lasting friendship with the band, with us recording a cover of the Inspirals' classic *This Is How It Feels* for the B-side of *After The Watershed.* Many people think it's the best song we ever wrote.

Our Reading Festival shirts got us into trouble when we took them to America, over a linguistic misunderstanding about the slogan on the back: *Come On Baby Light My Fag.*

The *Posthistoric Monsters* shirt which featured the album sleeve picture of a dinosaur got us in trouble with the *BBC* who claimed we had copied the picture from a cover of the *Radio Times.*

And we had to stop selling the Carter *Road Rage* shirt which featured a picture of the *Michelin Man* holding a baseball bat after we received legal letters from the French tyre company. We were just too darn postmodern for our own good.

We did manage to get away with the shirt with the picture of the Pet Shop Boys from their sleeve for *So Hard* but with a Carter logo and the words *More Hard*. That's one of my favourite Carter shirts, although I suppose it's really a Pet Shop Boys shirt. And our *Rock'n'Roll Is The New Comedy* shirts featuring Bono, Morrissey and Axl Rose with red noses passed without legal heartache. Until now of course.

Without doubt our biggest fashion *faux pas* of all was the Carter cycle cap. Looking out at two thousand people all wearing the same hat was so *Village Of The Dammed/Stepford Wives* that I was almost too scared to look.

BIG NIGE
AND HANDSOME DAVE
THE MAGNIFICENT 7 RIDES AGAIN

Once you've remembered Doc and you can name all of the seven dwarfs you can now have a go at the actors who played *The Magnificent Seven*. Everyone remembers Yul Brynner, Steve McQueen and James Coburn and film buffs can easily make it to six with Charles Bronson, Robert Vaughn and even Brad Dexter. But Horst Bucholz will have most people scratching their heads. Horst is the Doc of The Mag Seven. I'm having the same trouble now remembering the names of all seven members of the West Country security team who went on tour with us and kept us closely protected from nutters, stopped us getting crushed by autograph hunters and made sure we didn't get our heads blown off by T-shirt bootleggers. To be entirely honest, I'm not even sure there were seven of them, but the following movie synopsis doesn't work if there wasn't, so...

THE PLOT

A group of seven hard and highly trained heroes from Somerset ride into town to guard an indie pop group from a bandito gang of T-shirt bootleggers who came to sell their shoddy wares in the streets outside the venue and to steal from the poor peasant Carter folk. The seven, who are magnificent, will teach the Carter townsfolk how to defend themselves and together they will try to rid themselves of the evil gang. Night after night there is a showdown, a gun is pulled but bloodshed and fighting is avoided and eventually the frustrated gang of unofficial tour merchandise banditos move on to the next town and the now more lucrative T-shirts of the rock group Oasis. The seven men and the villagers are at odds, do they stay on? Can the Carter people fight for themselves and if so, at what cost? And most importantly - are the seven men ready to stand in the pit at the front of the stage catching crowd surfers, dressing up in gold thongs and Father Christmas hats, leading the crowd singalongs, squirting water from enormous multi-coloured water pistols and in June of 1992, going on holiday with us.

Newquay, 1992. A rare Phew what a scorcher of a British summer weekend in Cornwall with Fruitbat, Wez (pre Carter drummer days), some Crazy Crew members, our friendly mosh-pit security, two Jeeps, a Land Rover and a seven-man Canadian canoe. It was supposed to be like

Baywatch - beach volleyball, surfing, kicking sand in skinny kids' faces - by day two we were so sunburned that we couldn't walk and spent the rest of the trip hiding under stolen hotel towels covered in aftersun and blisters. We never quite got the hang of the seven-man Canadian, we didn't have the up-the-backside bikinis for proper beach volleyball, how the hell does anyone ever stand up on a surfboard? And as for the skinny kids, they beat the crap out of us. Back at the hotel there was a Liz Taylor lookalike singing Frank Sinatra numbers accompanied by a cheesy organ and drum-machine player. They didn't know any Carter songs and when we asked for some more Frank, Liz Taylor told us to piss off. I bought a wetsuit especially - it cost me forty quid and it hasn't been wet since.

I wrote the above for a free *NME* supplement on pop stars' holidays. And I'm now guessing that, because they brought a seven-man Canadian canoe with them, that there may indeed have been seven of them.

Whatever. Big Nige and Handsome Dave, along with Bobby, Dean, Steve and Kevin and a rotating group of West Country muscle men who took on the Horst Bucholz role, would follow us around on tour, chasing away the bootleggers and keeping us safe from Eli Wallach. They'd also attempt to teach us to surf and to box and when the sun came out they'd let us pose in our sunglasses with the wind in our hair as we drove around town in the back of their open-top Jeeps. They'd get up to all sorts of mischief; every now and then one of them would be ambushed as he stepped from the hotel shower to be covered in shaving foam, pushed naked into the hotel lift and sent down to the ground floor to scare the other guests. If somebody was getting on our nerves they'd lift him up in the air like a baby and swing him around until he stopped getting on our nerves. They gaffa-taped The Family Cat's T-shirt man Matty spread-eagled to a wheelie clothes rail and wheeled him around the St Austell Coliseum where they left him helpless in the middle of the venue. They stopped us getting alsationed to death at the Bizarre Festival and chased Fruitbat around Michael Eavis' farmyard and they made us feel safe and appear a little bit harder than we ever were. But in all the time they were with us, they never took advantage of the fact that they could probably have kicked the crap out of pretty much anybody they'd wanted, including us. De de de der - de de de de der. De de de der - de de de de der. Durrr durrr![12]

<hr />

[12] The lyrics to *The Theme From The Magnificent 7*

IF YOU TALK ABOUT YOURSELF FOR LONG ENOUGH, CHANCES ARE YOU'LL EVENTUALLY HEAR WHAT YOU'RE SAYING AND IT'LL SUDDENLY DAWN ON YOU THAT YOU ARE AN EXTREMELY BORING PERSON AND YOU'LL WANT TO TELL YOURSELF TO SHUT THE FUCK UP.

In 1991 we came top in a table for 'the hardest working bands of the year' printed in the Polytechnics and University Students' Handbook. In 1992 we didn't play a gig until 9th April. We were too busy doing interviews.

We did them in hotels, at gigs, in pubs and on the phone. We were interviewed alone, together, by post and by fax. We chartered a plane to fly UK journalists to Brussels for a press conference and gave them free beer, cheese and photographs at *Mini Europe*. It cost us twenty thousand pounds. We recorded an interview CD which came with a list of questions for local radio DJs to ask us without us having to be there to answer them. They just had to read out the questions and play the CD for our mumbled replies. I've got it in front of me now. Although the questions were written by a good friend of ours, Tony Smith (the first man to ever play Carter on the radio when he played the demo of *A Perfect Day To Drop The Bomb* on GLR, slagging us off for sending it in on a cheap cassette) and I'm sure we probably approved them, but some of them are completely unanswerable. So I've listened to the CD and somehow we've answered every single one. And our answers are even more boring than the questions. If ever there were an argument for the music speaking for itself then this CD is it. If I was a local radio DJ back then I'd like to think that I'd have asked the questions and played the wrong corresponding answers to make us look like idiots and to teach us a lesson for not having the common decency to turn up in person.

These days everybody already knows the answers to the pop questions. Everyone knows how playing live is better than recording, because of the immediate connection between artist and audience. We all know that since the first album the band have matured and how there are a lot of different flavours and musical styles including rock, pop, ballads and R&B on the new record. And we're all surely aware by now that, in spite of the fact that there's a greatest hits album coming out next week, the band are stronger than ever. They're like brothers or sisters and in spite of all the nonsense in the media they have absolutely no intention of splitting up (just before they split up).

People should ask questions like:

1. **What's your least favourite road?**
2. **What did you dream about last night?**
3. **Have you ever vomited on stage?**
4. **Why should you never touch the fruit in EMF's dressing room, especially the limes?**
5. **Who invented the trouser press?**
6. **Have you ever been accused of murder?**
7. **Have you ever cut your own hair?**
8. **Are you left or right handed?**
9. **Have you ever tried to give mouth to mouth resuscitation to a mouse?**
10. **Can I come on tour with you?**

All of these questions have been or will be answered somewhere in this book. The first 25 people to send all ten correct - o.n.o. - answers to JIM BOB PO Box 709 London SE19 1JY will get some sort of prize.

No you can't come on tour with us. Because we've had a few music journalists on tour with us over the years and even if they've been friends and fans of the band, it was always uncomfortable and they were always treated as outsiders. While they were around we had to watch what we did. And anything we said could be taken down and used in evidence against us. Everyone had to behave so we didn't come across like The Macc Lads and occasionally deliberately misbehave in case people thought we were The Osmond Brothers. It was like taking our parents on tour. And they usually took a dump in the bus toilet.

In Steve Lamacq's book *Going Deaf For A Living* he writes about the time he came to Paris to write a live review of Carter and how he was really there to get a sneaky exclusive interview for the *NME* to go with a picture of us on the front cover in order to spoil the *Melody Maker's* exclusive Carter front cover the same week. The gig was with Nine Inch Nails and The Wonderstuff and there were three coach-loads of Stuffies/Carter fans over from Britain on a package trip. As I sat with Steve outside a Paris bar, griping and moaning into his dictaphone about how tough it was being a pop star, the fans walking past us on their way to the venue would look at us, double-take and then about face and come over to our table to say hello. The constant stream of tipsy Englishmen in shorts outside his bar was annoying the owner and he came out and threw a large jug of water over me.

Earlier in the day I'd visited my namesake's grave at Pere Lachaise, where somebody had added the words *'you fat bastard'* and *'Carter USM'* to the other cemetery graffiti. I wonder what it's like to have one of your family buried there and to have all these Doors fans writing all over their gravestones? I wouldn't like it. The gig itself was great and in the dressing room afterwards Fruitbat had a shower with Trent Reznor from Nine Inch Nails. There's no great significance to this fact and there are no more details, I just thought I should tell you. After the gig Fruitbat had a shower with Trent Reznor.

And then we took a taxi to The Locomotive Club which was next door to The Moulin Rouge, to see International Resque. I must have been drunk because I got up onstage with them to sing backing vocals on their song *Yeah!* I'd never done that before and I only did it again in New York at a Mucky Pup gig when they announced that 'we've got a couple of special friends from England in the audience tonight, let's welcome them up onstage now, Jim Bob and Fruitbat.. singing *Wild Thing!*' Neither me nor he knew the song properly and so we just did the same bit over and over again until the ground of the Big Apple finally did the decent thing and swallowed us up. And of course, every night of the second tour with EMF we all used to pile onstage for the encore of 'E - ecstasy! M - mother fucker mother fucker!'.

Steve Lamacq was also with us in America, Croatia and Germany, reporting back to the *NME*, *Q* magazine and Radio One. He was like Judith Chalmers without the tangerine tan.

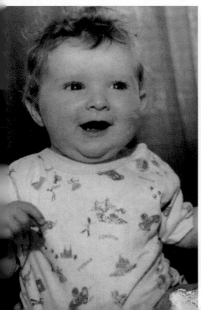

Above: Mum, Dad & Son, pre first shave

Far left: Look at the place names on my babygro, it's a tour babygro

Left: Hard as nails cute as fish

CARTER
■ THE UNSTOPPABLE SEX MACHINE ■

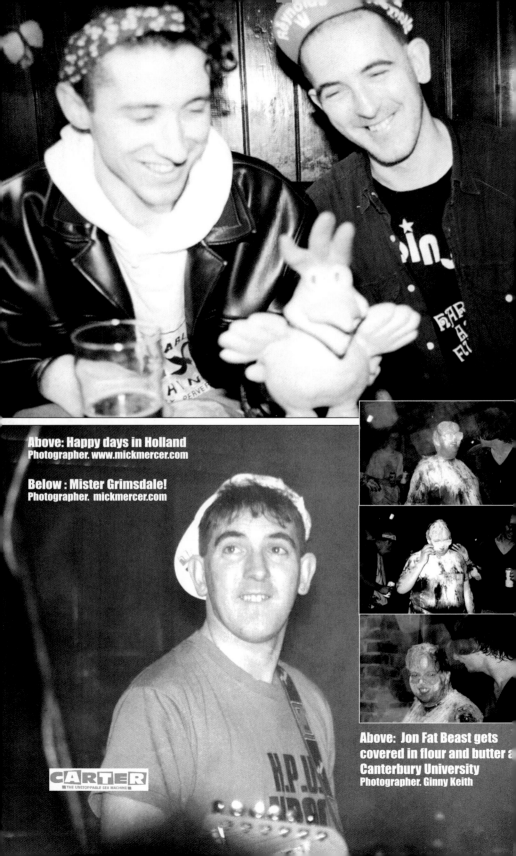

Above: Happy days in Holland
Photographer. www.mickmercer.com

Below : Mister Grimsdale!
Photographer. mickmercer.com

Above: Jon Fat Beast gets
covered in flour and butter a
Canterbury University
Photographer. Ginny Keith

CARTER
THE UNSTOPPABLE SEX MACHINE

Main pic: Goodnight Jim Bob
Photographer: www.mickmercer.com

Inset: Rolling Rock for toffs
Photographer: Ginny Keith

CARTER
THE UNSTOPPABLE SEX MACHINE

Rubbish launch party at Bull & Gate
Photographer: www.mickmercer.com

Left: Fruity, Jim &
Adrian Boss
Brixton Fridge
24.10.90. with the
setlist on my shirt
Photographer:
Ginny Keith

Below: After the
HMV 'riot', (Jelber
from The Family
Cat with back to
camera)
Photographer:
www.mickmercer.com

CARTER
THE UNSTOPPABLE SEX MACHINE

Beast prepares his rider
Photographer: Ginny Keith

30 Somethi
Photographer: Mark Ba

the
Corby trouser
press

Above: Tour manager Terry
& Fruitbat at Maastricht
mini airport
Photographer: Adrian Boss

Below: Reading Festival,
the audience
Photographer: Ginny Keith

CARTER
THE UNSTOPPABLE SEX MACHINE

Handsome Dave in a US mall car park
Photographer: Jim Bob

Yorkshire
fighting
with Dip
Photographer
Jenny Keith

On
May
the
10th
backstage
at
the
Carlisle
Sands
Centre
we
received
a
phone call
to
tell
us
that
1992
The
Love
Album
had
entered
the
charts
at
Number 1.

That surely should have felt a lot better than it did. I was cock-a-hoop head over heels as happy as a sandboy's dog with two tails called Larry when *101 Damnations* went in the Top 40 and even more so when *30 Something* went to Number 8. Straight in at Number 1 should have killed me. But for some reason it was a bit of an anti-climax. Maybe it was because we expected it. All the planning and marketing and not releasing it the same week as Iron Maiden's new album. I don't know. We opened a couple of bottles of champagne on stage that night and sprayed them all over the audience like the Schumacher brothers but it should have meant a lot more. And yet that Sunday evening in Carlisle I was almost disappointed. I was becoming a bit of a sourpuss. So we bought ourselves a *Winnibago* and went to France.

TRAILER TRASH

'LES HEROS SONT IMMORTELS' (the heroes are immortal)
ET LES FACILITES SONT NULLES! (and the facilities are rubbish!)
We had this idea which turned out to be bad. Instead of sleeping in hotels or on the bus. Lets hire a *Winnebago*. We can travel across Europe in it, Big Nige and Handsome Dave can drive, we can buy loads of tinned food and cook our own meals and we can park up wherever and whenever we want and go to sleep, it'll be like going on holiday and yet at the same time it'll be our mobile home. Our RV, our ute, our *Winnebago*.

Winnebago winneshmago. Me, Fruitbat, Terry, Handsome Dave and Big - that's *BIG* - Nige, sleeping in a bloody caravan. It was awful. The beds were small and uncomfortable, the cooker didn't cook and we could only pootle along at about 50 miles an hour, which on a German autobahn being overtaken by everything from *BMWs* to *2CVs* and milkfloats was embarrassing. Also, when you need to make a quick getaway from an angry mob of rain-soaked and disappointed English Carter fans, it's less than ideal.

And so, that was why, on a wet and windy Saturday evening in the North of France, our hitherto unstoppable heroes Jim Bob and Fruitbat were lying down in the back of Fruitbat's ex-girlfriend's car being smuggled past a currently miffed, soon-to-be furious crowd of unsuitably dressed for the harsh weather conditions alternative music enthusiasts. It hadn't looked good when we arrived earlier in the day. *The Calais Rock Festival*, or *Les Heros Sont Immortels* as it was grandly named, was to take place at Vieux Fort Nieulay Calais with us, James, Texas and The Young Gods on the bill for the weekend. It could have been wonderful if only it hadn't rained and rained so very hard. The fact that the organizers had only sold 700 tickets in the UK and none in France for an 8,000 capacity venue was annoying, but we would have got away with it. We could have asked everybody to move close together and pretended it was an intimate gig at an old derelict fort in England. Trumpton, perhaps. And the torrential rain and gale-force winds would have been so much easier to tolerate if there was a beer tent for the audience to shelter in and a roof and sides on the stage. But there wasn't. And the high-voltage electrical cables were ankle deep in Calais rainwater. It was decided that it would be suicide to plug our guitars in and we were forced to pull the gig.

We probably should have done the decent thing and stayed behind to explain the situation to the crowd, or played an impromptu acoustic set, done a few magic tricks and had a big group hug, but we didn't. Instead we left the *Winnebago* behind as a decoy and escaped on the back seat of Fruitbat's ex's car. Leaving our poor manager Adrian Boss behind to bravely announce that we sadly wouldn't be playing and to take people's names so we could send them free tickets for a compensatory gig (they got a T-shirt as well, with *I saw Carter in Calais* on the front and *NOT!* on the back.) The majority of the crowd were sympathetic and accepted the situation, while others were less so. Taking their frustration out on the only shelter there - the promoter's tent - they shook it till it collapsed. The festival security, unable to calm the fans' anger, tear-gassed them instead. Arrests were made (mainly the security for heavy handed use of CS gas) and a few people were taken to hospital. The trouble spread to the town, making the local TV news, and when Adrian returned to the hotel where we were hiding and told us what had happened we decided to get out of Dodge. We drove along the coast to another French port to avoid being, a) strung up by the locals (ouch) or, b) made to walk the plank by any disappointed homeward-bound Carter fans on the ferry. When we arrived at French customs we were questioned and searched by Johnnie Loi. This was when Adrian first showed us his 'how to get through customs by filling your pockets up with crap' trick. The following day, Big Nige and Handsome Dave drove our mobile home to Beachy Head where they put a brick on the accelerator pedal, took the handbrake off and watched it pootle slowly over the edge.[13]

[13] Of course, in actual fact we took the vehicle back to the rental company so as not to lose our deposit, but you should never let the facts get in the way of a good story.

NEVER LET THE FACTS
GET IN THE WAY OF A GOOD STORY

The border crossing that takes you from Canada into Detroit, Michigan is a frightening place. We'd been told a story about AC/DC's roadie who was asleep on the tour bus when they parked up at the border control and the police came onboard to check passports and look for rock'n'roll contraband. The story was that the slumbering roadie was having a particularly satisfying early-morning dream and when one of the Detroit police officers noticed a bulge in his continental quilt he shouted 'Concealed weapon!' and hit it with his night-stick. My French strip-search and JFK experience had left me so nervous when we crossed borders that I was prone to stupidity. Once when the US customs police came on our bus to check everyone's passports our sound engineer was asleep. The cop still wanted to see her, joking that he just wanted to see if Helen was as pretty as she was in her passport picture. Because I was nervous I tried to join in with the light-hearted rozzer with what I mistook for a joke, I said that he didn't really need to see Helen's face as she was as ugly as a **pig**..*horse!..cat*...hippopotamus...errr... (Helen looks like none of these animals by the way).

When we went into the Detroit passport control office I had a feeling of customs *déjà vu,* a French phrase coincidentally. The room was full of uniformed border cops and a lone plainclothes clerk who sat behind a desk asking the tourists trick questions and writing down the answers. Looking over her shoulder, checking her work like a bad schoolteacher, a big ugly bully of a policewoman kept interrupting the clerk and telling her off causing her biro hand to shake and her buttocks to lift slightly from their seat. I understood how she felt. I said that I had nothing to declare (other than my genius and my hatred for ugly lard-arsed bullies with guns) and explained my innocent and law-abiding business and promised that I had no drugs. I just wanted to get my visa stamped and get back to bed, so I tried not to be a wise-ass and just answered the questions. The woman with the gun warned me not to be a wise-ass and told me to just answer the Goddamn questions. All the time another customs clown kept whispering into her ear that we had some kind of a machine on the bus. He was obsessed. He'd read the name of the band and was totally convinced that we had 'some kind of a machine on the bus.'

'No, we've just got musical equipment.'

'What, no machines?'

'No, just guitars and musical equipment.'

'I think they've got some kind of a machine on the bus'... have you got any machines on the bus?'

'No, we haven't got any machines on the bus.'

'I think they've got some machines on the bus.'

And so it went on. Until in the end we had to unload the bus to prove that we indeed had no machines.

And they give these people loaded guns!

Everyone else must have been held up at the border, they must have been smuggling machinery and been rumbled by the fuzz because there was no-one at the gig in Detroit. It was at St Andrew's Hall at the rough end of town, we'd played there before with EMF and it was packed. But tonight everyone who hadn't been nicked for their contraband machines was across town at the State Theatre watching Faith No More. They were playing a lot earlier in the evening than us, Fruitbat and the crew went to see them before our gig and FNM's bass player Billy Gould came to watch us later on. I got on really well with him, he's one of my celebrity American mates that I never really saw again and he probably wouldn't know me if I said hello to him in the street today. Billy Corgan from The Smashing Pumpkins was another, I'd sat next to him on a panel at the New York New Music Seminar and we got on like a house on fire. We were both too shy for speech making and were completely upstaged by famous transvestite Ru Paul and Shitman, a man in a shit suit (no, seriously). I met Nirvana once.

The next couple of gigs were thankfully packed. Chicago was always great, the only place we'd really picked up some of the EMF audience and then the following night we were at The Palladium in New York, playing an AIDS benefit with The Disposable Heroes of Hiphoprisy, Gene Loves Jezebel and Mary's Danish. The security at the venue were much like those in the dickie-bows and white shirts dropping university crowd-surfers in England. On most nights The Palladium was a larger NY Latino version of a *Sparklers* or *Spanglers* discotheque with the security more accustomed to dealing with knife-carrying gang members than indie fans. Consequently, when the kids started moshing during The Disposable Heroes' set they thought there was a riot taking place and did what they were trained to do - they started throwing people out. And then they climbed on the stage and stood in front of the band, perhaps intending to protect them from audience attack but definitely blocking their view and buggering up the show. We were due on next and didn't want them stood in front of us. We asked nicely but that didn't work and somehow we managed to upset them to such an extent that they threatened to kill our tour manager Terry. We had to make another fairly hasty exit - shortly after Madonna, who was at the gig watching us - to hail a taxi back to the hotel.

While we got lost in a New York cab, the crew loaded our guitars and amplifiers into a stretch limo that had been hired for the day so we didn't have to take the bus into that part of the city where parking was a nightmare. The limo driver didn't have both oars in the water, he was king of the loonies. He was like a hybrid of Don Johnson and Peter Stringfellow, with his jacket sleeves rolled up to the elbows and his red plastic kid's sunglasses. Having spent the gig drinking our rider he was pretty drunk and on the way back to the Mayflower Hotel he wrapped his limo round a lamppost, knackering the exhaust pipe. He got out of the car, pulled the exhaust away from the car, stuck it in the boot, got back in and continued with the journey. If it had happened in Oxford Street or the Kings Road, the crew might have sued him or killed him and they definitely wouldn't have stayed in the vehicle, but because it was New York they thought it was hilarious. A big bloody adventure. Which it was.

ANOTHER DAY ANOTHER PALLADIUM

A couple of days later we were playing the Rocky Point Palladium in Warwick, Rhode Island. Me and Fruity took a cab ride to the venue from the Providence Holiday Inn and the journey was so traumatic that when we got back to Britain I wrote the song *Travis* about it. The lyrics of the song are pretty much verbatim what the cabbie told us that day as we made our way to Rocky Point. All the while he was turning round to look us in the eye to be sure that we understood exactly what he was trying to get off his troubled chest, his vehicle swerving across the road as he did so. When we reached our destination I was sweating buckets and it took me a while to calm down. We gave the taxi driver a big tip for his story, the future song and for not driving into a wall. Here are the lyrics (I've removed the middle eight which is me talking and I haven't added the swearing, which would have been every other word, but this is roughly what he told us about America.)

'I'm not a racist but I am I served my time in Vietnam I've got three jobs this is one sometimes I wish that I'd kept my gun this country's going down the tubes I can't afford to pay my dues unless you've got some sponsorship for Christ sakes buddy don't get sick don't grow old don't be poor do what you're told are you from Europe? So am I I came here

in 1955 half American, half asleep some day a rain will came and wash the streets the CIA, the KGB, it's all the same conspiracy etc etc, swerve, skid, screech of brakes...'

As we pulled into Rocky Point Avenue, I realized this was another amusement-park gig. Not like Universal Studios in LA though. Rocky Point Amusement Park had seen better years. It wasn't - as its owner Colonel Harrington declared in 1918 - 'New England's most beautiful amusement park' anymore. *The Looff Coaster, The Tumble-Bug, The Wildcat,* and The *Thompson Scenic Railway* could not compete with the might and muscle of *Disney* and *Daffy Duck.* Rocky Point was a metaphor for our taxi driver's America. Or is that an allegory?

The Rhode Island gig was a radio-sponsored event. We did a few of them while we were there. They were like mini indoor festivals with about half a dozen bands and a lot of interviews. At the radio gigs we usually got to go onstage a bit earlier, which just gave us more time to get inebriated and heckle the other acts and that's what happened the following night. We stood at the back of the Boston Avalon in the roped off VIP area and heckled Sean's singing brother Michael Penn by chanting, 'Who's your brother, who's your brother, who's your brother shagging now? Not Madonna, not Madonna, not Madonna anymore!' all the way through his set. The other very important persons must have thought we were the English soccer (football) hooligans they'd heard about and one by one started to leave until there was just us and two security men, who didn't know whether or not they were authorized to throw the 'artistes' out. Instead, they tried to contain our rambunctiousness by standing very close to us following us around and foolishly trying to confiscate Fruitbat's beer, which was *Rolling Rock.*

Before fame claims your soul and inevitably destroys it, it can be a bit of a giggle. You get to walk into places like you own them, or know somebody who does. There's no job like it for really giving it the large. Maybe the joker who spins the Waltzer (David Essex again), making the birds scream and giggle, showing up their boyfriends who are trying to remain cool and not puke. The guard on an old slam-door train, who's allowed to lean out of the window - and the door- when the train's moving, or likewise, the bus conductor hanging off the open back of a London double decker. But with the demise of the funfair and the introduction of automatic train doors and the one-man bus, it's been left to the rock/film/TV/fashion/cooking/gardening stars to fly the flag - and it's a bloody big flag - for the showoff. Fame gives you the oppoutunity to travel the world meeting interesting people and stay in hotels that are at odds with your hairstyle and clothing. And you can muck about.

The latter part of 1992 seemed to be mucking about season. Nine of us got stuck in a Pittsburgh hotel lift for 30 minutes after someone ignored the little gold sign and jumped up and down when they shouldn't have done. We managed to convince the hotel it was somehow their fault and they gave us free drinks and meals in their swanky restaurant. In the dressing room at the Fast Lane club in Asbury Park, Nick Ely practiced his lighting/pyrotechnics by letting fireworks off in the toilet. On the night off before our second New York gig of the tour we went to see Ned's Atomic Dustbin at the Irving Plaza and I cut my lip open attempting to stage-dive and then I won a gherkin-eating contest at 3 o'clock in the morning at an all night deli.

I don't want to suggest that we were crazy loons, or that being offensive from a safe distance or eating pickled cucumbers and staying up past our bedtimes is particularly hard or clever and quite a lot of the time we were either asleep, sitting in a corner reading or feeling sorry for ourselves. In between all the high jinx, buffoonery and horseplay I really was a miserable sod.

That was when I turned to my Walkman. There were a number of albums that I found comfort and solace in during the down times on a long tour. And none of them are by S Club Seven or The Archies. These were records that made me feel better, by making me feel worse. *The Bends* by Radiohead, *It's A Shame About Ray* by The Lemonheads, *The Holy Bible* by The Manic Street Preachers, *The Boatman's Call* by Nick Cave and the sad songs on REM's *Automatic For The People,* like *Everybody Hurts*, which nearly pushed me right over the edge when I heard it for the first time parked outside a shopping mall in middle America.

Going to see films in the afternoon at a shopping-mall cinema on a day off could also have a devastating affect on my emotional state if I got out of the wrong side of the bed that day. And considering that you can only get out of one side of a tourbus bed there was a 50/50 chance that could be every day. I saw *The Last Of The Mohicans* and *The Piano* in such circumstances and I still feel a bit weird when I watch either of them now. When Jodhi May jumps off the cliff rather than take Wes Studi's outstretched hand towards the end of *The Last of The Mohicans* it was almost too much for me and 'production assistant' Mole. We were both feeling particularly homesick and vulnerable at the time and were so distraught that we almost followed her. On the other hand, in 1997 we saw *Face Off* at a mall outside Chicago. We had no idea what it was about or why it was called *Face Off,* that particular movie was a different kind of emotional rollercoaster ride altogether.

MALL RATS

If you have trouble attracting women, here's a tip. Fly to America, hire yourself a big silver tourbus with air brushed murals of busty blondes astride Harley Davidsons down the side. Drive your bus to a shopping mall in the middle of nowhere and park up. Employ a moustachioed and handsome muscleman from Somerset, let's call him Dave for sake of argument, and get him to cover his bare chest with sun-tan lotion and sunbathe outside in the parking lot next to the bus. Then wait. There'll be a lot of rubber-necking from passing motorists and shoppers and then small groups of girls will appear to ask, 'who's the band?' and to get a good look at Dave. Obviously it helps if you're U2 or Bon Jovi and not some band who's name they've never heard of and have difficulty in understanding what it is you're saying. 'Caarrer?' But if they're not impressed by your band, they'll like your accent - which they'll presume is Australian - and they'll love topless Handsome Dave. They'll get you to sign something and go off to phone their friends, who'll steal their parents' car and drive down to the mall to take a look for themselves.

NB: I've never tried this at Brent Cross, the Hatfield Galleria or outside Croydon Purley Way *B&Q*. But I suspect it wouldn't work.

After our second date in New York, the crew went home while me and Fruitbat stayed on with our girlfriends who'd come over for the gig. It was Halloween and we went out for a meal in a restaurant where we were served by a waitress dressed as a cow. Udders and everything.

In 1996, Rocky Point fell into bankruptcy, a lot of the major rides were sold and in June of 2000 after a fire that started in the Dodgems caused major damage, the Mayor of Warwick called for the demolition of the remaining structures. You can find some of the old Rocky Point rides at other theme parks, such as the Freefall, which is now at Geauga Lake and is called Mr Hyde's Nasty Fall, and The Wild Thing at Enchanted Parks in Washington which used to be the Rocky Point Corkscrew.

YOU ARE WHAT YOU EAT

I'm a cheese sandwich. A Ploughman's cheese sandwich to be precise.

When we went to the US in 1992 we took our own chef Andy. We'd had our own catering in Europe for so long by then that we didn't know how we'd manage without it. We thought we'd starve to death or eat our clothes. We'd grown accustomed to arriving at the venue where someone would knock us up a fried-egg-sandwich for breakfast at one o'clock in the afternoon, we needed our three courses in the early evening and we liked to dictate - not so much what we wanted to eat - but what we didn't. In my case this was mushroom stroganoff, macaroni cheese, pretty much anything in a cream sauce and food that looked the same when it came out as it did when it was going in. I wasn't fussy, just precise.

I didn't want to go back to the days when all I ever ate were cheese ploughman's sandwiches and *Flamin' Hot Monster Munch* crisps bought from service stations. It was a bit different in mainland Europe where they're less keen on seeing unknown bands starve to death. Even if I didn't like the inevitable *vegetarische* pasta in a cream sauce dinner I could always build a pretty interesting sandwich from the *smorgasbord* of exotic breads, cheeses and euro veg that was always laid out in the dressing room. On the down side: no *Monster Munch* and just two flavours of crisp: plain or paprika. In certain parts of early-1990s Europe they'd only recently stopped locking vegetarians up in institutions for the culinary insane, we were what we ate, hence we were nuts. In Leipzig we had to return our cheese omelettes because they had ham in them; we were told it was only 'a little ham', it wasn't easy. The species and breed of animal or the way it's slaughtered is fairly key to making local delicacies local. So when vegetarians travel, our stomachs stay at home, eating salad.

I tried looking up 'national dishes of Europe' on the worldwide web, but found that most countries claim to have no such thing. For example, in France each region has its 'own gastronomic specialities', such as *gratin dauphinois* in the Grenoble region, the fondue in the Alps Savoie region and in Bourgogne it's snails and frogs. Germany too claims to have no national dish, but I bet Porky The Pig would take issue with such a claim. Yugoslavia was a bit more upfront about its national nosh and offered me *pihtije* (jellied pork or duck) and *raznjici* (skewered meat), as was Norway with its lamb and cabbage and Portugal with a plate of salted codfish, or *bacalhau*. The British national dish, is of course, mad cows. Whatever, all I know is that when we were on tour, there was no national dish that didn't involve at least a little bit of death.

But before I really sound too much like a little Englander - technically: half Scotlander (national dish Haggis, *Irn Bru*, deep-fried *Mars Bar*) - I'd like to stick up for the Italians who saved our lives with pasta and pizza and, of course, the Dutch with their hash cakes and brownies.

Still, the euro toilet circuit hospitality is a lot more hospitable than it is in the UK. The dressing-room fridge would always be full of beer, there'd even be an opener to save on dentist's bills. In Britain, one of the great battles fought between band and promoter is how many beers should be on the rider. Size is everything to us musicians: wily promoters will know this and they'll play optical illusionary tricks. They'll stack beer cans in front of the dressing-room mirror to fool the band into believing there are twice as many as there really are. They'll give you extra large - as well as extra cheap and nasty - bottles of wine. They'll hide a few beers in a lot of ice and you won't realize you've been short-changed until you've drunk half of them and you're scraping the bottom of the barrel which now only contains ice and cold water. But now you'll be unsure how many beers there were to start with and won't be able to complain with any confidence. A promoter in Sussex used to buy loads and loads of bags of crisps to make the rider look huge; it took me about three gigs before I realized his scam.

SMORGASBORD SHMORGASBORD

A band's rider is the part of the contract between them and the promoter that stipulates what they need to put on a show. It might be a simple request for a PA system, a few lights and a couple of beers each, but as the band grows in stature and popularity the rider will no doubt become more and more lengthy and unreasonable. And the requests will now be demands that, if not met, will result in the band pulling the gig. Once we'd hit the big time our rider became more extensive but it stayed fairly conservative. Aside from all the security, crowd barrier and St John's Ambulance clauses, all we asked for was a lot of quality bottled lager, a couple of bottles of quality French Claret (apart from when the French government carried out nuclear tests in the South Pacific and we boycotted French wine, replacing it quite often with *South African Shiraz*. Oh the topsy-turvy world of political correctness) and a selection of towels, soft drinks, water, nuts and crisps etc, etc. The only slightly unusual items on our rider were the two cycle caps that Fruitbat insisted on to replace the two that daring members of the audience would steal from off his head every night. It was a game. 'Nick The Hat From Fruitbat's Head.' They'd spend the whole gig trying to get onstage to get his hat and, if they didn't manage it, they'd hang around outside after the gig to nick his hat as he walked to the bus. He hated it more than just about anything else.

Aside from the cycle caps, it was a pretty boring rider and not much of a challenge for the promoters. It was no match for the extravagant and frequently ludicrous demands made by the monster rock acts of the 1970s and 80s. Like the miniature golf course that Pink Floyd insisted on, or the brand new black toilet seat that Janet Jackson needed underneath her before she'd sit down in the venue's ladies' room.

Perhaps the most famous and often copied rider request was that all the brown *M&Ms* should be removed from the bowls of sweets in Van Halen's dressing room. Legend has it that if singer David Lee Roth found an offending brown-coloured and initialled chocolate in amongst the reds, yellows and greens, he'd start throwing things around, stamping his feet and threatening to pull the gig. The Spandexed poodle claims that the seemingly childish request was actually a way of testing whether or not the promoter had read the rest of the contract. If there were no brown *M&Ms* then everything else (lights and sound etc) would probably be hunky dory - if not, then something more important was bound to go wrong. When Van Halen supported The Rolling Stones, the Stones gave them a fleet of brown Vee Dub Beetles with the *M&M* logo painted on the side and Mick Jagger added a line to the Stones' rider that all the unwanted brown *M&Ms* should be put in their dressing room instead.

These days everybody just asks for clean socks and pants and it's left to Maria Carey and Jennifer Lopez to fly the flag for the ridiculous rider with their demands for entire venue redecoration and cuddly puppies to stroke.

So, having our own catering on tour made things a lot easier and, like small only children, we pretty much got what we wanted to eat and drink. Unless the *BBC* were around. There was a series that they made for schools television about cooking, I think it might have been called *Food*. It's been on TV about a hundred times although I've never seen it. They wanted to film an episode that showed what it was like to cater for a rock band on the road and so they came along to a Carter gig at Trent University. That day the boss of the catering company turned up and - keen to look as good as possible on the telly - he changed everything. New tablecloths, cutlery and printed menus, no time to fry eggs in the middle of the day and for dinner that night they made my least favourite dish, mushroom stroganoff. Me, Fruitbat and Wez pretended we weren't hungry and hid in the dressing room eating spicy vegetarian bum burners smuggled in from the local *Burger King*. As I say, I've never seen the programme, but I know we were interviewed about what the catering was like and I'm presuming, that day, we lied.

But although we may have been a tad choosy with what we ate, our lighting man Pip was a chef and waiter's nightmare. In a fast food restaurant in Tokyo Pip returned his food because it didn't look anything like the picture on the menu. On a long-haul flight he was once so unhappy with his airplane food that he threw his tray down the aisle at the stewardess. On Pip's gravestone it should say *'I'm not eating that!'* (engraved in italics and a Yorkshire accent). And kind of on the subject of Pip and food; when we were in Tokyo, I wanted to buy something to bring home for my daughter but I didn't have any spare time because we were doing so much press. I asked Pip if he'd go out and buy something Japanese and cool that would impress a five-year old girl. Pip bought a giant pillow in the shape of a carrot. I had to carry the enormous novelty root vegetable with me for the rest of the tour, feeding it through airport X-ray machines as part of my hand luggage. A similar thing had happened in America when *über* roadie Daz bought me a kingsize *101 Dalmatians* continental quilt for my birthday. Again, I had to carry it with me for a whole tour, putting it through airport security machines and feeling like some kind of contemporary comfort-blanket-carrying Charlie Brown character. I tried to leave it behind in my hotel room a few times but Daz would always follow me on to the tourbus with the rolled-up quilt under his arm telling me I'd accidentally forgotten my birthday present again.

HOLLOW LEGS

Les has an allergy to canned beer. It turns his face red. If you're ever at a party with him, tip a can of *Carling Black Label* into his empty *Becks* bottle and watch him turn into a tomato. Whenever the rider was brought into the dressing room in cans we had to get it changed for bottled beer.

Before Wez joined Carter and was still playing drums with (International) Resque, we were in a restaurant in Rennes after the gig that both bands had just played for the mayor and the French big knobs (where I'd stormed off stage during the first song), when Jon beast challenged him to eat a dozen hard-boiled eggs.[14] It was like the legendary scene from the prison movie *Cool Hand Luke*, where Luke - played by Paul Newman - bets the other prisoners that he can eat fifty hard-boiled eggs in one hour. Beast said to Wez, if he could eat 12 eggs,[15] then he would drink a half-pint of neat vodka. We all - and I just typed this without thinking about it so I'm going to leave it in - egged Wez on, until he indeed, ate them all. Beast protested, saying he'd said *fifteen* eggs and not twelve and wouldn't drink the vodka until Wez ate another three. Wez couldn't face another egg and if he had I'm sure Jon would have claimed the bet was two dozen or that they had to be fried or scrambled eggs. Incidentally, Wez is as thin as one of his drumsticks and yet he can eat like a thoroughbred. Whereas Jon, like I said earlier, only ever managed a liquid lunch.

At hotel bars in America I liked to ask for a beer so that the barman would ask, 'Which brand would you like sir?' and I could say, 'What have you got?' and then wait five minutes as he named all fifty. Then I could order the first one he mentioned.

We once cancelled the last three dates of a European tour and came home early because, a) we were tired and emotional, b) we hadn't sold a lot of tickets, c) the promotion had been awful and mainly, d) an argument among the crew had got out of hand leading to tension, bad feeling and almost fisticuffs. The argument was over whether or not *café au lait* was a breakfast drink.[16]

When we were travelling by car, Fruitbat insisted on only travelling on A roads, and only the A roads that had *Little Chef* restaurants, so we could pull over for breakfast. He had a special map with them all marked out, we were like a couple of old wombles in our Morris Minor on a three-year day trip to Bognor.

Zac Foley, EMF's late, great bass player's party trick was to fit about half a dozen limes under his foreskin.

[14] It may have been more than a dozen eggs, maybe twenty, I can't remember the exact - or eggact - number, but I've just imagined the amount I think I could manage myself and doubled it. Anyway, it was a lot of eggs for a man so skinny to eat.
[15] Ditto 13.
[16] I've been told that *café au lait* may well have originally only have been drunk in the morning, before the milk went off. The same may be true for cappucino, I've heard the only people drinking it in the afternoon in Italy are tourists.

JESUS CHRIST!

Aside from all the finicky rider demands and arguments over sandwich size and content there are other things that go to make *This Is Spinal Tap* the most factually accurate documentary film ever made. We haven't had an end-of-tour party on the roof of the Hyatt Hotel in LA but we have eaten cheese toasties there. And although we've never supported a puppet show at a gig in an amusement park, we did play Cheltenham racecourse with Let Loose.

In case you've never seen the film, there's a scene where the band Spinal Tap decide to have an 18-foot-high Stonehenge built as a stage set. Guitarist Nigel Tufnel draws it on the back of a napkin and writes the dimensions next to it. Of course when he writes eighteen feet, it's mistaken for eighteen inches and when the band are on stage a one-and-a-half-foot model of Stonehenge is lowered from above.

Our Stonehenge was a reproduction of Tower Bridge, coincidentally also eighteen feet high. It was bolted together from two-inch diameter scaffold tubes, lighting trusses and industrial aluminium gantry mesh with a painted fascia Velcro'd to the framework (you can probably tell that I've found a copy of the plans.) It spanned the width of the stages of sixteen theatres, halls and leisure centres from Gateshead to Brixton in December of 1992 and the by now population of Lichtenstein-sized Crazy Carter Crew had to arrive at the venues at 5 am every day in order to erect it in time for the show. To make the cold and clinical leisure centres appear more warm and theatrical, a red- painted proscenium arch was made and hung above the stage. Up until then I thought a proscenium arch was the bit between your scrotum and your bumhole. On the front of both towers there were drawbridges which were lowered every night so that me and Fruitbat could make our dramatic entrance onto the stage to the theme song from the musical *Jesus Christ Superstar*. My mum always told me that you should make a spectacular entrance.

After the gig was over and the crowd had whistled along with *Always Look On The Bright Side Of Life* from *Monty Python's The Life Of Brian* showing on the wall of TV screens stacked up between the twin towers, the crew would un-Velcro and dismantle the bridge and load it back in the truck for the next gig. It was like the plot to the *The Bridge On The River Kwai* over and over again. Build - dismantle - rebuild - dismantle - re-rebuild - dismantle.

The idea for constructing a scaled-down copy of Wolfe Barry and Horace Jones' 1894 bridge was tour manager Terry's and guitarist Fruitbat's, I've just e-mailed Fruitbat and asked him why Tower Bridge? He's replied, 'Good question.' Too much brandy in the hotel bar.

By the way, near the end of the tour, as a joke on the band, someone had made an eighteen-inch-high version of the bridge out of foam rubber and during *GI Blues* it was lowered from the roof above us, just like in the movie.

In the NME End of 1992 Readers' Poll we were still Number two Best Band, once again behind REM. *1992 The Love Album* **had replaced** *30 Something* **as fifth best album and we'd moved up two places in the best single vote with** *The Only Living Boy In New Cross* **at Number 4.**

TWO LITTLE BOYS AND A DRUM MACHINE

In 1993 we were invited onto the bill for *The Big Day Out*, a festival that tours Australia. Because it was such a long haul flight to Oz some of us decided to go over early, the crew went scuba diving at the Barrier Reef and I went with my missus and daughter to stay with my Auntie Dorothy in Perth. Dorothy used to live in the house where I was born in Streatham, she helped the midwife bring me into this world and when I was growing up she was my agony aunt. Me and my best friend John (ex 'R'n'R Revival 1975') went to a party in West Norwood that consisted of four hippies getting it on on a bed while me and John - who were both about 14 - sat on the carpet and drank a *Party 7* [17] until John was drunk - teenage drunk - and I was too scared to face his parents who I was supposed to be staying with that night. So I left my best friend asleep in his front garden, where his mum and dad - returning home from an evening out - found their son, comatose in their herbaceous border, having not only been sick but also having shat his pants.

When his parents came looking for me they found me at my Auntie Dorothy's, she told them that I would be staying there and we'd sort it all out in the morning. This was just one of many times she'd saved my life since having a hand (literally) in starting it. It wasn't the pressure of sorting out her nephew's adolescent problems that made Dorothy escape to Australia but that was where she went to live, so we stayed with her there for a week or so before I flew across the country to meet Fruitbat and the crew in Melbourne for what was my most enjoyable tour ever. I wrote a diary about it in the *NME* and it seems to sum up the experience fairly well and it's going to do wonders for my word count, so I'm going to copy it out for you now. It begins on Saturday 23 January.

SATURDAY, 23 JANUARY

Melbourne, Australia, Other Side Of The World. Flight number TN009 from Perth drops me off at 'work' after a week visiting my Auntie Dorothy. Hotel, photoshoot, beer, bed.

[17] A large can, most popular in the seventies, that contained seven pints of usually warm, flat and difficult to open beer. Which has given me a great marketing idea: 'S Club Party 7' - A large can containing seven pints of usually warm, flat and difficult to open alcopop.

113

SUNDAY 24

Big Day Out Number One (a kind of Lollapalooza travelling festival-type thing with Iggy Pop, Sonic Youth, Nick Cave, Mudhoney, Disposable Heroes of Hiphoprisy, loads of local groups... and us. Despite the heat it's pissing down with rain and the thought of printing 15,000 'I SAW CARTER AT MELBOURNE... NOT!' T-shirts does not improve my hangover. 2.15pm: Our short, obnoxious set in the rain is of course the best thing since sliced bread and we go to bed happy.

MONDAY 25

Flight AN26 to Sydney for a gig at the Dee Why Venue, which will close down after tonight's Carter show; the two things are apparently not connected. Anyway, it was the usual stuff: two old farts in short trousers obviously miming to a badly-recorded karaoke cassette... totally brilliant of course. The cockroaches particularly enjoyed it.

TUESDAY 26

Big Day Out Two, Sydney. I seem to have lost this day completely, it has disappeared from my memory. Needless to say, I'm sure we were very sexy onstage, etc, and that's good enough for me. I do recall dancing badly to the Disposables who were wonderful, and I think this was the day Fruitbat gave himself a skinhead haircut and discovered Pantera!

WEDNESDAY 27

The days off are always the hardest. You have to sign some autographs in a record shop, drink as much as possible, and then there's always the obligatory boat party in Sydney Harbour with a couple of hundred pop celebs and assorted loonies. And then, of course, you always have to round off the evening pissed off your face without any shoes on singing *The Green Green Grass Of Home* in a Japanese karaoke bar in the middle of the red-light district. Ho hum.

THURSDAY 28

BLEEAAUUURRRGGHH!!!
HANNGGOOOVVEERRRR!!
Sydney East Leagues Club is some sort of rugby club, there's dress restrictions and not enough electricity. Not perhaps the

ideal venue, but at least there weren't 150 Sydney pensioners playing bingo during the soundcheck - which of course there was.

FRIDAY 29

Another bloody airplane...
Oh good. I hate flying on the same flights as other bands; it always reminds me of Buddy Holly, you know... 'IGGY POP AND SONIC YOUTH IN AIR DISASTER... London punk rock duo also involved.'

Anyway, flight AN27 lands safely in Perth and we drive to Fremantle (Hull with sunshine) where I meet up with long-suffering girlfriend and daughter. Day off.

SATURDAY 30

Big Day Out Three, Fremantle, Western Australia. Phew, what a scorcher! Another 43 minutes of abusive synth-pop from token Pommie bastards Carter USM, the highlight of the set being the small pyrotechnic fire display and the stage invasion during *Sheriff Fatman* by two blokes dressed as a bear and a chicken.

SUNDAY 31

AN84 to Adelaide, where I sat in the hotel and watched the film *Single White Female* and no doubt got drunk because it was a Sunday.

MONDAY, FEBRUARY 1

Pinched and punched for the first of the month, then went down to Big Day Out Four, the last one and the hottest stage I've ever been on. It's 43 degrees celsius, which is about 14 million degrees in English money... HOT! Our sex god king roadie Daz sprays the audience with a firehose for the whole gig, washing off their factor 15 sunblock and giving them all skin cancer.

Dance badly to Sonic Youth, Nick Cave, the Disposables and Iggy Pop, who has now made a surprise appearance with almost every band here except for us. Tonight Iggy sings 'Foxy Lady' with the Hiphops while the Brits on the piss do their Garth from Wayne's World dance at the side of the stage.

TUESDAY 2

AN20 to Melbourne. We're back, Ronnie Corbett and Donald Sinden are still on at the theatre over the road and all is well. We have a Mexican meal in a 'bring your own' (alcohol) Mexican restaurant. We bring our own and the waitress steals it. Day off.

WEDNESDAY 3

Last night Guns 'N' Roses played Melbourne Enormamegabigdome and something like ten per cent of the Melbourne population went. Food and drink was confiscated at the door so you could replace it with the expensive stuff inside, it was hotter than hell, cost a million dollars to get in and there was no transport home. Tonight we played in a pub called The Prince Of Wales.

THURSDAY 4

Get your kicks on AN66, which lands on the Gold Coast of Australia. Today the sun reaches our brains and we go bungee jumping and get our picture in the Surfers' Paradise Bungee Jumpers' Hall of Fame, along with Julian Lennon and a bunch of heavy rock legends.

Of course, I didn't really do it. Three of the Crazy Carter Crew did, but I am in the photograph. Come on, let's be honest, after the bungee jumping it was margaritas by the pool and free beer at a Sonic Youth gig. We're on fucking holiday!

FRIDAY 5

Tonight's gig was a tad empty, what with the Sonics playing last night etc. Still, we do *Surfin' USM* because we're in Surfers' Paradise. Whacky eh?

SATURDAY 6

Short drive to Brisbane for the last Oz gig. It's the best one and that's the way we like it. Thank you, whoever you are.

After that, my *NME* diary takes us to Japan to get a Gilbert O'Sullivan album. The gist of the days in Japan seems to be that I'd been plunged into a pit of despair somewhere between Brisbane and

Tokyo. I haven't included the Japanese diary entries because, aside from the stuff about Gilbert and how we gave all the Japanese record company people we met new English names like Trevor, Colin and Susan, it's not very amusing or interesting.

As far as the Australian trip goes. I would like to add that the hotel we stayed at in Surfers' Paradise bore the name *Travelodge*. I don't know if it's part of the same chain, but there was no slow-boiling kettle, pay phone in the hall, complimentary Tory newspaper, *Corby Trouser Press* or *Little Chef* restaurant next door. Just swimming pools (indoor and out), frozen margaritas and sunshine.

I should probably also mention that Iggy Pop also missed the party boat when it set sail from Sydney Harbour and he had to board mid trip from a smaller boat that chased after it and pulled up alongside.

Fruitbat became very friendly with Iggy's guitarist Eric and also Sonic Youth's Lee Renaldo, swapping guitar chops and licks.

And Mudhoney are the worst-behaved rock band I've seen in my entire life. Trashing their way through the hotel and dressing rooms of Australia and on at least one occasion (Fremantle) throwing the hotel manager in the pool. They eventually annoyed the festival promoters so much that when the band turned up at the Big Day Out in Adelaide, they found a notice stuck in the earth next to a bush with the words 'MUDHONEY: DRESSING ROOM' written on it.

And finally, not only did Iggy Pop perform with just about every other band on the bill, I've just read on a Mudhoney fan website that in Sydney, Mark and Matt from Mudhoney sang 'I Wanna Be Your Dog' with Sonic Youth, Iggy Pop and Nick Cave. Which has reminded me that I was aware at the time that everybody came onstage and sang with everybody else. Except for us.

Dear Mark and Matt from Mudhoney, Sonic Youth, Iggy Pop, Nick Cave, Disposable Heroes of Hiphoprisy etc,

I've just read on a Mudhoney fan website that in Sydney, Mark and Matt from Mudhoney sang 'I Wanna Be Your Dog' with Sonic Youth, Iggy Pop and Nick Cave. Which has reminded me that I was aware at the time that everybody came onstage and sang with everybody else. Except for us.

Why?

Yours sincerely,

James Bob

IT'S ALL BOLLOCKS

Crikey, that was an eye opener. A revelation, a burning bush, an epiphany. A rock'n'roll epiphany, to paraphrase the Manics. *It's all bollocks*. Nothing will be the same after this. It's like finding out that Father Christmas, the Tooth Fairy and the Easter Bunny are all your Dad, that magic tricks are just that - tricks. Or how Milli Vanilli, the pop duo responsible for such classics as *Girl You Know It's True* and *Girl I'm Gonna Miss You* were in fact a German producer called Frank Farian who was also Boney M. Little fibs and big lies. Like when my Grandfather explained the scar across his nose by telling me the story of how he was running down the street with his hands in his pockets and he tripped and fell headfirst into the spinning wheel of his daughter's bicycle, chopping the end of his bugle off. And how it was only when I was well into my thirties and I was passing my Granddad's story onto my own daughter that it suddenly dawned on me it was a morality tale about not running with your hands in your pockets and probably wasn't true.

And then there was the day that it was brought to my attention that the button that closes the doors of a lift doesn't really do anything, it's just there to make you feel like you're getting somewhere and you're in control of your life. The same person who told me about lifts also told me that some of the push and wait buttons on traffic lights, that you push to turn the red man green don't do anything, other than switch on a light behind the word 'WAIT'. I'll never cross the road or take a ride in a lift in the same innocent way ever again.

But mainly. The biggest whopper of all turned out to be the music industry. I don't know when I realized it was entirely testicular. I'd always had my suspicions, but a number of things that happened around 1993 left me in very little doubt.

1. Henry Rollins told me:

It was at the Astoria on his spoken word tour. I went along on the day I got back from Tokyo, I was probably jetlagged and definitely tired and emotional. Henry seemed to know this and ignored the other fifteen hundred people in the audience, basing his entire show on my recent life. He did a bit about jetlag and touring Japan and also the stuff about what people presume rock stars are doing on a Saturday night - immersed in a mad mad world of drugs and debauched, promiscuous and wanton sexual activity - when in actual fact Henry was at home alone, pacing around his bedroom agonising how he should best reply to a difficult letter from a fan.

THE BOLLOCKS FILE

At *Rough Trade* they had a file that was called the 'bollocks file' where they put all the letters from Morrissey fans. We didn't have a bollocks file, we replied to everything and if my name was on the envelope then I'd write back personally. I know a few people didn't believe this, like this geezer (I know it's a bit unfair to reproduce the letter here, but he'll probably never read this and I've changed his name and removed any details that might embarrass him or set him on a lifelong path of bloody vengeance if he does. Besides, I want to get across what I'm trying to say and I really couldn't make a letter like this up):

Dear bloke with typewriter and photocopier who pretends to be Jim Bob,

The reason I wanted to join the 'CARTER" club was so that I could hear about tour news, new releases and club news. Although, after months of preparation by me and my friends so that we could see our favourite band play live in ——— on ——— ——. I was rather annoyed to find out five days before that the dates had been rearranged. As a member of the club I should be informed of any rescheduled dates in hand.
Could you please tell me how I could purchase the new single as I live in a small town and it will be difficult for me to get hold of it.

Yours sincerely
——— ———————

P.S. Am I going to get a reply or a photocopied letter to all Carter fans (members) which probably won't have anything to do with this letter!

You see, the problem is, our fan club was completely free of charge, it was run by me, my girlfriend and my sister, not a *'bloke with typewriter'* at all. It was bound to be a bit rubbish at times and in the days before everyone had e-mail it was impossible to write to twenty thousand people every time a gig was moved at the last minute. Most of the letters we received were lovely and a pleasure to reply to and I know this particular letter isn't that bad, it's just one I found when I was looking for clues for this book. It's by no means the worst snotty letter we received, nor is it the only one, but as far as I know we never wrote back to anyone to tell them to go fuck themselves or stick their letters up their arses.

So like Henry Rollins, I was spending my time off at home replying to letters and aside from the snotty ones there were some that were getting more and more disturbing and difficult to reply to. I suppose it began after we'd released the single *After The Watershed* and an alarming number of people wrote to tell me how they had been abused in one way or another and that they had no-one else to turn to.

There was a bloke who I'm going to call Michael (that wasn't his name) who'd written to me quite a bit and once while I was away, he sent me a long letter to tell me his life was a mess and so he'd decided to end it just as soon as he'd finished writing the letter. It was his suicide note. Because I'd been away the letter was over two weeks old and so I presumed the worst. I wrote back straight away - if I'd had a phone number I would have rung him up - and I contemplated driving the two hundred miles to his house but I didn't. I felt terrible, I presumed he was dead, this wasn't what I'd joined a band for. We spoke to *The Samaritans* for advice and help in how to deal with the ever increasing desperate letters I was getting and they gave us some leaflets to send back with our replies. About a month later we received an order for T-shirts from 'Michael' and a week or so after that I saw him at a Carter gig and he said hello as if nothing had ever happened. Now I'm not saying that if he was going to write such a heavy letter to me threatening to kill himself and scaring the hell out of me that he could at least have had the decency to go through with it, but, fucking hell. I wrote *Lean On Me I Won't Fall Over* all about him. Actually, now that I think about it, once he'd written the letter he would have had to find an envelope, buy a stamp, stick it on the envelope and take it to the post box. Possibly too much for someone so close to the edge.

2. Chrysalis Records was taken over by EMI

We had our first meeting with the new head of marketing. He said that we needed to sell a lot more records and that there were no singles on the album we'd just spent two months recording and what singles there were would need to be formatted if we wanted to compete with everyone else in the charts. We'd have to release two CDs with different B-sides - or 'bonus tracks' - one CD released a week after the other so that people would buy both and keep the single in the chart. We hated the idea, writing a load of extra songs or filling the CDs with acoustic songs, live tracks or remixes and we felt like we'd be ripping the fans off. We'd rather shoot ourselves in the chart position foot and we refused to give in. The (dick)head of marketing then informed us that this was the music *business*, disagreement turned to heated debate and heated debate to argument. In an attempt to win the argument he claimed the gold discs we'd received for our previous Number 1, *1992 The Love Album,* were 'worthless'. I tried to climb across the table to squeeze the life out of his cynical body, but he was already dead.

It was difficult to have any confidence in the label after this and we always felt they were under-selling us. I suppose it didn't help that we kept slagging them off in the press and in song.

For example:

Commercial Fucking Suicide Part 1

'The 1970s are great / Four and twenty years too late
Prejudice and racial hate / The dismantling of the welfare state
And just to keep you on toes / A soundtrack to go with the clothes
Created by computer kids / And marketing executives
If you buy this record today / It's not true what the advertisements say
Your life won't be greatly improved / But Christ, you've nothing to lose And we've got so much to gain
So satisfy your heart's desire / Throw your Gameboys on the fire
Bono ain't the new messiah / Michael Jackson is a liar
We need a hit to keep us warm / In St Moritz and Benidorm
So we can split and then reform.'
    and...

Sing Fat Lady Sing

'Everything is sponsored from the sea to the sky / this chorus will be brought to you by EMI.'

As a penultimate stand against formatting - we finally gave in with *Glam Rock Cops* (when we also gave in to remixing) - we advertised our *Lean On Me* single as *'Part one in a one-part pack'*. And then we Insisted on releasing *Lenny And Terence* as our next single. We were convinced it was a Top 40 hit (it was... Number 40!) *Chrysalis* felt we'd proved them right by releasing such a radio-unfriendly single, while we thought they'd deliberately let the record fail just so they *could* be proved right. The relationship between band and label did improve slightly when the marketing antichrist moved on to crack the whip at another record label, but when the *EMI* takeover really took over and most of the *Chrysalis* staff were downsized to make way for Robbie Williams' impending arrival, we became more and more disillusioned and paranoid.

3. I heard what I was saying and it suddenly dawned on me that I was an extremely boring person and I wanted to tell myself to shut the fuck up.

I'm not Archimedes or Carol Vorderman but I've calculated that of the 100% of days in 1993, 14.8% were press days and 20% were gig days (when we also did interviews). Compare this with 1991, when our gig percentage was 35.5% of the year whilst 14% was taken up with interview days. Which means in 1993 we were gigging 15.5% less and doing .8% more interviews, we were becoming more like after dinner speakers or professional chatshow guests. At this point all the mathematics and percentages caused my head to implode and I had to go and lie down with a cold flannel and twenty minutes of *Richard & Judy*.

We were getting way too much off our chests. Whole weeks booked into a hotel in Notting Hill explaining the album *Posthistoric Monsters* and its songs about killing Nazis, ethnic cleansing, starvation, suicide, murder and being abused by my cub-scout leader. Add to this my unhealthy preoccupation with the negative aspects of television adverts, the deterioration of the music industry and the gratuitous use of the saxophone in modern TV themes. And we were constantly having to defend and justify ourselves. Certain music writers had grown tired of us and the British music press - as cliché and tradition demands - had stopped building us up and started knocking us down. *Melody Maker* in particular had to run a piece about us every week just so they could demonstrate their hilarious comical versions of our name. Here are a few (make sure you're wearing your incontinence pants)...

'Carthorse The Uninteresting Something Or Other' - 'Dumpy's The Unstoppable Rusty Nuts Machine' - 'Cart Off The Unstoppable Drum Machine' - 'Jimbat and Fruitbob' - 'Fruitcake' and so on.

Once I'd realized that interviews were stupid, it was difficult to ever take them seriously again. I didn't believe anything I was saying, I was talking in clichés, a lot of the time answering questions by instinct without thinking about what I was saying. I'd explained where we got the name of the band so many times that I couldn't remember the truth. Two words into the question, 'Where did you get the name of the band?' my heart would sigh and sink very deeply into my chest, of which I'd got so much off of that it had nothing left to give. It had reached the stage where I was being interviewed about how much I hated being interviewed. From now on, at every interview it would be there at the back of my mind... It's all bollocks. And I knew that every time I opened my mouth the people who hated us hated us that little bit more.

'Now hatred is by far the longest pleasure / Men love in haste, but they detest at leisure' - Lord George Gordon Byron (1788-1824)
'And the goth girls are even worse' - (Lord Jim Bob Morrison (1960-?)

When bands tell us - as we did ourselves on many occasions - that they'd rather be either loved or hated and never merely liked, it's a bunch of nonsense. Hate and love are fickle emotions and in the hands of pop fans, who are the boss of fickle, kaboom! With hindsight I would have loved to have been liked - the bands that are merely liked tend to stick around a bit longer and seem happier. Being hated isn't that cool after all. I went to see Depeche Mode and The Sisters Of Mercy at Crystal Palace Sports Centre that year and, as I walked through the crowd during the day, about ten different Sisters Of Mercy fans swore at me and told me Carter were shit. It was actually pretty intimidating, especially as they were all girls which made it harder to know how to react. Being beaten up by a gang of blokes is heroic and romantically attractive, as I proved early on in life at my girlfriend's party. Getting done over by a gang of goth girls on an athletics track is just embarrassing. It reminds me of the time when I was stood in the crowd at a ULU gig having a chat with Mike Edwards from Jesus Jones when a girl came up to us and got all excited, telling me how great Carter were etc. She then turned to Mike and said, 'Are you the bloke from Jesus Jones?'

'Yes?' the bloke from Jesus Jones replied, preparing his autograph hand.

'You're shit!' and she walked off into the crowd.

A similar thing happened to the Wonderstuff's Miles Hunt when a girl threw a pint of beer in his face when he was standing with me at a gig having a cha... hang on, it's me isn't... keep away from me, I'm a looney magnet.

The funny thing is that I once met Sisters Of Mercy singer Andrew Eldritch at a Carter gig in Hamburg where he told me he thought we were the best band in the world. At the Crystal Palace gig I should have said, 'You may hate me but I know Andrew Eldritch and he thinks I'm great' and then stuck my tongue out and ran away very quickly. An amusing thing about meeting Andrew Eldritch in Hamburg is that Big Al, who was selling shirts for us that night was the Number 1 Sisters Of Mercy fan and he came into the dressing room about five minutes after Andrew left. He didn't believe that his goth idol had been sitting with us talking about football for the past half-hour. Neither did he believe us when we told him about a year later that his other all time favourite singer Ian Astbury from The Cult had been having a beer with us backstage at a gig in Vancouver - where The Cult were recording - again about five minutes before Al came in from the T-shirt stall.

So anyway, I was feeling a bit disillusioned. I'd lost faith in my chosen religion and become a non-believer. Like Millwall Football Club I thought that no-one liked us but unlike Millwall Football Club I cared, I really cared. We went on a UK arena tour with Madness, we thought it would be great, we loved Madness and felt we had things in common with them and so the Madness fans would probably love us. Wrong. The gigs were already sold out before we were announced as support, so nobody had bought a ticket because they wanted to see us and every night we'd go on to the huge cold stages, where for forty minutes we'd be booed, heckled and have things thrown at us. Not by the whole crowd, obviously - the majority of the audience were there for a good time and a sing-song. It was like a huge wedding reception every night, with us as the world's most unpopular wedding band. But 1% out of a crowd of ten thousand throwing stuff at us was enough to make us fear for our lives every night before we went on.

I thought we would have been alright by the time we got to London but on the first of two nights at Wembley Arena a pound coin hit me just above the eye on the first verse of the first song, cutting my head open and - on the positive side - making me look really hard and cool for the rest of the set. I wanted to tell the crowd every night, in a tongue-stuck-out ner ner ner ner ner way, that Madness had asked us to play and that while they were standing in the rain waiting for a night bus we'd be back at the hotel bar with their favourite band listening to Suggs take the piss out of us for being from South London where we all live in caravans with pots and pans hanging from the windows.

It was the Madness tour and the *Radio Live 105 Listener Appreciation Show* that we played so badly at in San Francisco a week earlier that led to a loss of onstage self-confidence and caused Fruitbat to believe the only way we could save the band was to do what we had always up until then considered to be the absolutely unthinkable...

GET A DRUMMER

The gig in San Francisco was with Duran Duran and The Cranberries, both huge in America. Duran Duran were headlining but had decided they didn't want to go on too late so we were moved to the top of the bill. Top of the bill meaning one in the morning when all the audience who've seen the bands they came to see have gone home and taken the sound and lighting engineers with them. By the time we walked onto the stage of the San Francisco shopping centre (yes) with no lights and nobody to do the sound to an audience of about thirty seven people, we'd had enough time to get incredibly drunk, insult everyone from our latest American record label, call Simon Le Bon a fat bastard and then sober up again. As for the gig, we were awful.

Fruitbat was convinced that if we'd had a drummer we could have just rocked out and got away with it. Likewise, when we did the Madness tour we wouldn't have looked so lost on the big arena stages if we had somebody behind us banging away on a drum kit. So at the end of 1993 we drew up a short list of suitable drummers. It looked like this:

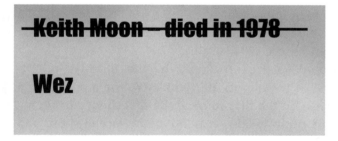

Keith Moon died in 1978

Wez

Wez Boynton was the drummer with International Resque and later just Resque. We first met Resque when we supported them at a Christian college in Southampton. It was one of the first times we had a rider in our dressing room, we had beer, crisps and sweets and we swapped our sweets for some of Resque's beer because they were either a) not thirsty or b) on non-liquid stimulants. It was a sugar/alcohol exchange that would lead to a long relationship between the two bands. We toured right across Europe together, entertained by bass player Roger's puppetry of the penis (long before it was theatrically viable) and Wez's appetite for eggs and hedonism. When Resque split up, Wez started working with Carter selling T-shirts, setting up the lighting rig and mixing us cocktails for the encore.

When Christmas and New Year were out of the way we gave Wez a ring at his home in Gosport and on the 14th of January we had our first rehearsal together. Within two months we'd played our first gig as a three-piece, secretly supporting The Sultans Of Ping at The Kentish Town Forum, filmed the video for *Glam Rock Cops*, recorded a *Radio One* session, appeared on a couple of TV programmes, had our photo taken for the *NME* standing on the big white 'H' of the helicopter pad on the roof of the Royal London Hospital and dressed up as coppers on *Top Of The Pops*. Wez had been happily sitting at home watching the telly and we'd turned his life upside-down. His first Carter tours were in America and Japan.

THE OSMONDS

Salt Lake City has got a bad reputation. Bad meaning good meaning bad.

When we went there in '94 it had been snowing heavily and we thought we were going to be stranded there for a couple of days and were terrified. We'd been to a big restaurant for breakfast and everyone there was wearing starched and striped Gordon Gekko businessman shirts and braces. Was this a town entirely populated by bank managers? We weren't looking forward to the gig, we'd heard all the rumours about Bible-bashing teetotallers, we'd seen the Osmonds. But let's not forget, the Osmonds recorded *Crazy Horses* Ooweeow! Ooweeow! The gig was great. Yes, there was a certain amount of achy breaky line dancing going on and there were quite a lot of Stetsons and not many Carter fans but we really had a good time. They didn't lynch us or round up a posse to chase us out of town and we left Utah the same alcoholics heathen non-believers we were when we drove into town earlier that day.

APRIL FOOL'S DAY AND OTHER NOTABLE DIARY DATES

We played San Francisco on Saint Patrick's Day and we spent the afternoon visiting various local radio stations to do short interviews and mainly to say, 'Hi, we're Carter The Unstoppable Sex Machine and you're listening to WWBBMBRGGTT999.8 FM'. We once did a whole week of these radio IDs, sometimes driving a hundred American miles to do so; we must have recorded about fifty thousand different versions of the sentence all over the world. But in all my years on this planet I've never heard myself once on the radio saying, 'Hi, we're Carter The Unstoppable Sex Machine and you're listening to WWBBMBRGGTT999.8 FM' or any other radio frequency. Anyway, we were at a radio station in San Francisco and the DJ - commenting on the City's obsession with the Irish day of celebration - asked us if St Patrick's Day was big anywhere else apart from America. 'Uh, yeah...um, Ireland.'

We played in Providence on Good Friday, which was also April Fool's Day and in honour of the latter, at Lupo's Heartbreak Hotel in Providence, high on tequila[18] at another one of those radio festivals, we really gave the Crash Test Dummies a hard time. They had that humming song single out that I hated at the time and to us back then they were the most boring and criminally dull band we'd ever seen. We had to let them know. So we stood in the crowd for the whole gig hurling an unreasonable amount of abuse at them until we were nearly ejected from the venue.

We also played on Easter Saturday, Easter Monday and on both the day Kurt Cobain shot himself and three days later when an electrician installing a security system at his house found the body. We didn't know about the tragic event yet when we parked the bus outside the Masquerade club in Atlanta, we were more concerned with whether Fruitbat would make it to the gig or not. The previous night we'd played in Augusta, where we'd stayed behind afterwards ordering drinks by colour. You should never drink by colour, the vomit is too vivid. The Bloody Mary is a great tipple until you've thrown up a pint of scarlet sick. And if you take a trip to the Markthalle in Hamburg you may still be able to detect a blue tinge to the venue's staircase, left there by a member of Cornershop after we drank blue there together in 1993.

The green drinks we'd been given in Augusta had a bizarre affect on our legs, more potent than any scrumpy. We'd had one final green shot, said goodbye to the barman and left the venue to walk across the parking lot to the bus. Our soundman John Gibbon had to crawl on his hands and knees, laughing all the way and it could've been the green drinks or just carelessness but, as we drove away in the direction of Atlanta, we left Fruitbat behind.

He'd had no money with him and only an equally skint roadie Daz for company, but somehow they managed to make it the 157 miles across Georgia to Atlanta before us. They'd stayed the night with someone from the gig and

[18] Tequila, like *Rolling Rock* is another drink that Fruitbat uses as an excuse for bad behaviour. He also claims it makes him hallucinate and once when we were sitting outside a cafe by Lake Como in Italy on a day off, he said that the previous night's tequila binge was making him see chickens. Then we all saw the chicken. If you're ever at a party with him, tip some tequila into his empty Becks bottle and watch him turn into a tomato, literally. Or a chicken.

convinced them that it would be a great idea to go to see Carter just that one more time. And seeing as how they were going that way anyhow, could they have a lift?

WHO'S KURT COBAIN?

8th April 1994 was a bad day to be driving around American radio stations to plug your new album, it couldn't have seemed more trivial. We found out the news about Kurt Cobain taking his own life from the rep from *IRS*, our new US label, who'd come to take us to our radio interviews for the day. All the radio stations were taking phone calls from distraught Nirvana fans and also a surprising number of sickos ringing in to say how much of an arse they thought Kurt Cobain was and to try to be the first to tell a tasteless joke about him. There was nothing to talk to us about, nobody was interested where we got our name from or why we'd got a drummer. They didn't even want to record a quick 'Hi, we're Carter.' We went back to the venue to soundcheck and to spread the bad news to the crew and the local in-house sound man said, 'Kurt who?' so his friend said, '*You know*, that Nirvana guy.'

Kurt Cobain wasn't as well known in the States as we might have imagined. He'd have to die dramatically and young to be really famous in America, which he'd obviously just done. Much like James Dean, Marilyn Monroe, JFK and honorary American John Lennon, from that day everyone would know who Kurt Cobain was. At our Atlanta gig I'd either crassly or touchingly dedicate *Suicide Isn't Painless* to him.

The next day we were in Phoenix, Arizona for the last date of the tour at the Phoenix Edgefest and we had a drink problem. We couldn't get one. Our passports were at the Japanese Embassy awaiting the glueing-in of visas for the following week's Tokyo gigs and without ID they wouldn't serve us any booze at the festival site. I don't know why we didn't have a ryder, maybe we'd drunk it already, but never let it be said we weren't resourceful. We managed to get served at the frozen margarita stall which was great up until they got nervous about serving us any more and also when we started to feel nauseous; there's only so many alcoholic ice lollies you can take without throwing up.

For people from a country where the licensing laws let us drink in pubs from the age of 18 and where we do it from about 14, the strict over 21, no ID, no drink laws in America were a bit of a culture shock. When The Senseless Things first toured the States they were still under 21 and at some of the venues they were only allowed in for the soundcheck and the time they were onstage. A similar thing happened to our underage roadie Mole in Seattle. He had to sit on the bus from the minute the doors opened until when we went onstage when he was allowed in to do his job of assisting the production before having to leave again. The ridiculous thing was that while he was sat on the bus Mole got incredibly drunk and the beefy security guard on the back door who had to let him back in the venue pissed off his face wasn't happy. The doorman was a knob anyway, his alcohol-policing powers had gone to his fat head. At the end of the night he wouldn't let us walk the twenty yards from the back door of the gig to the bus because we were carrying beer. He said he was only doing his job but it was obvious he was also showing off to his corkscrew-haired girlfriend who was with him. When he stopped Adrian Boss from leaving the gig until he got rid of his beer, Adrian obliged by throwing it in his face and just before we drove away, Handsome Dave said goodbye to him and kissed his girlfriend which almost made the doorman cry. In the words of Alan Partridge, needless to say we had the last laugh.

At the Phoenix Edgefest as we took a break from our quest for illicit booze and Mexican ice lollies, we borrowed another band's dressing room to do a short interview. We asked the band's tour manager if it was OK and he said yes but not for long. Then he kept interrupting us, acting like he was a big-shot American rock manager and I had to promise Wez that I'd write a song about him when I got home if he agreed not to hit him. When I got home I wrote *Me And Mr. Jones*. More people thought that song was written about them than Carly Simon's smash hit *You're So Vain*. Everyone from the marketing man at *Chrysalis* to Jon Beast.

I forgot to say - and he'll hate me for doing so - but Wez looked a lot like Rowan Atkinson. Weirdly, Salv who'd play bass with us later also looked like Rowan Atkinson and, as you know, Fruitbat and Tony Robinson are never seen in the same room. If you haven't got a television, both Rowan Atkinson and Tony Robinson are actors who appeared together in four series of the *BBC* comedy *Blackadder*. Television is an electronic system for transmitting still or moving images and sound to receivers that project a view of the images on a picture tube or screen and re-create the sound.

Adrian's Magic Pants

Fruitbat first met his girlfriend Crissi when she interviewed us for music and fashion mag *Buzz*. Crissi brought Adrian Boss along to The Clarendon in Hammersmith to see us play and a month later, at the *Buzz* magazine party at Heaven, he asked us if we wanted a manager. We said yes.

Up until then we'd been alternating between The Cricketers in Kennington and The Clarendon in Hammersmith. We were both phone phobic and not very good at selling ourselves, we really needed a manager. If you look again at the photo on the sleeve of *30 Something* you'll notice that in his right hand Adrian is holding an early example of a mobile phone. Adrian was the first person I ever knew who owned one, it was the size of a Second World War walkie-talkie and it never left his ear. You can't imagine how hard it must have been for him to keep it down at his side like that while the photo was taken, hence the gritted teeth. Unlike me and Fruitbat, Adrian Boss did not have a phobia of phones - quite the opposite, he bloody loved them. And so Adrian became our fifth Beatle, driving us to gigs, getting us a record deal, booking us tours, finding us an agent, getting himself arrested for putting Carter stickers on public property, stencilling our logo all over the UK, putting fake 'unstoppable sex machine' prostitute cards with major record label phone numbers in phone boxes, giving up the warmth of his car interior to sleep in a field, aggravating Northern gig promoters and, most of all, astounding us with his magic pants.

FOREIGN PLUMBING

There are two big Adrian's Magic Pants stories, 'The locked door' and 'The blocked bath'. The first one involves Adrian locking himself in a hotel bathroom in Holland (the one with Norman Bates and the parrot) and, in attempting to free himself, pulling the door handle off. With no locksmiths or carpentry tools to hand, dressed only in his pants - his magic pants - he ingeniously shaped his undercrackers into a key/handle and poking them through the hole in the door managed to open it and free himself. The second more elaborate tale took place in the Prague flat that we'd been given for our stay there. During the night Adrian had woken in desperate need of a dump. Unable to find a light switch in the bathroom or the toilet and not wanting to wake up his band who were sleeping nearby, he decided to do his business in the bath. Next problem: no toilet paper. In an alien environment, perhaps confused by the darkness and under the influence of too much Czech bubbly, Adrian turned to an old friend for help. Having - and I'm starting to regret telling you this story now - used his magic pants for toilet tissue, Mr Boss attempted to send the offending jobbie down the plughole with the aid of the shower. It was no mean feat. Waking up the band with the relentless showering, flooding the downstairs flat, causing the irate lower neighbour to come upstairs to bang angrily on the door and complain in Russian for half an hour. Eventually all was calm and in the morning we tidied up, Fruitbat did the washing up and we left. In the back garden of the downstairs flat, snagged in the top branches of a tree, there was a pair of pants. In the confusion, Adrian had chucked them out the window. They may still be there now and, a bit like Jack's beans, maybe they've caused a bigger tree to grow and at the very top there now lives a giant with a huge pot of gold. Or maybe there's just a sad old tree that's died. Killed by a pair of pants. Adrian's Magic Pants.

THE END

KARTER USM

Here's a condensed version of extra curricular activities or 'additional information' included on the itinerary for the two days that we weren't onstage during our return three-day trip to Croatia in 1994. It reads more like the itinerary for James Hunt or Donatella Versace.

Thursday 19 May

8 PM:	PRESS CONFERENCE AT RADIO 101
9 PM:	DINNER - THEN MAYBE ONTO A CLUB

Saturday 21 May

11 AM:	GO-KARTING IN ZAGREB
LUNCH:	AT OLD CASTLE AND SPEND THE AFTERNOON THERE - HORSE RIDING?
EVE:	PARTY @ THE CASTLE AND THEN OPENING OF AN ART GALLERY

And the build up to the gig had been more like something you'd expect for The Pope or The Beatles. There'd been previews and reports on Croatian TV weeks ahead of our arrival and the ball boys in the Croat equivalent of the FA Cup Final had worn Carter shirts. The Croatian tourist industry had been one of the many victims of the recent war and they were keen to get some positive publicity - if it was to come from a South London indie band whose star was slowly on the descendant back at home, then so be it. The gig was organised by Radio 101 as a part of their 10th anniversary and it was their singles chart - compiled from listeners' votes - that our single *Glam Rock Cops* was currently sitting at the top of. (Stupidly, or rather because we weren't aware of this chart-topping fact, we didn't play the song at the gig. Nor did we play *The Impossible Dream,* which had also been a Zagreb Number 1.) Doh!

"On behalf of Croatian Airlines and Radio 101 we would like to welcome on board members of Carter The Unstoppable Sex Machine and wish them a pleasant stay in Zagreb." They could have just let the air stewardess say 'USM'. This is what came over the aircraft tannoy system of flight OU491 as it took off from Heathrow in the direction of Zagreb. We really were starting to feel like the Pope; maybe we should kiss the tarmac when we arrived. At the airport we were met by Damir Tijak from *Radio 101,* a lovely guy much respected on the alternative music scene in Croatia. Damir hadn't managed to get us a van to take us from the airport to the radio station for the press conference. So he'd had to get a white stretch limo instead. He claimed it was the same price anyway, but I did feel a bit strange driving through the poorer parts of town in such a flash motor. Still, as we pulled up outside the radio station and stepped out of the car to the flash guns of the awaiting photographers (that's never happened before) I couldn't resist flicking the Vs,[19] much like I imagine (no pun intended for a change) John Lennon would have done. Or maybe The Pope.

The gig was at the Doma Sportova sports hall and was a triumph, in spite of the fact that the 19 songs we played didn't include the two that the 4,000-capacity crowd particularly wanted to hear. Afterwards we were whisked away to the national television studios to do a live midnight interview to accompany the concert footage that had been hastily edited and was now showing.

The following day was packed with jam. Steve Lamacq and the *BBC* were with us to record a week of shows for *Radio One* about the effects of the war on the lives of Croatian music fans. So they went with Fruitbat and The Red Cross (weren't they a band in the 80s?) to visit a refugee camp. There were three and a half million refugees or displaced people in the Former Yugoslavia - when we went up on the roof of the Hotel Panorama where we were staying to have our photo taken for a magazine, we found that the whole top floor was taken up by people made homeless by the war. And in the lift on the way up we noticed somebody had written on the wall, *'Carter sex and drugs and rock and roll. Without condoms!'*

No, no, always condoms, always condoms.

If it wasn't for the top floor guests, the trip to the camp and the white Landrovers parked outside the hotel with the U and the N on the side, you wouldn't have known there was still a war on not a million miles away. Zagreb had remained - physically at least - untouched. And I got the impression that the crowd who'd had to fork out three days wages to get a ticket for the gig just wanted to get on with their lives, listen to some music, show off their home made Carter shirts, shout 'you fat bastard' in an exotic accent and dance.

Aside from the trip to the Red Cross camp the rest of the day that had been lined up for us was better than a trip to Alton Towers. First off we went go-karting. We had the track to ourselves apart from some professional karters - 12-year-old girls who kept repeatedly lapping us - I drove my kart like a *Morris Traveller*, figuring

[19] The picture became the front cover of the live Carter video, entitled *Flicking The Vs*.

that I might not win any races but at least if I didn't crash then if I wouldn't look too ridiculous on the TV cameras that were filming our every move during the three days, Big Al won the go-karting and Steve Lurpack spectacularly crashed into a wall of tyres.

After that we were driven to a castle in the countryside for what seemed like a 47-course meal. I'm the type of person who sits at home in front of the telly with a plate on my lap and I only ever eat one course (unless a piece of cheese, a pickled onion or a *Twix* counts as dessert). Every time I thought I'd eaten the main course, another one would appear, each accompanied by a different bottle of wine from the castle's extensive cellar. If you've got the *Flicking The Vs* video you can see us being interviewed shortly after the meal and you'll understand what such a Henry the Eighth type meal and accompanying booze does to you. The final course was a dessert presented on a plate for each of us with the words 'Welcome Carter' written in chocolate. After we left the castle, we were taken to a famous Croatian artist's show at a swanky gallery in the centre of Zagreb and we finally ended up back at the Apple club where we'd played a couple of years before under armed guard and we were treated like we really were The Beatles. Practically everyone at the club had been at the gig the previous night and they wanted to say hello, get their faces signed and ask us why we didn't play *Glam Rock Bloody Cops*. I spent most of my time at the club talking to an incredibly intense skinhead poet who had spent a lifetime writing incredibly intense skinhead poetry and had then taken it all to a cave and burned it. If only some of the people writing songs in Britain were that dedicated to their art. I'm willing to supply the matches.

THE FASHION VICTIM
SUPPORT GROUP

What possessed me to walk into Debenhams department store in Croydon and buy the pair of blue and white checked pyjamas that I wore onstage at The Phoenix Festival in 1994? Did I think I was Johnny Fingers from The Boomtown Rats, Doris Day or Wee Willy Winkie? If only I'd looked a bit more objectively in the dressing-room mirror before going onstage. Maybe there wasn't a dressing-room mirror. Perhaps it was hidden behind a stack of 48 lagers that looked like 96, or maybe I'd tripped over my long fringe earlier and smashed the mirror, giving myself seven years' bad luck. Which was about how long the gig was on television for. ITV had filmed the festival and they were showing a different song from our set pretty much every night of the week for ages reminding me of my jim-jam *faux pas* over and over and over again. The ponytail was a bad idea as well, I don't know what got into me that day. Strange, because as you know, I'd always been revered and lauded by the press for my sartorial elegance.

When I was just ten years of age I used to go and stay with my cousin Ian in Hemel Hempstead. I realize I might have been high on *Tizer* and *Spangles* and this may just be an antacid flashback, but I have this very vivid memory of being treated like a Martian because I had authentic bottle green *Levis Sta-prest* trousers. Kids in the 1970s used to mug other kids for their *Levi* jeans' tags and labels. They'd tear them off so they could stick them onto the back pockets of their own less cool *Tesco Bombers* jeans. I suppose Hertfordshire must have been a lot further away from London back then than it is now and the young smooth arriving in his flash London trousers was equal parts, popular: with the local girls who, in spite of being a lot older than me would want to kiss me and show me their chests and, unpopular: some of the local boys were keen to kick my poncy big-city teeth in and tear the tags off my trousers.

From then on, via my cheap pale blue teddy boy's drape suit mail ordered from the back pages of the *Melody Maker* in the 1970s for a five spot. On through the more mod suit and pink footwear of my Jeepster years. (I know the pink shoes were cool because I was walking through the West End once when Poly Styrene from the punk band X-Ray Spex passed me on a pushbike and said, "Cool shoes".) And on up to the first time I walked onstage in a pair of short - and yet long -

tartan trousers round about 1991, I was a dedicated follower of both fashion and anti-fashion.

It's said that in every band there's at least one member who is 'the plumber', the one who looks like he's moonlighting and may be called away from behind his drum kit at the Wembley Arena at any minute to unblock a sink or bleed a noisy radiator. There are also a few bands who consist almost entirely of plumbers, but whatever you say about Carter you couldn't accuse us of that. And if you think I ever resembled a plumber I'd like to think it was a famous plumber, a fashion-conscious plumber, maybe Italian.

THE SUPER MARIO BROTHERS

In spite of the fact that I only wore short trousers on stage for a period of about 18 months and Fruitbat kept his head warm with a wooly bobble-less tea cosy more often than a cycle hat, we were always known as a cycle hat and shorts-wearing duo, even when I was in a suit and tie and there were six of us. Of course there was a period of time when we looked a bit ridiculous but at least we made an effort, at least we took our coats off before we went on stage. I'm always a bit suspicious of a band who look like they may have to leave very shortly. Big anorak zipped up to the chin = going in a minute. Short trousers, T-shirt covered with cartoon characters, middle of December = not going anywhere just yet. Pyjamas, in an airfield in Warwickshire = ditto.

On the drive home from the Phoenix Festival our car broke down. It was the orange VW Beetle that's featured on the front cover of our B-sides album *Starry Eyed And Bollock Naked*. Me and Mrs Jim Bob were stuck on the hard shoulder of the M40 for what seemed like forever waiting for the RAC man to turn up to push our poor old orange banger onto the back of his equally orange rescue truck and drive us home. This was when I discovered the answer to one of the two great questions of the modern age. How do the men who drive the snowploughs and the staff at motorway service stations get to work? I don't know about the snowplough drivers, but when the RAC mechanic turned off the M40 and onto a 'secret' service road leading us away from the motorway and into a town, I realized that the woman who sold me my ploughman's cheese sandwich and my *Monster Munch* probably got picked up by a special service-station minibus and driven to work along one of these secret service roads.

When we did finally get home our toilet exploded, flooding the bathroom, the hall and the kitchen of our house, and I had to get my

Reader's Digest big book of home DIY off the bookshelf to find out how to turn off the water. If only I'd been more suitably dressed.

THE MAN WHO INVENTED ACID HOUSE

I know it's fairly obvious, but I used to cut my own hair. I haven't been to a professional hairdressers since I was about eighteen. When I was at school I used to get my teddyboy hair cut by an old Greek barber in Tulse Hill, because he hadn't learnt a new haircut since the 1950s and he was ideal. Me and my Rock'N'Roll Revival 1975 band-mates Nicky and John used to spend hours at home dressing our hair. We used to pile on half a tub of *Brylcreem* and then comb and mould the sloppy mess into a quiff at the front and a duck's arse at the back. Then - keeping very still - we'd cover our heads with *Cossack* hairspray to hold it all in place. I even had a go at a Bill Haley kiss curl to be different for about a month and, let me tell you, keeping one of them in place on your forehead is no mean feat. I think I chose Bill because John was Eddie Cochran, Nicky was Gene Vincent and I didn't want to be Elvis.

After my Ted years I moved from the Tulse Hill barber's chair to a more up to date seat in front of a sink at one of the few unisex hair salons in South London, it was called Oliver's and although it's seen better days it's still there today.[20] I used to like the fact that it was a girl who washed your hair before Oliver - I presume it was him - would pump up your chair and start feathering and cropping. At the end of the haircut, as he held the mirror behind your head, there'd be the inevitable question, 'hairspray?' to which only the bold or the obviously gay would reply, 'Yes please'. (As a Ted I only ever sprayed my hair in private.)

I wasn't the only big-haired one at my school who visited Oliver's on a Saturday afternoon. *Radio One* DJ and inventor of acid house Danny Rampling had the barnet of a man who was partial to a bit of product. He went to the same school as me, there's a plaque in the Dunraven School dinner hall dedicated to me and Danny. Don't bother going there to look though, I think somebody must have nicked it.

After a period of doing my own barbering, I discovered my girlfriend could cut hair and I haven't had to pay a professional since. This has made the more experimental and the just plain mental hairstyles much more of a possibility. I could never have gone into Oliver's or Keith's - my post-school barbershop in West Norwood - and asked for 'everything off the back, the top and sides but leave the fringe really really long' -

[20] Between finishing writing this and finding a publisher Oliver's has had a makeover, including a shiny new sign and shopfront.

'and something for the weekend sir?... a straitjacket perhaps?'

Once again, I know it's fairly obvious, but my famous long fringe began its life as a relatively unknown short one. I did meet people who asked me whether I had really long hair which I had cut off except for the fringe. My crazy barnet actually started out like a rockabilly haircut, or a skinhead girl's, cropped all over with just a little tuft of hair at the front. And then it just grew. In length and in stature. In the *Smash Hits* Polls of 1993 when they ask the famous to fill in their own readers poll voting form, Howard Donald from Take That nominated me for 'Most Tragic Haircut'. My fringe almost got me deported from New York before I'd even arrived, it used to fly into my mouth when I was singing, making me gag and, although imitation is the sincerest form of flattery, meeting fans with the same haircut as me began to freak me out a bit. By 1994 my front barnet had grown so long that one afternoon I was on the top floor of Tower Records at Piccadilly Circus looking for bargains. As I browsed I hummed the tune to our Number 7 in the charts hit *The Only Living Boy In New Cross* and a local prince, hearing my beautiful voice, climbed up my luscious locks to the top of Tower Records, where he asked me to marry him. Although once again I was flattered by the prospect of such a fairy tale happy ending, I sensed there were about another ten thousand words left of my story and decided to get the scissors out.

So during the recording of the *Worry Bomb* album at the huge country house in Oxfordshire where Mike Oldfield had recorded *Tubular Bells* setting Dickie Branson on the road to global Virginalism, I passed some of my down time by chopping off my bangs. I had the fringe framed and we gave it away as a prize to the person who completed the sentence, 'I would like to win Jim Bob's bangs because.....................' in the most imaginative or amusing way. The lucky winner was Robert Cotter from Cabinteely, Ireland with, 'I would like to win Jim Bob's bangs because I want to start up a fringe theatre group (badum-bum ching!)' Let's hope that Robert wasn't a witch who merely wanted my hair to put into a big cauldron to complete the recipe of a terrible spell he was working on. 'Eye of newt and toe of frog, wool of (Fruit) bat and hair of Jim Bob.'

Oh Christ. And what about Samson? Samson and bloody Delilah!! What if I'd just lopped off the source of my powers? Was it all a Philistine plot to sap my strength? Was my girlfriend hairdressing for the *Melody Maker*? Had she just taken her scissors to my punning muscle? Would I never pun again. Oh God! Oh God !Oh God! Oh God!!!!!!!!!!!!!! !!!!!!!!!!!!!!!!!!!!!!!!!!!!!!!!!!!!!!

VICTOR IMMATURE

Phew!

When we were in East Berlin in 1990 repainting the town red, we played a game of knock down ginger, the popular street game of our misspent youth where we'd knock on people's doors or ring on their bells and run away. We also played the running over the bonnets and roofs of cars - in this case *Trabants* - game and I expect we would have had a go at kiss-chase and conkers as well. But although I wouldn't mind chasing Fruitbat up and down Friedrich Strasse, I wouldn't have been quite so keen to catch him. And it wasn't conker season. I'm not proud of this Brits-on-the-piss juvenilia and I can't apologize enough if we knocked on your door and got you out of bed in the middle of the night just in time to see us running away down the street and over the top of your fibre substitute car.[21] I wasn't proud either when, after a night out in Atlanta, Georgia - having stumbled across a ye olde Englishe pubbe complete with ye olde beer garden, ye olde pints of ale and a larger than ye olde lifesize wooden Beefeater (that we tried to steal) standing guard outside - we were involved (well, mainly our manager Adrian was involved) in yet more running over the tops of cars, this time the capitalist Western version. It was all too much for Handsome Dave. And when Adrian took a long run-up ready to go over the top of a particularly cool sports car, Dave stood in front of the vehicle with his arms outstretched shouting, *'Not the Porsche! Not the Porsche!'*

When you return home after six or seven weeks of such infantile and immature behaviour and you try and tell your wife or your mum or worse still your kids - who are now a lot more grown-up than you - all about it, they just stare at you blank faced and tut. (There's a good infantile game: see who can tut the loudest, it's nigh-on impossible.) Your friends and family

[21] Fibre substitute: *Duraplast*: a fibre substitute used by East German car company *VEB* to build their *Trabant* cars. *Trabants* were 2-stroke-engined cars with a top speed of 30 mph, loathed by their East German owners. Up until the collapse of the Wall and the Curtain, when they could sell them to Irish rock group U2 and to Western yuppies, who'd have them re-fitted with three-litre V6 engines, six-speed gearboxes, anti-lock brakes, electric windows, side-impact protection, sunroof, cruise control, satellite navigation systems, cup-holders, metallic paint, DVD-player, airbags, child-proof locks and air-conditioning. Making them worth £12,000, an increase of about 12,000 per cent on the original value.

don't understand you because they weren't there to experience what it's like to be cooped up in a sixteen-wheel steel hotel with the same dozen hotel guests talking crap for two months. So these other childish acts and stories may be nonsensical to you, but that's probably the point.

SPORT
When a particularly annoying member of the audience came backstage after a gig and drank too much of our rider and started to overstep the mark, insulting other people in the room and trying to steal things, we used to get Mole to tell them the fascinating story of his 'football injury'. The punchline to his tall tale was for Mole to drop his trousers and pants to reveal the long vertical scar down the centre of his backside that he sustained in the said soccer accident.

INTERNATIONAL JOURNALISM
During an obviously too long tour of Europe, I was reading a copy of *The International Guardian* when I noticed that if I removed part of the newspaper's front page masthead logo, because of the way it had been designed I was left with a piece of paper that said *International Ian*. I decided this must be some sort of a sign and I changed my name to International Ian for the next few gigs. I found that I could go onstage with a completely different personality to that of Jim Bob; it gave me a whole load of new things to talk to the audience about and Ian was a lot funnier than I was. When I got back home and started to design my International Ian T-shirt and Fruitbat was talking about becoming Continental Colin I realized that it wasn't amusing anymore.

CULTURE
Something I always wanted to do, but sadly didn't. When people used to come backstage after the gig I would have loved them to find us in dressing gowns, smoking pipes and enjoying a large brandy, listening to opera. Just like Morecambe and Wise.

POLITICS
During the general election in 1997 we played a gig at Farnham Maltings in the safe Tory seat of Surrey South West. During the day, Conservative MP Virginia Bottomley drove through the venue car park with a megaphone telling everybody to 'Vote Conservative! ' and Steve Boynton (Wez's brother and new Carter guitarist) climbed out onto the roof of the tour bus and mooned her. Luckily her love-child Mad Dog

Bottomley wasn't with us by then, as he would have killed us.

On the night of the General Election Virginia Bottomley managed to keep her safe Tory arse on her safe Tory seat, she was one of the few to do so. We stayed up all night in a car park outside Stoke watching the election results on the tour-bus telly, cheering wildly at the look on defence secretary Michael Portillo's usually smug face as he lost Enfield Southgate to Labour's Stephen Twigg. It was the end of eighteen uninterrupted years of Conservative rule. And the beginning of another eighteen.

INTERNATIONAL POLITICS

During the US democratic Party Convention in New York in 1992 we used a picture of Georgian Nobel Peace prize-winning peanut farmer Jimmy Carter with the words 'THE UNSTOPPABLE SEX MACHINE coming any moment' underneath. The posters were mistaken for an ad campaign related to the Democratic nomination - either an amusing pro-Democrat gag or a dirty tricks scam on behalf of the Republicans - the Democratic nomination was ironically won by the *real* unstoppable sex machine Bill Clinton. Or George Clinton, as I mistakenly and embarrassingly called him in one of my rants to the US music press.

So, you see, childish and yet still politically active. Art terrorism at its most stupid. We've taken petitions to Downing Street on behalf of fee-paying students, we've played benefit gigs for CND, *The Big Issue*, Shelter, The Terrence Higgins Trust and The Liverpool Dockers, we helped get a 'men only' roadie competition changed to a men and women event. Just as Jiminy Cricket had advised us, we always let our conscience be our guide. And when we weren't sure whether or not a cause was Kosher, we'd ask Billy Bragg's manager what Billy would do. That's actually true.

Then there was the easy sixty grand we turned down for having our music used in a *Lucozade* advert because the recovery-aiding glucose drink was made by enthusiastic animal testers Smithkline Beecham. It got us into the tabloids and the publicity led to requests from various anti-vivisection groups to support their cause. So we wrote letters of support, modelled their T-shirts and had their stalls at our gigs. And then in 1992 I was asked to make a speech at the end of the big animal rights march *World Day For Animals*. In spite of my apparent self-opinionated and loud-mouthed nature on stage I'm actually a shy guy, not a great public speaker at all, just a self-opinionated loud mouth. I'm also not very good at saying no. So I found myself on a stage at Earls Court in front of eight thousand animal activists and about two hundred Carter fans who'd come along to see me hopefully play a couple of songs - which with hindsight would have been a more sensible idea - but instead, after being completely blown off stage by some moving poetry from Benjamin Zephaniah, an attempted stage invasion by the Animal Liberation Front and a show-stealing, house-bringing-down to rapturous applause, foot-stamping, screams and cheers articulate speech from Ken Livingstone, I ambled up to the microphone and mumbled something inane like, 'I'm not very good at speeches I'm just here to stand up and be counted.' And then I ambled off again, the silence of Earls Court broken only by the rustle of tumbleweeds scuttling across the vast hall. Those who came to see Carter play *Sheriff Fatman* were disappointed that we didn't and everybody else was just plain disappointed. I felt like a halfwit. As I walked away from the stage a small crowd gathered to ask for my autograph which just made me feel worse, like I was cheapening the whole day with my vulgar pop stardom I should have been happy, I was finally like David Essex in *Stardust*. (The scene where he goes to his Mother's funeral and the hearse gets mobbed by screaming fans.)

Before I sneaked out the back door of Earls Court into a taxi to Beachy Head I was introduced to Ken Livingstone who blanked me completely. And although I went on to later vote for him at the London Mayoral Elections, was grateful that when I was very young he successfully stopped a road being built through my house and although I enjoyed all the free gigs he put on in London's parks when he was boss of the GLC. In spite of all that, a part of me hated his newt-keeping, geography teacher-suited, how dare he bloody ignore me guts.

THE FAT CONTROLLER
AND JAMES THE CHEATING RED ENGINE

Childish acts and political gestures were thin on the ground for the rest of 1994. We spent the latter part of the summer twiddling our thumbs, playing the occasional date in Switzerland and miming at the *Radio One Roadshow*. Me and Fruitbat had 'played' our first roadshow the year before in Swansea and in '94 we did three more with Wez in Edinburgh, Birmingham and on Blackpool Beach. *Radio One Roadshows* began in the 1970s when a couple of DJs would drive round Britain in an old caravan with a box of records to play to small crowds of holidaymakers, but by the time we performed at one it had blossomed into a huge free event with a convoy of trucks, charabancs, cars and vans, attracting thousands of screaming pop fans, some of whom had planned their holidays around the event. They'd become so popular that The National Association of Head Teachers asked the *BBC* to reschedule the shows in the mid 1990s because classroom attendance dropped by fifty percent when the Roadshow was in town. The Roadshow line-up usually consisted of a big-name boy/girl band, an up-and-coming boy/girl warm-up band who travelled around with the roadshow and a couple of more alternative acts like us so the holidaying indie kids didn't feel left out.

The night before the roadshows - which started early in the morning - too early in the morning - we'd sit up all night in the bar of a nearby hotel getting arseholed with the *BBC* DJs and staff. The boy/girl bands would usually be sent to bed early and it would be left to Fruitbat to instruct the new head of *Radio One* Matthew Bannister how he should be running his radio station and where he was going wrong. All the time, accidentally on purpose referring to him as Roger Bannister and congratulating him on his four-minute mile. I really quite enjoyed this part of the event, it was the standing on the roof of a lorry at eleven in the morning, miming to our latest single while ten thousand girls tried to cure my hangover by screaming at me that I found so difficult. The Roadshow was replaced at the start of the noughties by the *One Big Sunday* which I've never been to but I think it's exactly the same as the Roadshow, except on a Sunday.

KNOCK KNOCK? WHO'S THERE? BOYZONE

We've played with all the great boy bands. At *The Smash Hits Poll Winners Party* with New Kids On The Block, on a Spanish TV programme with Take That - when Gary Barlow had bright blond hair and Robbie Williams could still get his head through the door without major deconstructional building work - and at the filming of *Super 50,* the Belgian equivalent to *Top Of The Pops,* where we began another year of high jinx by almost getting into a fight with the just-about-to-be famous Boyzone. I exaggerate enormously. I've told myself a zillion times to stop. All that happened really was that a member of the 'zone asked us if we were - and I may well have got this wrong as well but to complete what's becoming a really awful anecdote - The Sultans Of Ping? Wez replied, 'No, are you Take That?' and I could see it turning very rapidly into a big ugly showbiz scrap, but it didn't and, Jesus, that really was a rubbish story wasn't it? Shall I leave it in? It's up to you. If you don't like it, tear it out of the book.

By the way, have I told you that when I was a boy I kept pet mice. They bred like rabbits. I woke up one morning and my two white rodents had become twelve. Sadly however, one of the newly born baby mice wasn't breathing and I was so overcome with sorrow and distress that I attempted to bring it back to life by blowing into its tiny mouth. I hate to say this, but my comedy rule-book insists that I do: I tried to give it mouth-to-mouse resuscitation. It was to no avail and I buried it in the back garden with all my hamsters, guineapigs and funfair goldfish. This story has got nothing to do with being on the road with a rock'n'roll band but I like to think its inclusion tells you something about what a nice, kind-hearted guy I am. It also gives something for *The Daily Mail* to blow out of all proportion for book publicity purposes. Oh, go on.

Inside industry secret Number 2: During a game of the guess the song game Bits And Pieces at the Radio One Roadshow in Swansea, I managed to score more points than everybody else and won. The ugly truth is I didn't win at all, Radio One DJ Mark Goodier just said that I did because he was a Carter fan. Shocking.

THE PEDANTS
ARE REVOLTING

Our first tour of 1995 was a tour of local radio stations. The three of us piled into a non-recoupably-hired car with a *Chrysalis* rep behind the wheel, on this occasion I think it might have been Adrian Boss's future wife Vanessa. We'd drive up and down the country to fill all the local DJs in on where the name of our band came from and we'd explain how we were now a three-piece, introducing our new member Wez who'd been with us for over a year now. It wasn't easy for Wez, he'd always be the new one. There'd always be two chairs, two microphones - and, at record signings, two marker pens - waiting for us when we arrived. It used to infuriate him. Usually the frontman gets all the attention while the rest of the band slag him off behind his back. But with Carter it was doubly bad for Wez as there were two frontmen. It was difficult for him to not feel neglected. We tried our hardest to involve him equally; we got him to stand in-between me and Fruitbat for photos so editors couldn't crop him out of the final picture. We endeavoured to make sure journalists spelled his name with a Z and not an S, which - like Liza Minnelli - he hated. In the same way that Fruitbat couldn't stand it when they called him *Fruit Bat* instead of Fruitbat. I didn't care when they called me *Jimbob* instead of Jim Bob although the S that everyone (including Fruitbat) always added to *Bloodsport (s) For All* was annoy ing. Today of course, I could console Wez by telling him about the *BBC's 100 Great Britons* poll in 2002 that featured John Lennon at Number 7, Paul McCartney at 19 and George Harrison at Great Briton Number 62, but no Ringo Starr. How must that have made poor Ringo feel? To compound matters, when the votes were counted up even Brunel was in there at Number 2! I mean, I know he's a great bass player and I love The Stranglers but surely he's French?

Anyway, we toured more radio stations in Paris and Germany shortly after which I only want to mention because, while we were there, the French record label took us to The Zenith venue in Paris to see the Beastie Boys. I love seeing bands abroad. We went to see Status Quo in Germany once and we were the only people in the building not wearing denim. The Quo played all their hits in the main set and then finished off with a medley, of all their hits... again! Genius. We also saw The B52s in Cologne and Ice Mutha Fuckin' T in an old deserted airport in Munich. We were playing in the smaller hall next door to where Ice was performing with his thrash-metal band Body Count and after his set he came in to see us. Some people have an aura about them when they walk into a room and Ice Mutha Fuckin' T certainly did. Although he was a bit of a shortarse.

I also went to see Morrissey at The Hollywood Bowl; we got a lift there on the back of someone's truck and had to walk home afterwards. I heard that as his band were still rocking out on the last song, Mozzer was already in a limo on his way back to his hotel. Encore, shmoncore. Anyway, I digress (all the sodding time). Back at the Zenith we went backstage after the gig to be introduced to the Beasties. Mike D was about as impressed to meet us as Ken Livingstone had been meeting me a couple of years earlier. We tried to make embarrassed small talk by dropping the name of our mutual friend Angus Batey - our first roadie who was now hip-hop correspondent for the *NME* and wrote the Beasties' book *Rhyming And Stealing* - but it didn't break the ice or the silence and we were as relieved to shake hands and get the hell out of there as Mike Mutha Effing D was to see us Mutha Effing leave.

As a punter without a major record label chaperon I've never tried to get backstage to see a band after a gig; I even feel guilty and intrusive if it's somebody I know personally. I wouldn't want to invade the band's space. They'll need time to get their breath back, change into a dry pair of trousers and carry out a gig post-mortem. So I'll go home, maybe leaving them sat in the corner of the dressing room with a towel over their head, feeling lonely, wondering why that unsocial bastard Jim Bob didn't come back to say hello.

HEADBANGING IN ATHENS

We first played in Athens, Greece in the Christmas of 1991. The journey there would have jazzed up a dull episode of *Airport* or *Airline*.[22] A whole load of us flew to Greece during an airport industrial dispute via a six-hour wait at Amsterdam Airport, a night in a hotel in Dusseldorf and a brief stopover on a runway in Thessaloniki. We eventually arrived in Athens and we had a blast, playing two victorious dates at the Rodon club where we experienced a slightly stereotypically fantastic thing about Greek audiences. They clap along to everything. But they gradually speed up their clapping tempo throughout the song. Which is very exciting, but when you're playing to a drum

[22] Both are reality TV shows about airports telling the day to day story of the staff that work there and the passengers who want to get on television by complaining about the outrageous delay of the flight from London to Majorca that they've just forked out almost fifteen pounds for.

machine that's sticking to its own rigid British stiff-upper-lip tempo and is also being drowned out by the sixteen hundred hands of the Athens audience, the results are hilarious. Particularly on the slower, quieter songs like *GI Blues*, where the only chance we had of keeping in time was to listen to the gentle tip-tap of the drum machine hi-hat. We were all over the shop.

When we returned for our second trip in '94 we took a drummer. It was Christmas again and this time we didn't get further than Heathrow Airport, where a wheel fell off the plane and we had to rearrange the date for February the next year. On the first night of our rescheduled return trip we went out for a quiet meal with the promoter Kostas outside a restaurant in a narrow but busy pedestrian street. Somewhere between the starter and the main course, we noticed that every time somebody walked past they'd hit one of us over the head with a squeaky plastic club or an inflatable Pink Floyd hammer. We ignored it for a while and just presumed it was revenge for all the football hooliganism, *Club 18 to 30s* and the theft of The Elgin Marbles. But then it started to get out of hand and we had to go and buy ourselves some clubs and hammers and even club hammers, to fight back. It turned out that it was all part of a Greek festival called *Apokria* which, according to Fruitbat's Greek friend Ilias, is *'a mixed celebration, part based in Orthodox Christianity ('Apokria' means in way 'without meat', and it is the pick of the season that according to Or Chris we should starve and not eat meat) and part based on some ancient Greek pagan celebrations. Basically, let apart the Christianity thing, what we are doing during this season is dress up, like Halloween but not only with scary costumes, or wear masks and go around and hit people with these plastic sticks, especially around the Plaka area... It is quite fun, but it can turn out really nasty, lots of serious street fighting and stuff.'*

Thanks Ilia. Of course, to us veggies, every day is Apokria, but at least we don't get hit over the head with a knobbly truncheon every time we go into *Holland & Barrett*.

Our three days in Greece were wonderful – we were treated like Posh and Becks (all eight of us), taken out clubbing (absolutely no pun intended whatsoever) every night after the gigs and given our own roped-off VIP area with free and increasingly more exotic flavours of alcohol throughout our stay. We boogie oogie oogied till we just couldn't boogie no more and then we played chicken with the crazy taxi drivers on the wide main roads between nightclub and hotel. In the morning we went to the Acropolis, soaking up centuries of history and crumbling architecture and felt so good we started enquiring about house prices and decided that we'd record our next album somewhere in Greece. The studios were cheaper, the weather was nicer and the people - even when they were beating you about the bonce - were so friendly.

When we got back to England we sat in a northbound traffic jam in the pouring rain on route to a working man's club just outside Blackpool, where we were filmed miming our latest single *Let's Get Tattoos,* alongside Les Gray's Mud and the show's host (ess) Lily Savage to an audience of drunk old couples who had no idea who the hell we were and were waiting for the bingo caller to come on and put them out of their misery. Luckily we had the dancers from the *Tattoos'* video with us and they seemed to keep the women happy and distracted with their shaven chests and six-pack ribs long enough for their husbands to not glass us and we escaped back to the traffic jam - now heading southbound - to London, for pancakes. Because it was Shrove Tuesday and as the Bible will tell you, Shrove Tuesday is Pancake Day, or *Jif Lemon Day.*

THE NIGHT OF
THE LIVING DEAD

Service stations. Service stations at three in the morning, when the only customers are rock bands, acid-housers who've been looking for some bright lights in a field since July of 1987 and insomniac compulsive gamblers who can't close their eyes without seeing the bells and cherries of Newport Pagnell's fruit machines and just have to come back for that £14 jackpot. At three in the morning the *Burger King* is closed, the all day breakfast is finished and there's no staff. Just one woman sat behind the counter in the mags and fags shop and another making the coffees and hot chocolates in the Country Kitchen / Pantry / Barn / Cottage over the footbridge on the Northbound stretch of the motorway. We'd pull in there looking like zombies, caught in the no man's land between drunk and hungover, in search of a tray of vastly overpriced food and coffee and a WC that accepts solids. When the soup of the day is now the soup of the night, and the badly EQ'd service station soundtrack is the music of the 1980s, always, even in the 1960s and the 1970s. Songs that you know but can't remember who's singing them - it might be Glen Medeiros, or is that a make of Scottish cooking sherry?

I think the staff that worked at these places in the middle of the night were as sleep deprived and bored as we were. We once visited a services restaurant for a very early breakfast, all eleven of us wearing moustaches. It wasn't a Freddie Mercury night, it had been our busdriver Eric's birthday. He'd taken us to Blackpool Pleasure Beach for a day out on *The Big One* (I didn't go on it), *The Grand National*, *The Revolution* and *The Log Flume*; he was a lovely man and we liked him, he was in our Top 5 of all-time great bus drivers. Oh, and he had a moustache. But the point is that the staff who served us our runny eggs and stewed beans and took our money at the till didn't bat an eyelid. It was as though a busload of men with ridiculous moustaches often popped in at four in the morning for breakfast.

We had our favourite services. Farthing Corner on the M2, purely because it sounded a bit like Farting Corner, anything with a Little Chef restaurant, and there used to be - may still be - a services in the Lake District that was the only one in England that was independently owned. We always used to visit when we were on our way to Scotland, because we felt we were doing our bit for anti-globalization when we bought a cup of splosh and a jam doughnut.

And then there'd be the tough decisions: stop at the next services toilet one mile ahead, or cross your legs and hang on to the next in 26 miles. You want to get to your destination as soon as possible and no matter how quick you are it always takes at least an hour for a services stop, so is it better to hang on a bit longer while the traffic's clear but running the risk of wetting yourself? Or stop now and psychologically make your journey 25 miles longer than it actually is? So you split the difference and pull off at the nearest one but only go to the garage to use the toilet and get yourself a cheese ploughman's and a bag of *Hot Mega Monster Munch*, super heartburn flavour. (Do four mentions qualify me for some sort of sponsorship deal with *Walkers Crisps*?) And while you're there you fill the hired diesel motor up with unleaded petrol, seizing the engine and upsetting the AA man who can't believe anyone could be so stupid.

DIDDLEE DIT DE DE...
TWO STAGES

Somebody had the brilliant idea of holding a rock festival in a huge tent near Brighton. They'd erect two stages inside the tent, one at each end and what would happen is that, when the band at one end of the tent has finished playing, the audience can simply about face and watch the next band on the stage at the opposite end of the tent. In theory: genius. It would save a fortune on tent hire. Of course, unless you build a couple of hours into your schedule for all the technical difficulties, power cuts and other things that are bound to go wrong throughout the day, then your plan is going to be bollocks. What will happen is this: as the last chord of The Charlatans' encore is still ringing around the big top's canvas, the MC / DJ / bastard will already be introducing Carter USM, who will have no choice but to go on. There are now effectively two bands on at the same time, the audience have their backs to the one that's just come onstage or they're leaving the tent to get another pint of warm, flat lager and a pancake, they're confused. The whole thing will be filmed for TV, Jim Bob will be drunk and angry, ranting and swearing throughout his band's set and then after the gig he'll go off in search of the festival's promoter, probably carrying a chair.

OPATIJA

Opatija - a town where the royal families and the world's A-list (Wilhelm II, Franz Joseph I, Gustav Mahler, Isadora Duncan (worked at Telefunken) and Anton Chekhov among others) used to take their winter hols. Opatija has a tourist tradition that is as old as the town itself. In numerous restaurants along the Riviera you can taste the national dishes of the world, whether it's a cheese fondue, salted cod or Porky The Pig, the choice is up to you. You can be served by candlelit waiter or relax in the rustic ambience of the pub. You can chit-chat in cafes and coffee-houses, you can dance on terraces, in discotheques and in night clubs and then you can lose your shirt at the Casino. Or why not take a boat to the famous Postojna caves, ski or ride a horse on Ucka or on the nearby highlands and then return to the bosom of Opatija, where you can moor your yacht in the marina?

While finding out the above tourist info on the beautiful coastal town of Opatija, just fifty klicks from Trieste I was diverted via various pop-up ads and Internet marketing tricks and managed to spend £10.39 (saving £2.60 on the list price) on a book about Spiders From Mars guitarist Mick Ronson and 38 quid on a flight to Barcelona.

All that *Judith Chalmers*[23] holiday brochure stuff is pretty accurate though and it should give you some idea why when we went to Opatija to play at a rock festival with The Stranglers in 1995 and had to wait for three days sat on the beach in the Istrian Peninsulan sunshine drinking cold bottles of *Coca Cola* and swimming in the Jacuzzi-warm Adriatic, waiting for The Stranglers and our equipment to turn up. It should give you some idea why we didn't want to leave.

Me, Fruity, Wez, our sound engineer / tour manager Derek Fudge and Leeds band The Pale Saints - who were also due to play at the festival - had flown out ahead of everyone else. After lounging around in the sun for a few days, getting really used to the beach-bum lifestyle, it transpired that there'd been some trouble with the festival - what festival? Oh, *the festival* - and it was cancelled. Both us and The Pale Saints were told we'd have to leave immediately to catch a plane from Zagreb back to London. We didn't want to go home, we were having a lovely holiday for God's sake. We hadn't been skiing or horseriding yet, I had a shirt to lose at the Casino, I wanted to park my yacht in Opatija's bosom. Instead, we had to pile onto a coach and drive as fast as we possibly could up and down the narrow mountain roads towards Zagreb, it was like the last [23] Steve Lamacq

154

ten minutes of *The Italian Job*. After about half an hour's rollercoaster ride swerving round blind corners, narrowly avoiding approaching vehicles and almost driving over the edge and ending up in the beautiful briny shivery shiny, somebody with The Pale Saints said, 'Is it just me or has anybody else left their passport back at the hotel?' Aaaaarrrrrggggghhhh! The coach driver had to do a U-ee and bomb it back down the mountain to Opatija to get the missing passport, leaving us even less time to get to the airport - where they were now holding the plane on the tarmac for us - hence an even madder near death-bus ride.

People in bands are always forgetting their passports. Every time we ever toured abroad and had to meet up at the airport, someone would invariably arrive without their passport. In fact getting any more than four people in the same place at the same time is a logistical nightmare. At the airport when there's about thirteen of you travelling together and your flight is boarding soon but you can't check in yet because somebody is late, and it's the person with the tickets. And then someone forgets that you need a passport to get from West London to North America. Well.

Not as bad as eating out with a big crowd on tour though. Table for thirteen? Smoking or non-smoking? And what does everyone want to eat? Let's look in the *Yellow Pages* for a local Chinese/Indian/Italian/Thai/Mexican/Vegetarian steak house and book a table for a baker's dozen in the non-smoking smoking area of the restaurant and could we have thirteen different bills please, apart from some, because not everyone's brought any money with them. It's okay, I'll get a sandwich when we get home.

WE ENJOYED OUR CROATIAN HOLIDAY SO MUCH THAT WE DECIDED TO TAKE ANOTHER HOLIDAY STRAIGHT AWAY, THIS TIME IN SPAIN

Benicassim is a coastal city 80 Kilometres north of Valencia and the Benicassim Festival Internacional that takes place there every August is the *Ferrero Rocher* of indie rock festivals. When we played there in '95 there was a swimming pool backstage, a beach down the road, a free bar for the bands, a shuttle bus driving back and forth between the hotel and the festival all day and night, a bloke in a penguin suit walking around with a pyramid of sickly golden chocolates, etc, etc. And I bet we moaned about it.

So there you go, Benicassim is a wonderful festival, as was the one the following weekend in Cardiff, where the whole crowd sang *Delilah* at the end of our set and the sky lit up with *Blue Frosts, Moon Cakes, Super Barrages, Mega Super Monster Barrages, Space Crusaders, Devils Crashes, Whistle Rockets, Big Boys* and *Pulsar Rockets*; don't let anyone ever tell you that I don't know about fireworks. And then I went to *Disneyland.*

MICKEY MOUSE HAS GROWN UP A COW

My family trips to *Disneyland Paris*, or *Eurodisney* as it was called in them there days, could be used as a metaphor for my pop career. I first went in 1992, which was the year we'd topped the album charts, and I was booked into The Newport Bay Hotel, a nautical-style hotel with indoor and outdoor swimming pools, just ten minutes' walk from the Magic Kingdom or five minutes on the shuttle bus. There's a lake and a lighthouse outside the hotel and if you put on a sailor's cap you could be mistaken for thinking you were Tony Curtis in *Some Like It Hot.* The Newport Bay is the third most expensive place to stay within the grounds of the Disney resort.

For our next trip in 1995 our latest album had made Number 9 in the charts and we checked into The Sequoia Lodge, an American National Park-style establishment - indoor and outdoor pools again, but with used plasters in the water and possible risk of veruccas. The Sequoia was eight places in the album charts cheaper than the Newport Bay and, although we were still only a five-minute shuttle bus journey away from the rides, it was now *fifteen* minutes to walk. We were steadily working our way down the hotel food chain to three days' self-catering at the Davy Crockett Ranch: just fifteen minutes *by car* from the theme park because the bus doesn't shuttle that far and there's only the one swimming pool.

I knew that from there it would soon be' *buy one, get two in for free'* coupons, cut out and collected from *The Sun* newspaper for an afternoon in the rain at Chessington World Of Adventures. It was the reverse snowball effect and we'd soon be back in that Brummie B & B finishing off the game of *Monopoly* we'd started in the winter of 1989.

But, as the American deadpan comic Steven Wright once said, 'You can't have everything...where would you put it?'

I had to think positively. So when I got home from Disneyland and the tune to *It's A Small Small World* was almost out of my head I told myself that we were about to turn the shrinking snowball round again and send it trundling back down the hillside with our new single

Born On The 5th Of November and another show-stealing set at Reading Festival. Everything was going to be alright... And then Fruitbat decided to clean his bath.

FRUITBAT CLEANS HIS BATH

According to *The Royal Society for the Prevention of Accidents*, over 2.8 million people in the UK have to go to hospital each year as a result of an accident in the home. Of these 2.8 million, an estimated 28,000 are bath-related mishaps. And that's *bath* not bathroom. I'm ignoring the 11,000 toilet injuries, the 630 sponge and loofah accidents, the 200 talcum-powder problems and don't even get me started on the 9,000 casualties inflicted on the United Kingdom by cotton bud abuse. So, just bath accidents. Baths are dangerous. Especially the French ones. My American namesake and singer with The Doors died in one in Paris in 1971. He'd woke up in the middle of the night coughing and complaining of chest pains and had decided to run himself a bath. In the morning Jim's girlfriend Pamela found him still in the bath-tub, having died of heart failure.

Then there was the French revolutionary and scientist Jean Paul Marat, who's number came up in in 1793 when he was murdered in his bath by young Girondin conservative Charlotte Cordayd 'Armont. Marat pretty much lived in his bath because it helped to relieve the terrible skin infection that he suffered from. REM mention him in their song *We Walk*.

A COUPLE OF OTHER BATH-RELATED FACTS I FOUND BY TYPING THE WORDS BATH INJURIES INTO A WEB SEARCH ENGINE:

Both mine and the other Jim Morrison's rock relative Van Morrison lives in Bath, Somerset and something that I didn't really understand: hot blonde in **bath** all wet and slippery tasty blonde angel teases ... nasty slut with buried deep into her butt deja hot blonde in **bath** all wet and slippery free porno two young sluts on their knees licking like a ...

I almost managed to get through that whole chapter without saying that, for both Jim Morrison of The Doors and revolutionary prune Jean Paul Marat, French baths had been the *bain* of their lives. Almost.

I don't know why Fruitbat decided to clean his bath. It was pretty clean already, it was practically brand new. I remember him having the old one ripped out and replaced with the shiny new one, but, a few days before Reading Festival in 1995, he leant over - perhaps to remove a tiny tide mark that he thought he could reach with ease - and something in his spine clicked, leading to an injury that would plague him on and off for the next three years of his life.

He had to play the Reading gig sat in a chair; he really was in a lot of pain and we should have pulled out. He'd aged about thirty five years in less than a week and it was cruel to make him go through with it. But he insisted. He'd played Carter gigs injured before, like after the time he broke his arm falling off his pushbike when he swerved to avoid a dog two days before a tour. He had to keep his arm in a sling all day until he went on stage, when Daz would remove it and place his guitar into position so he could play, I think he probably enjoyed it. I could hear the mischief in his voice when he rang me up about the dog bike incident or the time he phoned me on the night before a tour to say, 'Hello Jim, don't panic...but I fell down the stairs last night and I've fractured my finger...it's bent sideways but I can play the guitar.' And then of course - just as when the top Harley Street doctor had told me that I had acute laryngitis - it was once again my comic duty to reply, 'Wow that's incredible, because you couldn't play it before!'

But this latest injury wasn't that funny and, whether it was heroic, bloody-minded or because we knew it might well be the last chance Carter would get to play at Reading, we went ahead with the gig, just like Elton John would have done. Ask the very important people of Portugal. In 1999 Elton was booked to play an exclusive VIP show at a Portuguese casino. The £150 tickets sold out months in advance and, as the audience of Portugal's high society and European Community ministers waited eagerly in the casino's concert hall, Sir Elton told the promoter he was just going outside to take some air and he'd be back in fifteen minutes. He walked outside, climbed into his limo and drove to the airport where he boarded his private jet and flew home. After about an hour the venue management realized the superstar wasn't coming back, an announcement was made and the disappointed audience were refunded their cash. The Portuguese media were outraged and, although Elton offered to reschedule the gig, he didn't give a reason for his runner. Two weeks later he had a few hundred *I saw Elton at a posh casino in Portugal...Not !* T-shirts printed.[24]

Had the muddy Berkshire field been full of Euro MPs and stuck up socialites, then we might have sneaked out and took the first train back to Paddington, but it wasn't, it was Reading Rock Festival '95 and the show must go on. *Awwlriigghhttt!*

[24] Doing a runner is relatively easy for a solo pianist with a hired piano, try sneaking out the back when you've got an 18 foot Tower Bridge with you.

And then Wez sat in a draught for too long and buggered up his leg.

WEZ BUGGERS UP HIS LEG

So we'd gone ahead and played the Reading show, making Fruitbat's back worse. We had to film the between-song links for our *Straw Donkey* video collection as 'Carter USM *forty years into the future*', because that's how Fruity was looking at the moment. Me and Wez covered ourselves in talcum powder and facial fuzz and cobwebs and put on cardigans and tartan slippers while poor Fruity just stayed in his pyjamas not really needing to make up, looking uncannily like my Grandad. He'd tried all the popular treatments and pain-relievers, he'd had acupuncture, aromatherapy, massage, osteopathy and chiropractice. He'd applied heat and cold and swallowed steroids and *Paracetamol* and enough *Ibuprofen* for a lifetime of headaches but the pain persisted. It moved down his Mark Morrison[25] into his leg and onwards to his foot - I'm no doctor, but I suspect his intervertebral disc may well have prolapsed and his *nucleus pulposus* was very likely herniated. That's right...sciatica. He wanted to go to bed and sleep for a hundred years but that's no good, you have to keep moving otherwise the wind will change and you'll be stuck there for ever, so during the filming of the three old codgers from Carter video, Fruitbat had to lie down on a lilo - in between takes (but not for too long).

Here's a little tip I picked up about sciatica (pain down the leg, caused by irritation of the the sciatic nerve). Aside from cleaning the bath it's thought that sciatica in men might be caused by 'wallet-itis'. This is brought on by persistent sitting on your wallet in the hip pocket of your trousers, causing irritation to the sciatic nerve. Here's the trick; either swap your wallet to the opposite pocket from time to time or put your money somewhere else, thus relieving the potential pain and irritation to the sciatic nerve. That's my big tip for avoiding back problems - also, if you have to lift anything, don't bend your back, get yourself a good chair and be aware of your posture. And don't sit in a draught, which is how Wez hurt his foot.

Just as Fruity's back started to get a bit better and we went into the rehearsal studio to practice for our *Straw Donkey* tour, we found out that there was something wrong with Wez's foot. I couldn't tell you exactly what it was because I am, strictly speaking, a back specialist. But the doctor told Wez that his injury might have been caused by sitting out in the cold for a long period of

[25] From *Jim's Family Related Book Of Rhyming Slang* for 'back', as in 'Mark Morrison - The Return Of The Mack.'

time at the Reading Festival. All I know is that when he played the drums it really hurt his right foot. Why was Wez playing the drums with his feet, you might be thinking? Here's why: the drumkit is basically a car and you need all four limbs to drive it. Besides hitting things with handheld sticks, you're gonna have to - if you're right handed, vice versa if you're a southpaw - operate the hi-hat cymbals with your left foot and the kick drum with your right. That's why it's called a kick drum, because you kick it. The hi-hat was invented by a man in a ten-gallon titfer, the snare drum is used for catching things in, the tom was named after a bloke called Tom and the tom tom after the piper's son. Then there's the kettle drum which is for boiling water in, the cymbals named after the artist formerly known as the Artist Formerly Known As Prince and so on and so forth.

Again, I see what you might be thinking. It's not very glamorous or rock'n'roll. Fruitbat puts his back out cleaning his bath and Wez hurts his foot by sitting in a draught. Compare this pair of namby-pamby mummy's boys to Gloria Estefan whose bus crashed on a snowy highway in 1990 near the Pocono Mountains in Pennsylvania, leaving the Latin pop star with a broken vertebra in her back. Surgeons repaired Gloria's spine by inserting two eight-inch steel rods and, although it was thought she might never walk again, Gloria Estefan made a miraculous recovery. Or how about Def Leppard's drummer Rick Allen who took a corner too fast in his black Corvette, ploughing it into a wall, flipping it over and severing his left arm at the shoulder? After just four weeks in hospital Rick had returned to the recording studio and dedicated himself to mastering a custom-built electronic drum kit that allowed him to play the left-handed stuff with his feet.

Maybe if I add the phrase 'high on drugs'. As in, 'Keith Moon drove his Rolls Royce into his guitar shaped swimming pool, high on drugs' or 'the Doors vocalist got his tummy banana out on stage and waved it at the police, high on drugs.' Let's see: 'Fruitbat puts his back out cleaning his bath...high on drugs.' 'Wez hurt his foot sitting in a draught for too long...high on drugs.' Yes, that works for me.

Anyway, high on drugs or otherwise, it was all very frustrating for Wez and the only real joy he got out of it was when he went to see a physiotherapist who'd also been Keith Moon's physiotherapist (just like being treated by Tony Robinson's Osteopath had pleased Fruitb... no, I'm joking now.) Wez's foot problems deteriorated throughout the UK part of the tour and halfway through the German leg (sorry) we had to give up, cancel the remaining gigs, come home and take the rest of the year off. The day before this happened we were in Stuttgart, it was a bank holiday and we were booked into the worst hotel in Germany. Because of the bank holiday there wasn't a lot to do and I imagine that's why we ended up in a Stuttgart karaoke bar; And not just any old Stuttgart karaoke bar. This one was run by a man with a mullet haircut from the North of England, his name was Gary Oaky and - you guessed it - tonight was Gary Oaky's Karaoke Night. There aren't many things worse than being a singer in a karaoke bar, everyone expects you to get up and do a few numbers. People at parties have often said to me, 'Go on sing us a song.' I usually get out of it by asking what they do for a living, 'Carpenter? build us a wardrobe.' This once backfired when heavyweight boxer Lennox Lewis asked me to sing him a song and I ended up spending six weeks in hospital.

I didn't sing karaoke that night in Germany; not many other people did either as it became fairly clear that the only other reason that Gary Oaky ran a karaoke bar (apart from his name) was so he could get up on stage himself, it was vanity karaoke. I did sing in a karaoke bar in Melbourne, though there weren't many people there apart from me, a couple of Australians I was with and seven or eight drunk Japanese businessmen. I sang The Green Green Grass Of Home. I've also stepped up to the mic and video screen at a party in Fruitbat's back garden (The Lady In Red) and at his brother Bam Bam's birthday in a pub in Thornton Heath. I sang a duet there with Fruitbat; it was Everybody's Talkin' At Me and it was the first time we'd been 'onstage' together since Carter split three years previously.

Footnote: If we hadn't cancelled the end of the tour we would have played at Shepherd's Bush Empire on 24th November 1995, instead of rescheduling for 2nd March the following year. It was at the Shepherd's Bush gig in March of '96 that my sister Vicky met her future husband Neil and I don't know how fate works but I presume that, if Wez hadn't sat in a draught at Reading Festival in 1995, then Neil wouldn't now be my brother in law. The fickle foot of fate, eh?

STAGEFRIGHT

Apparently, stagefright is a natural phenomenon. An overdose of Adrenaline as a result of a conditioned reflex that's universal throughout the animal kingdom - ask Basil Brush or Skippy The Bush Kangaroo - it's known as the 'flight or fight response'. The reflex is automatically activated when your emotional and physical wellbeing is perceived as being threatened and as a result you experience physical, mental and emotional discomfort. It's the negative perception of the experience of performing that sets off the 'fight or flight response'.

It starts off as soon as you think about the fact that you've got to go onstage which, for me, could be the moment I woke up on the morning of a gig or three weeks before. Many stars including Marilyn Monroe, Elvis, Cher, Rod Stewart, Larry Olivier, Barbara Streisand and Benny Hill suffer or have suffered from stagefright; there's always some old ham being interviewed on television, proclaiming the positive nature of stagefright and how crucial those butterflies are to a good performance. They'll tell us how the minute they didn't feel scared before going on...that's when they'd *really* be terrified. Stagefright is all part of the fun.

Bollocks. The retching and the vomiting, not being able to eat, never being able to stray too far from a toilet, the fear of crowds, the fear that there won't be a crowd, the inability to hold a conversation as showtime approaches, the irrational panic attacks, the incredible urge to run away, wishing you were Elton John with a limo ticking over outside and a private jet sitting on the nearest stretch of airport tarmac. And the endless pacing back and forth, back and forth across the dressing room waiting to go on to the stage that you're so damn terrified of. I could personally do without all of that to enhance my performance thank you very much.

There were so many butterflies in my stomach it was like New Year's Eve at the Syon Park Butterfly House in there - there must have been millions of the buggers partying hard or holding the butterfly Olympics or something. And it was getting worse. And the shrinking audience was making me nauseous.

LESS IS LESS

You'd probably think that playing to forty thousand people at Reading Festival would scare the bejazaus out of someone with chronic stagefright, but you'd be wrong. It was the empty gigs that really made me nervous. Standing backstage at Reading with a large portion of the crowd out front chanting 'You fat bastard! You fat bastard!' made me feel empowered, excited rather than scared, raring to get up there and do the business. And the empty gigs didn't bother me so much at the start of Carter, I loved the three men and the dog that had chosen to leave the warmth of their homes to see my band. I loved them and I wanted to have their children. But when the month's flavour had changed from us to somebody else and we couldn't rely on putting a SOLD OUT sign outside the venue two weeks before we arrived to soundcheck, I'd be sat in the dressing room wondering whether anyone at all would turn up. And if it was just the three men and the dog, I didn't love them anymore. I hated them for turning up just to rub my nose in our box office failure. I was embarrassed.

Every so often someone who knew me and knew what I wanted to hear would walk into the dressing room and when I asked how it looked out front, they'd say 'steady flow'. A steady flow being the diplomatic term for empty. Two people arriving at a gig over the course of ten minutes can be interpreted as a 'steady flow'.

I've consulted a statistician about other audience number terminology and he told me this: a couple of people is two, a few is a couple more, several is some, many is a lot, a lot is plenty, plenty is more than enough etc, it's not scientific.

Something I really hated was when I was sat at a bar at, say a 1997 Carter gig in Glasgow with 250 people in the audience, the thing I really hated was when someone would ask me how I felt about having previously been able to sell out two nights at the 4,000-capacity Barrowlands. It felt really great, I was really, *really* very pleased.

I've always had an irrational fear of numbers - arithmophobia or numerophobia, they call it - but it used to be the big numbers. When I was a boy my three most recurrent nightmares were: **1.** A very difficult to describe nightmare, it involved being surrounded and suffocated by terrifying shapes; sometimes I couldn't close my eyes without seeing them and this was way before they invented the *Gameboy* and *Tetris*. **2.** The second nightmare was the witch that used to climb through my bedroom window to stick a sewing needle in my eye. **3.** And the third and most awful was counting, not sheep or money, just counting, to infinity and beyond! If you asked me to imagine counting to five million I'd probably be sick - I nearly threw up then just thinking about it. Now I had a whole new terror...small numbers. The fear of the finite. I suppose we could always get a few more people on the stage.

LITTLE HOUSE ON THE PRAIRIE

When we were out playing silly buggers in Atlanta Georgia, running over cars and attempting to steal beefeaters, we happened upon a bizarre housing phenomenon. In amongst all the high falootin' skyscrapers and office-blockery there was a little old house, all alone out of place and time. People would enquire - much like they did of the old crumbling Gothic windmill I once saw by the side of a motorway in Bremen[26] - why did they build such a little old building so close to all this modern stuff? Ho ho. Of course, it was there already. In the same way it was back in 1899 that Cornelius J Sheehan had built the Atlanta house as a two-story, single-family home with the fashionable 806 Peachtree Street address. Since then it's been moved back and forth to make way for the latest commercial developments, had a ground floor added, moved its front porch to the back and changed its address to 17 Crescent Avenue and then later again to number 979.

And then when Margaret Mitchell moved in and wrote the classic novel *Gone With The Wind,* turning her apartment into a literary salon and meeting place for bohemians, it would eventually lead to the building being declared a city landmark, so they couldn't bulldoze it and build a *McDonalds* or a *Toys 'R' Us.* Two attempts at arson in 1994 and 1996 caused serious damage to the property but it still stands defiant and, in 1997, it was opened to the public as *Margaret Mitchell House And Gone With The Wind Museum*, complete with gift shop. There's a small parking lot but it's best to visit on Saturday or Sunday morning if you're driving, group discounts are available and all major credit cards are accepted.

Carter were a bit like that little old defiant building on Peechtree Avenue... while all around us the exciting new concrete and tinted glass of Oasis, Suede and Blur scraped the sky we didn't move...we simply added a floor, moved the porch and opened a gift shop. We became a six-piece.

Initially it was just supposed to be a bit of fun for the encores, we'd play as a three-piece and then we'd unplug the tape machine, bring on some real musicians and play like a proper group. The German bloke looking for the hidden drummer would be pleased. 'Where's the drummer?' he'd shout.

[26] It may well have been an old church, a castle or even a lighthouse. The point is, it was a lot older than the road.

'He's over there', we'd reply.

The woman who worked at the York Barbican when we played there in 1992 who thought it was not only fair to the audience, but also her moral obligation to put up a sign next to the 'STROBE LIGHTING WILL BE USED IN TONIGHT'S PERFORMANCE' sign, saying, 'PARTS OF TONIGHT'S CARTER USM PERFORMANCE WILL BE ON PRE-RECORDED TAPES' would also be able to sleep peacefully at night. It wasn't long before we found ourselves checking our wristwatches during the main set,[27] wishing the time away so that we could get to the three songs we enjoyed playing with the full band at the end. The main set got shorter and the encore longer. And longer. So before the encore became the main set we threw the tape machine out of a hotel window and we played our first full gig as a **sex**tet on 7th September 1996 at The Sheffield Leadmill, it was fucking excellent. On the downside, I could now end the gig with the punk-rock no-no of introducing all the members of the band individually...

On bass...the man who bit John Major's penis off in the video for his previous band S*M*A*S*H*'s single *I Want To Kill Somebody* (it turns out that it wasn't the trapeze-artist Prime Minister at all, but our future tour manager Gary Robinson wearing a plastic John Major mask.) In a certain light he looks a bit like Rowan Atkinson...which means he looks like Wez, it's a small world after all. People will occasionally say to Salv, 'Hi Wez' ...please put your hands together...on the bass guitar...the Italian Stallion[28] **Salv!**

On guitar... he used to have a big beard and he smoked a pipe and he looked like Billy Crystal but now he's shaved off his big beard, he's seen the film *The King And I* and he's become obsessed with its Oscar winning star, Russian baldie bonce Yul Brynner. Now he's forever shaving his head to look like Yul, usually near food which annoys his brother Wez and so they argue constantly with each other in that way that only brothers in rock bands can do, et cetera et cetera...Give him a real Carter USM welcome... **Stevie B!**

On keyboards...I've had to ask Ben himself how he ended up playing keyboards with Carter and as far as he can remember - and I have to tell you that Ben should wear a T-shirt with three pictures of himself on the front with the words *'one and a half second*

[27] This is just a turn of phrase, I would never wear a watch onstage, Fruity did but I always thought it looked too un rock'n'roll. Did Elvis wear a watch? Elvis probably didn't even know what day it was.
[28] Technically Salv is Sicilian but it doesn't rhyme so good. Now if he'd been half Brazilian or his name was Maximilian...

166

memory' written underneath - Ben says, *'When was I in Carter???'* He's the youngest member of the band, he's actually bunking off college to be here tonight and when he first came on tour with us he told his parents he was somewhere else so as not to disappoint them with his choice of career... ladies and gentlemen...**Ben Lambert!** By the way lookalike fans, Ben has been lookeelikened to a long list of people, including Jonathan Creek, Joseph Feinnes, Kevin Keegan, Welsh heartthrob actor Ioan Gruffydd, a couple of *The Hair Bear bunch*, and Shergar. Ben is the lookalikee king.

And prior to **Ben on keyboards...** this next man is insane. In the nicest possible way. He's a Cadbury's fruit and nutcase. We recorded every single Carter album with him whether in the ten-star comfort of an Oxfordshire manor house or in a small brick garage in a back garden in the middle of a council estate in Mitcham. I could go on all night about all the funny things that he's said or done but as with Frank Carson it's the way he tells 'em. A herd of cows? Yes of course I've heard of cows. *No, a cow herd*, So what if a cow heard, I've got no secrets from a cow.' that's one of his party pieces. Welcome on to the stage please... not funny on paper...**Simon Painter!**

There you have it, the all new six piece Carter. Luckily no one was either willing - and I didn't say able - to play a little solo when I announced their name.

So,

For the first time in the group's history there were more people in the band than there were in the crew. I liked the freedom I now had from no longer being strapped to a guitar. I had both hands free to climb up the PA and dive into the crowd at will and I could entice roadies onstage to fix things that weren't broken just so I could then wrestle them to the floor and get a big cheer from the crowd for being such a crazy rascal. But all was not well, we had no record deal and we were spending a lot of time in the recording studio with no money to pay for it, we also had a large outstanding tax bill backdated to a time when we were earning enough money to pay it. We needed to get some balance into our bank balance very quickly or go to jail. With hindsight I wish I'd gone to jail.

A LOAD OF BALLS

We reluctantly agreed to play some of the lucrative black tie student balls we'd always turned down. It could have been fun, it was supposed to be. That's why there was a fun fair there, and an electric bucking bull, a laser shooting game, a bouncy castle and fireworks. There'd also be a comedian on, or maybe an old children's TV ventriloquist and his puppet who'd both fallen on hard times, unable to get bookings for kids' television anymore the ventriloquists would put swear words and innuendo into the mouths of their dummies and tour the universities of Britain. The black-tie ball-room music would usually be provided by one or two tribute acts, we played twice with No Way Sis (Oasis), Bjorn Again (Abba), a britpop covers band called Supersonic (Oasis again - and Blur, the singer used to argue with himself in-between songs) and a Tom Jones impersonator. And then there were the bands with outstanding tax bills, including Let Loose, Bananarama, Big Country, Louise Nurding, Gabrielle and us.

The audience of drunk, overdressed and over-educated future world leaders and *Big Brother* contestants would have much preferred it if their social secretary had booked Sooty And Sweep (blue version) ('What's that Sooty? Fuck off?' ho ho ho) or *Fake That*, *The Gay City Rollers* or *The AC/DC Bee Gees*. Anything other than those grumpy sourpuss has-beens Carter USM, *they weren't even playing all their hits for God's sake!* For me, playing at these gigs was like being trapped inside a particularly grim episode of *The Hitman And Her* (see 9) and the only real moments of enjoyment I had at any of these shitty gigs were: **1.** When Louise's single that she was miming and dancing to kept stopping and because it was a CD she had to keep starting from the top again. She performed two songs and was on stage for about half an hour. **2.** We were mistaken for Let Loose by a load of drunk women as we were leaving the gig at Cheltenham Racecourse where we'd both been playing. **3.** The bit during Let Loose's set when the singer was telling the audience a great between-song spur-of-the-moment anecdote about all the sexy ladies he's been with and the guitarist played a wolf whistle *wit weeow* on his guitar, they so obviously did the same thing every night. **4.** When we played the blackest of all these black-tie events at The Inns Of Court in the centre of London and we managed to clear the entire hall of future high court judges by the end of our set. And **5.** When we got the money and left.

It would have been a much better idea for us to hire two blokes - one with a cycle hat and shorts and the other with a long fringe - teach them the hits and send them out on tour as a Carter tribute act. They would have got paid twice as much as the real thing and would have been a lot more popular. We could have stayed at home living off all the PRS royalties they generated, plus our very reasonable forty per cent cut of their fee. For an extra £500 we could supply either a half-naked fatso to introduce the band or a tribute children's TV presenter to be attacked by the tribute 'the Fruitbat.' We could give the band one of the hilarious names *Melody Maker* had come up with a couple of years earlier.[29]

1996 was our quietest gig year since we'd started the band. We only played twenty five gigs, seven of them were balls and some of the others weren't so hot either boom boom! It took us fifty two weeks to play just over three weeks worth of gigs, 1991's 'the hardest working band of the year' were now 1996's laziest. The most exciting thing that happened all year was when we played at the Passau Festival in Germany and the drug squad raided the backstage area, arresting the promoter and the main band. It was the first year since 1988 that we didn't release a record; the Carter golden goose was going through the menopause and we were skint.

In April my Dad died. I had to go to the hospital to meet with the patient affairs and family bereavement rep for a cup of tea, some softly spoken advice and to collect a pile of leaflets on what to do when somebody close to you dies. Me and my Dad hadn't really been that close for years - I didn't know where he'd been living until I went to clear out his flat - but over the next week or so we made up for lost time. If you've ever had to arrange a funeral for a loved one you'll probably know what I mean.

I sat in a lowercase h-shaped waiting room at the Kensington and Chelsea Registrar for Births, Deaths and Marriages in London's swinging King's Road waiting for a death certificate. I don't know if I would have noticed it if I was a proud new father or about to marry the love of my life, but why do they send people who've just become parents to the same place as those who've just lost theirs? The mix of emotions thrown together in that h-shaped room was cruel.

I organized the funeral, I chose a coffin (elm) from a catalogue and, as I mentioned earlier, I'm almost certain the singer from 999 helped carry it into the crematorium. I recorded three cassettes of music to bring to the service, one for the entrance of the mourners, one to send the coffin on its way and another for the mourners' exit. My Dad was an opera fan and all three cassettes played Verdi arias. Once again death was cause for a big family reunion. I got

[29] There were at least two Carter tribute bands that I know of. One was 'Low Fat Custard', named after a slogan we had printed on the back of our Crazy Carter Crew shirts as a hint to the audience to subtly change their You fat Bastard chant now that Jon Beast had long since moved on. It didn't work. Low Fat Custard's drummer Arran became one of Fruitbat's lodgers at the start of the 21st Century, he's a dead ringer for Tom Hanks' son Colin. People agree with me on that one. There was also - obviously - an Australian Carter. Sadly I never saw them

to meet all my cousins, aunts and uncles I hadn't seen since God knows when and - too late maybe - I was once again very close to my Father.

In a speech in November 1992 the Queen referred to that particular year as her *annus horribilis*, I know how she felt. 1996 was my *annus horribilis*, my horrible fucking year. It was probably a pretty good time to throw in the towel and split the band up, quitting while we were marginally behind but we carried on. Perhaps for our shrunken but still loyal fan base. The ones who'd had our logo tattooed into their skin and named their children after us, the least we could do for them was stick around a bit longer than Hear'Say and The Sex Pistols. And then just before Christmas we signed a record deal with Cooking Vinyl for the exact amount we needed to pay off that funny little bowler hatted cartoon character at the Inland Revenue. Out of the thirty or so songs we'd spent half the year recording we had a great six track mini album which we'd call *A World Without Dave* and with it we'd stage a spectacular comeback. There's no point starting a new year without optimism. So fuck 1996, maybe 1997 would be a great year, a really fantastic year...my *annus fantasticus*.

I consulted my Oriental mysticals for encouragement: 1996 was the year of the rat, which seemed fairly accurate. Rat children become angry easily and although they are good at saving money they don't like sharing it. 1997 would be an ox year and, although I was first heartened to read that ox kids are calm and laid back, I also found out they can be short-tempered and mean. So, the same as the rats then. Mmmmm.

I checked my horoscope.[30] It told me that '97 would be a busy year, I'd be spending a lot of time brainstorming with others, sharing ideas and coming to a group consensus. Just what we needed. My stars also told me that I had a date with destiny.

[30] I was a Scorpio right up until sometime in the 1990s when experts decided to move the astrological goalposts and I became a Sagittarius overnight. Had I taken any notice of my horoscope up until then, I would have been living my entire life under false pretences.

DESTINY WAS WASHING HER HAIR

She said she was bent over the bathroom sink rinsing out the shampoo with cloudy water from an old long stemmed cracked wine glass when the phone had rung. Someone had broken the giant *Central Perk* coffee mug she usually used for rinsing; she suspected Chance and Fate who'd stayed round her flat at the weekend - she thought they were probably also responsible for the crack in her wine glass. I didn't believe Destiny was really washing her hair, there was something in her voice that told me liar liar pants on fire. Then Destiny said she really had to go as her hair was dripping all over the telephone receiver and she feared electrocution - she told me to remember what nearly happened in Calais - so I said goodbye to my destiny and hung up the phone.

BRAINSTORMING, SHARING IDEAS AND COMING TO A GROUP CONSENSUS

1997 began in Belfast with Chris Evans and Meatloaf, moving on to Dublin where Stevie B threatened a coach driver with his loaded penis and, finally, back to Brixton for a family feud and a bloody punch-up in the street outside Fruitbat's house. Along the way we were involved in a couple of airport incidents that in today's terrorphobic times would've got us arrested, handcuffed, footcuffed, blindfolded and daisychained together in death row orange boiler suits on a one-way flight to a Cuban naval base, it was a long weekend. Okay so it was a Thursday and Friday but long weekend is more poetic.

We'd been booked to make our TV debut as a six-piece band for a BBC Northern Ireland programme that on paper sounds like the line up for one of those black tie student balls that I'd enjoyed so very very much six months earlier. Aside from us playing a couple of numbers (mimed music and live vocals, here we go again), there was a comedian (in inverted commas) and two lookalike celebrity impersonators – 'Chris Evans' and 'Meatloaf'. The show took all day to film but passed without incident apart from the confusion about how many members there were in Carter nowadays - they had to take our word for it in the end - and the programme's director insisting that I sing...

The Only Living Boy In New Croooooooooooooooooooooooooooooooooooooooooooooooooooooooooooooooos, exactly like I do in the video as they'd worked out camera shots to the precise length of the word 'cross'. They may think that I did exactly what I was told that day but if you can get hold of a copy of a videotape of the show you'll notice that I actually sing 'Crooooooooooooooooooooooooooooooooooooooooooooooooooooooooos.'

TV people? Telling me what to do? I don't think so.

After the show there was an aftershow. Two things astounded me there, firstly that 'Meatloaf'. stayed in character to pick up women. The second thing was that the women seemed to fall for it; he was surrounded. I don't know if they were lookalike groupies or if they couldn't see just how fine the line was between a man who looks like international rock superstar Meatloaf and a sweaty fat bloke.

Believe it or believe it not - and our record labels in both London and Dublin believed it not - the following day there was only one train from Belfast to Dublin and we missed it. We were supposed to be there by midday for interviews and so we took the coach. Time was tight and so Stevie B ignored his mother's advice and didn't go to the toilet before a long bus journey. He then compounded the effects of this fatal error by spending the time he should have used emptying his bladder filling it up with coffee and orange juice. I sat on the bus seat opposite Steve for the long and what would have otherwise been tedious journey and watched him become more and more desperate and anxious to go to the toilet. It was worse than a tourbus: no number twos *or* number ones and, by the time we hit the traffic jam on the outskirts of Dublin, he was practically in tears, pleading with the driver to stop for just one minute so he could relieve himself behind a bush. But the driver said no, probably tapping his watch to signify the importance of bus-driving time. The nearer we got to our destination the worse it became until literally five minutes away from the bus terminus when Steve really couldn't hold on any longer and told the driver if he didn't let him off the bus now he'd piss all over him. The doors swished open, just like on the *Starship Enterprise* and Captain Stevie B Kirk stepped off into Dublin to relieve himself. If I hadn't felt so sorry for him, the hilarity of the situation probably would have made me piss myself as well. And we all sang:

The wheels on the bus go round and round, round and round, round and round.
The wheels on the bus go round and round, all through the town.
The guitarist on the bus says I'm gonna piss on you, I'm gonna piss on you, I'm gonna piss on you. The guitarist on the bus says I'm gonna piss on you, all through the town.

The Dublin branch of our new record label appeared to be based in the disused classroom of an old abandoned Eastern Bloc primary school; there was no coffee machine, teapot, coffee, tea, kettle, electricity or indeed a toilet. It was lucky Steve had departed the bus when he did or he'd really have been in trouble. We turned up about three hours late having run from the bus station; we were hot and sweaty, hungry and thirsty and in big trouble with Sir. Dublin had been on the phone to London all morning wondering where the Christing heck we were and they'd both decided that we'd obviously stayed up all night getting wasted with Chris Evans and Meatloaf and then we hadn't bothered to get out of bed in the morning to catch our train. All in all we'd behaved unprofessionally, we'd set a bad example to any young kids hoping for a career in pop who might be watching.

After the interviews we had quite a bit of time to kill before our flight home and so we went to the pub. We picked the kind of place where we'd feel the most unwelcome and intimidated by the regulars who were keen not to reinforce any stereotypes about good-humoured and welcoming Irish people, I ordered a lager to increase the tension - I've never really liked Guinness, I've tried to acquire the taste but haven't succeeded - and we sat in a corner of the pub where everyone had a clear view of us in case we tried to sneak out before Christopher Lee turned up with the *Esso Blue* and the giant wicker statue. Instead of finishing our first drink and moving on to a pub for tourists we drew straws and the loser went to the bar to order another round, and then another and another until the pub had become our favourite local, full of all our friends, reinforcing the stereotypes about good-humoured and welcoming Irish people. We got into a long conversation with a minicab driver - in job description alone because he was enormous - he claimed to have driven all the big rock stars around Dublin and told us some unrepeatable stories about them. When it was time to leave we promised him a job as our chauffeur if we were ever in the position to afford one and he offered to go home and get his cab to drive us to the airport - luckily we weren't quite as drunk as he was and declined his kind offer.

Our flight back to Stansted was heavily delayed and we ended up sitting in a Dublin Airport bar drinking Irish whiskey and talking crap for two hours. Mild-mannered Ben cornered me in the toilet and threatened to kill me if I insulted his family one more time and Salv found a microphone that was connected to the airport tannoy system and started to make announcements. 'Mister Steve Miserable Boynton to Gate Number 7, Mister Steve Miserable Boynton to Gate Number 7.'

Which was where me and Fruitbat were sitting when we heard the pirate broadcast. By the time the airport staff realized something wasn't quite right with their PA system Wez and Steve had both made their own comic announcements. If we'd had a TV camera with us we could have filmed the whole thing, called it *Trigger Happy TV* and sold it to Channel Four. But instead of a 10 o'clock slot on a Friday night we were called idiots, morons and a serious risk to passenger safety and informed that there was absolutely no way whatsoever that we would ever be allowed onto the plane and then we were allowed onto the plane. I suppose they'd weighed up the pros and cons of letting us on, the pros being us getting the fuck out of their country and the cons...us staying behind. We were escorted to the steps of the aircraft by security, having sobered up very quickly, and would have sat in silence all the way home if only snooker player Steve Davis hadn't been booked onto the same flight. He seemed to take all 352,000 'interesting' jokes in the good natured way they were intended though.

As we said goodbye to Steve Davis back at Stansted and waited for our guitars by the baggage carousel we were surprised to see our bass player Salv come through the rubber curtains on the conveyor belt. I could have sworn we'd taken him on the plane as hand luggage. Salv was always doing things like this. Stealing eggs from a German service station to throw at rich-looking *BMW* drivers, asking *Pizza Hut* waitresses if they had any olive oil and, upon being brought a small bowl of the stuff, putting it in his hair and saying thank you. If you've ever served Salv in a restaurant, a coffee house ('have you got any tea?') or a shop, I'm sorry. There's a picture of him somewhere in this book, memorise it. Better still cut it out or photocopy it and keep it with you when you're at work. If you recognise Salv coming towards your till, take a teabreak. Anyway, pretending to be a suitcase was something Salv had always wanted to do; he knew it was frowned upon by the airlines and had there been any staff working that night perhaps he would have been arrested. But in 1997 Stansted still

[31] If you live anywhere near Crystal Palace you'll know that getting a black taxi home from the centre of London is not easy. The only time you're likely to see a licensed cab driver round my way is on the back of a moped with a clipboard and an A-Z revising for the 'The Knowledge'. The part entitled *Algebra, Latin And The Periodic Table* – or – *Stuff I learned at School And Never Needed Again*. I touched upon it in our hit single *Glam Rock Cops* with the following lyrics: *I can't even get a taxi to the safety of my house / the driver gets a nosebleed if he travels that far south.*
[32] Contemporary slang for a guitar, originating in1950s jazz (when the groovy jazz cats used to chop wood during the day with their Gibson Les Pauls).

seemed to be something of a ghost airport so he got away with it and we made our way back to London. We took two taxis and I was in the wrong one. The taxi going to Crystal Palace - that's a *taxi to Crystal Palace* [31] - the other cab was the one with the argument in the back, the one that pulled up outside Fruitbat's house where a fight broke out in the road between the Boynton brothers and, like Fruitbat attacking Phillip Schofield so many moons before, I missed it. And apparently it was a good fight, full on, fists and blood and everything. The next day - apart from the cuts and bruises - it was like it had never happened and they were the best of friends, like brothers in fact.

It was the first real Carter fight since I tried to put an axe [32] through Fruity's skull at the *NME* party but, like buses, accidents and celebrity deaths, Carter fights tend to come in threes.

ANYTIME ANYPLACE
ANYWHERE BUT SWINDON...

People of Swindon, don't take this the wrong way it's nothing personal. To Billie Piper, Melinda Messenger, Mark Lamarr, Diana Dors, Julian Clary, Desmond Morris, XTC and my old mate Gilbert O'Sullivan...and all Swindonians past or present I apologize for the cheap title but as I say, it's nothing personal. It's just that every time I pass through Swindon on the train to visit my family in Devon I get the jitters. Like Charlie Sheen in the movie *Platoon* I feel like I'm returning to the scene of a crime. I feel the same when I go near Calais or when the *Smash Hits* Poll Winners Party is on the television. It could have just as easily been Anytime Anyplace Anywhere But Coventry or Northampton it's just that it happened to be Swindon where things came to a head. Quite lidderally mate.

We'd been on the tourbus for too long and we hadn't had many days off; we were playing 12 and 13 gigs in a row without a hot hotel bath and a *Corby Trouser Press.* We couldn't afford to stop. If we didn't have a gig we still had to pay for tourbus hire, food for ten growing men - make that nine, I used to lose a stone when I went on tour - we didn't get a rider on a day off and we were fast becoming alcoholics so our need for one was practically medical. We booked more shows, we played forty gigs in forty nights - forty five actually but, once again, more poetic - spending our after show time either driving to the next gig or more often than not parked up in a service station. And we didn't have a CD of *Queen's Greatest Hits.*

We'd been touring round Britain for thirty eight days when we got to Swindon. It was the thirty-third gig, we'd experienced closed-down venues, power cuts and the first change in government for ten thousand years. We'd been in direct competition with Supergrass and football for bums on seats for most of the tour and we were booked to play some unusual venues. Such as The Kidderminster Market Tavern, a gig that had been one of our favourites on the way to the top back in 1991 and we were nostalgically looking forward to seeing what it looked like on the way back down. The main change was the name...*The Cage,* named after the cage that now enclosed the stage to protect the band from the audience at the heavier metal gigs. Everyone said it was just like the country and western venue in *The Blues Brothers;* I've been put off by the hype so I've never seen the film but, if it helps, I have played in Salt Lake City. We convinced the landlord of the pub that it would be safe to keep the front gate part of the cage open tonight and we were right because nobody came anyway. Which is weird because it was advertised. About two hours before we went onstage I saw somebody write 'TONITE CARTER THE UNSTOPPABLE SEX MACHINE' on a blackboard and stick it outside the pub.

The highlight of the tour so far had been when an infamous gang of bikers came to see us at a particularly rocking gig and gave us their seal of approval, inviting us back to their lodge for "drugs and women". We declined their kind offer, obviously because we had some crazy shit of our own planned already anyway. That was the night we sat up till four in the morning watching the general election on the telly.

U.G.L.Y.

There's a great history of throwing things at the stage, rotten fruit and veg if the audience doesn't like you and underpants if you're Tom Jones. People had always chucked stuff at Carter, everything from crisps, peanuts and chocolate bars to toilet seats and coins, and pints and pints of lager hurled towards Jon Beast when he was introducing us. I've seen some spectacular audience throwing displays: EMF when they played with us at London ULU, Australian band The Beasts Of Bourbon at The Big Day Out Festival in Melbourne when they were pelted with more mud than was in the UK pop charts in 1974 - the band eventually had to leave the stage, only to return five minutes later when the singer walked up to the microphone and said, 'Is that the *best you can do?*'[33] and disappear under an even bigger deluge. And at Reading Festival, in the same year that Oasis and the Stereophonics were on the bill, the audience chose to throw things at Daphne And Celeste instead.

It was about seven gigs in to what we didn't know was our last UK tour when people started throwing bottles at us. The first recorded missile was in Wolverhampton, in Fruitbat's website tour dairy he wrote this: *'The gig itself was ruined for me by a stupid wanker throwing bottles at the band.'* And the last missile was the full beer can which hit me on the head at The Astoria five weeks later causing the whole band to walk off and then back on again when the rest of the audience started singing 'Who's the wanker with the can?'

Fruity's diary also says that on the day of the Swindon gig,' *My fears of a return to the bad old days*

[33] Re-read that line in a comic Australian accent, it works better that way.

of my bloody back were confirmed when I dragged myself to the service-station showers. By the time I had finished showering and ordered my breakfast I was in too much pain to eat and had to get back to the bus for a lie-down. I didn't get much sleep as my joints were aching too much. Luckily the promoter had found a chiropractor for me go to at short notice and he drove me there in his sporty Honda. The chiropractor was very nice and helped me relax and eased my pain.

I was feeling a whole lot better by the time that I left the clinic, but decided to take it easy and went for a lie down. Unfortunately, I was in serious pain again by the time it came for us to do soundcheck and actually had to do some of the check lying down. Our set. Well, I had a real problem coping with standing up and even sitting down was a big problem. I spent the first 5 songs in agony and had to scuttle off during Nowhere Fast to lie down. Wez had a really bad time too, a full can came flying out of the audience and hit him on the forehead which prompted him to grab hold of JIm's microphone and challenge the offender to show himself. Of course no-one admitted to throwing it. Then some bloke started shouting out that Wez was boring and even continued after I asked him to shut up. Wez lost his temper and bloodied his nose. This is very unlike Wez – although he is a bit of a grumpy git, he is generally a peaceful person and normally turns the other cheek. After 6 days without a break, tempers do tend to fray.'

Christ yes.

It didn't help that the stage in Swindon was such a high one and that there was no barrier. If the audience didn't have their noses resting on the edge of the stage like 'Kilroy was here' cartoons, perhaps when Wez swung his foot out it wouldn't have made such a mess of the bloke's face. And if only the next song in the set hadn't been *Bloodsport For All.* I couldn't look, not because I'm squeamish - which I am - but because I was embarrassed and because I knew right then in that split second that this was a big turning point in my life. I left the stage and the venue as soon as the last song was finished and went onto the bus, followed by Wez and Fruitbat who argued for a bit and then had a fight in between the bunks. Although they shook hands, hugged and made up afterwards, I knew then that I didn't want to be in the band anymore. It would just take me twenty three more gigs to pluck up the courage to tell anybody.

THE BIG YIN

I hate confrontation and conflict. I'm a big softy, they named the ice-cream man after me. Now I don't know exactly what I'm talking about here - why start now? - but applying the ancient Chinese philosophy of yin being passive and yang active, I have a ch'i imbalance. I'm way too yin for my own good. For example, If I'm walking towards somebody in the street I'll step aside to allow them to pass, even if I have to leave the pavement and risk being run over by a bus. If the person approaching me too, however, has the same more yin than yang imbalance it can be embarrassing. We'll both sway from side to side attempting to pass each other for about ten to twenty seconds like a couple of over-polite fridge magnets until we eventually managed to escape and continue on our separate ways. Yang-heavy pedestrian meetings on the other hand can be disastrous. As the two over-aggressive yangers get closer to each other, a game of pavement chicken will commence, neither willing to give way to the other until they meet - an irresistible force meeting another irresistible force - ending up in a row, a fist-fight or until one of them pulls a gun. To maintain the pavement and the planet's equilibrium we need a little bit of yin and a little bit of yang, presumably in equal proportions and then everything will tick along just fine. Lately I've noticed the scales tipping in favour of the more active and aggressive yangers. Those people love a fight. We need to practice a bit of universal *feng shui* or the species is finished. I suggest, we remove the conduits of negative energy and put them in the garden by the compost heap.

I'll do anything for a quiet life me. I've broken up more fights than Arthur Mercante.[34] I understand all my disputes and near death experiences with venue security and promoters might not seem like the actions of a non-confrontational hippie, but I was only trying to protect my audience and my band and at the risk of sounding like a ten year-old kid in a playground...*they started it.* All my other acts of trouble-making, such as heckling bands, tripping up roadies and my persistent shit-stirring were more mischief than malice. I can be a bastard when I'm bored, worse when I'm hungover and even worse still if I'm bored and hungover. If I've got an audience I'm insufferable. I'm a big showoff and shouldn't be encouraged. Still, most of the victims of my spiteful

[34] Arthur Mercante, known as 'The Dean of Boxing Referees' stood between Muhammad Ali and Joe Frazier for 'the fight of the century.' Mercante has refereed over 120 world title fights.

wit are still - I think, I *hope* - my friends.

All the recent agro was stressing me out. It compounded my stagefright and because the dressing rooms on this tour were either small or non-existent there was nowhere to hide, so I spent a lot of time in bed on the bus. I was getting up as late as possible in the morning - usually about 2pm - and going back to bed between the time the venue doors opened and the time we went onstage. I was wishing my life away, I wanted the tour to finish so I could go home where I wouldn't have to worry about what mood everyone was going to be in from day to day. Which side of the bed - and as I said earlier there's only one side - they'd get out of in the morning. In a purely selfish way I was concerned about the happiness of my mates. Lying awake at five in the morning hoping the loud music on the bus didn't wake Fruitbat up, or that Steve didn't get up early and drink the last of the coffee, putting Wez in a bad mood for the rest of the day. And I didn't say anything, till now.

In the beginning was a word. And the word was mum. The longer I kept my feelings to myself the harder it was going to be to share them with anybody else. And then something good or funny would happen and everything would be alright again, like when Eric the bus driver took us to Blackpool Pleasure Beach, or we put some disco on and Wez showed us the hand movements to *sunshine moonlight good times boogie.* And then there were the days when people were nice, like at Middlesborough Arena when they not only gave us our full rider, they also made us vodka jelly, jam sandwiches and a cake with our name on it.

The moments of nostalgic Carter anger, when people weren't nice, when there was no cake and little else, when it was us against the world again instead of us against ourselves, felt good as well. Anger is an energy, Johnny Rotten said so. It had always been the main driving force behind Carter but lately I wasn't that angry and I was knackered. My get up and go had - you guessed it - got up and gone and at the back of my mind I kept hearing David Bowie saying 'a change is as good as a rest Jim...a ch-ch-change is as good as a rest.'

David Bowie also said: 'I think it's the most derogatory thing I can say about somebody or something: "God, it's so fucking *Croydon*!"'.

SO FUCKING CROYDON

After a six-and-a-half-week tour of the UK that had left me feeling confused about my future, the last thing I wanted to do was a gig in Croydon. Once again, Croydon, nothing personal. I don't want to slag you off with a load of cheap jokes at your expense but I do virtually live there; my house is bang smack on the cusp with Lambeth, it would be like Woody Allen telling Jewish gags. So here's a few.

It wasn't Croydon's fault, I didn't really want to play anywhere at all at the moment, even if it was - as proclaimed by the signs that welcome you to East Croydon Station - the home of *Nestlé UK*. I would have felt exactly the same about a gig in Glendale California: home of *Nestlé USA* or even in Vevey: home of *Nestlé Switzerland*... the big daddio of mass-produced chocolate. It's just that in the mood I was in I'd rather stay at home in bed with a good book and a *Kit Kat*, an *Aero*, a *Lion Bar*, a *Milky Bar*, a *Drifter*, a *Yorkie*, a *Toffee Crisp*, a *Caramac*, a *Walnut Whip,* a box of *Black Magic* and maybe a *Cadbury's Creme Egg* (for corporate impartiality). And besides, what if the gig went badly. I didn't want to be shit on my own doorstep, I have to go there a lot, I do my Christmas shopping in the Whitgift Centre, somebody might recognise me.

Croydon's number one fan and chairman of the Croydon Tourist Board Sir [35] David Bowie played at The Croydon Fairfield Halls in 1973. He did two shows - a matinee and an evening - and announced his retirement a week later. I couldn't say if it was the double Croydon that did it. There was only one way to find out.

A jumble sale was booked in for the afternoon of 22nd June 1997 so a matinee show was out of the question - we had to just settle for the one in the evening. It's a weird venue, the Fairfield Halls, they have possibly the only octogenarian rock gig security staff in England. There are three main halls: the big concert hall where all the orchestras play, the Ashcroft Theatre where I saw Jimmy Webb (the man who wrote everything) and the Arnhem Gallery where we were on. There are plenty of other rooms available for conferences and wedding receptions, the whole place smells of school dinners circa 1972 and in the foyer you can have a drink at the smallest, most understaffed bar in the whole of 1960s communist

[35] It's only a question of time.

Europe where the Croydon Fairfield Halls is currently stuck. Like I said, sorry Croydon it wasn't your fault, I just didn't really want to play anywhere at the moment.

FAME COSTS
AND RIGHT HERE'S
WHERE YOU START PAYING...IN MONEY

Carter fights tend to come in threes. The promoters of the festival in Pully, Switzerland, had been ever so nice; they'd hammered a tap into a barrel of beer backstage and told us to help ourselves. And if we wanted some wine, hey, they had their own supply and we could have as many bottles as we wanted, all we had to do was ask. Contributory factors perhaps to fight number three as Wez attempted to stagger away up a slippery grassy knoll with a carrier bag full of wine whilst I chased after him trying to hit him over the head with a carrier bag full of wine.

FAKING ORGASMS

In July I took the band on holiday to America. We had an eleven-date tour of the East Coast and Canada booked and no money to fund it, Fruitbat had been spending for England and all his Carter money was gone, pissed up the wall on cats and bicycles. I, on the other hand - being the indie Rod Stewart - had been more prudent with my dosh. I transferred enough money from my personal account to the Carter account to pay for a tourbus and nine tickets to Boston, Massachusetts, I put all thoughts of splitting up the band to the back of my head and decided to give it one last shot, as we set off to rediscover America.

We had two dates booked in New York, one at the start of the tour and one at the end and both were at The Mercury Lounge in East Houston Street just a few doors down from Katz's Deli where we went for sandwiches and cawwfee. Katz's Deli is New York's most famous deli, the one where the fake orgasm scene in *When Harry Met Sally* was filmed and where Johnny Depp met with his FBI contact in *Donnie Brasco*. Loads of celebs have been there for some pastrami or corned beef, or a combo of sour and half-sour pickles and a *Dr Browns* black cherry soda. Every table has a little sign on it informing you of the famous people who sat there before you, including Barbara Streisand, Kathleen Turner, Bruce Willis, Dan Aykroyd and various US presidents and international political heavyweights. I sat at the table where US Vice President Al Gore once won a gherkin-eating contest while Russian Prime Minister Viktor Chernomyrdin faked an orgasm in the seat opposite.

Following both shows at The Mercury Lounge we swapped lounges and walked round the corner to The Luna Lounge, a bar where our friend Jim, the guitarist from New York band Lotion, worked. The thing that struck me about both The Mercury and The Luna Lounge was the way Iggy Pop, Debbie Harry or Dinosaur Junior would be sat at the bar having a beer with nobody batting an eyelid. It was so cool that I couldn't stop staring. If you are in any doubt about the cool credentials of these bars I should tell you that The Strokes played a fair bit at both The Luna and The Mercury and in December 2000 they played The Mercury Lounge every single week. The big drawback with cool is that the audiences that packed out both of our New York gigs were really, *really* boring. And like Meg, at both New York gigs I faked my climax.

With the exception of New York and New York - so good we played it twice - and Chicago, the venues on this tour were depressingly empty. The new US record company weren't that hot and the promotion was a bit lacklustre, it was a long way to come to find that out. The second grimmest attendance was Upstairs At Nick's in Philadelphia, a fairly small bar that we should have sold out twice over and where there were more people watching *The Way Out Wacky Races* on the television above the bar than there were watching us - Penelope Pitstop drove her *Compact Pussycat* past The Slag Brothers in their *Bouldermobile* to win, by the way. I'd become jealous of our support band Thin Lizard Dawn who seemed oblivious to the poor turnout and just looked happy to be playing: most distressing of all, I thought they were better than us. I used to believe we were the greatest band in the world and now we were only the second best band in Philadelphia, home of the spreadable cheese. When Fruitbat had a similar inferiority complex on tour in Germany with The Senseless Things, he blamed it on the drum machine and we reinvented ourselves with Wez. We upsized. We found safety in numbers. Salv, Ben and Steve helped get us through our next crisis of confidence, we could always get a few more band members. Here's the sum: 2 (me & FB) + **1** (Wez) = 3 + **3** (Salv, Ben and Steve) = 6 + **5** = 11 + **7** = 18 + **9** = 27 + **11** = 38 + **13** = 51+ **15** = 66 + **17** = 83 + **19** = 102 + **21** = 123 + **23** = 146. In just eight more moves we'd have enough musicians to change a light bulb. We were going to need a bigger stage.

I knew musician multiplication wouldn't get us out of this one, though. I obviously hadn't pushed the thought about breaking up Carter or me leaving - there's an option I hadn't considered, the band continuing without me - I hadn't pushed it far enough to the back of my head, spending every waking hour thinking about how to tell the others how unhappy I was. It seems ridiculous now, but ten years is a bloody long time. what would Fruitbat say? Was he fed up as well? How about Wez, would he feel betrayed? Would I be pulling the rug out from under everyone's feet, or would they breathe a collective sigh of relief? I should have said something ages ago, if only I knew how. Every band I'd ever been in had been split up by somebody else, usually Fruitbat; I didn't have any experience in man management. I could always lie my way out of it, 'We've had a letter from a Swedish psychedelic band also called Carter The Unstoppable Sex Machine - they had a big hit in Scandinavia in 1969 and are going to sue us unless we change our name to Carter The Unstoppable Sex Machine UK. I don't want to change the name so unfortunately we'll have to split the band.' Or maybe I could just run away like Joe Strummer did when The Clash were in a hole, or Elton John when he remembered he'd left a fork in his spoon drawer back home in England. The next day I got up early and went for a coffee with Fruitbat to tell him what was on my mind. He wasn't shocked or traumatized, he didn't throw his double espresso in my face; I think he might even have felt the same as I did. We agreed to finish the tour first and talk it over properly with everyone else when we got home. At least part of the huge weight was lifted from my mind.

HELLO CLEVELAND!

I've got a T-shirt that says on the front 'Cleveland Rock'N'Roll Capital Of The World'. It's secondhand and I don't know where I got it from, a joke shop perhaps. The same place where they sell the 'Beijing Free Speech Capital Of The World' baseball caps and the 'Falkland Islands Home Of The Bikini' pen and pencil sets. I couldn't tell you why Cleveland is the rock'n'roll capital of the world. Alan Freed, the DJ credited with inventing the stuff had a radio show there, the Rock and Roll Hall of Fame is there (Big Al bought an autographed guitar pick in their gift shop when we visited in 1992) and Spinal Tap got lost backstage in Cleveland - oh if only, if only. But hey, Alan Freed was a DJ way back in the 1950s and the Hall Of Fame is full of old farts, perhaps it's time for a rock'n'roll rethink. Constantinople isn't *still* the capital of the Eastern Roman Byzantine Empire, it isn't even called Constantinople anymore and Memphis ceased to be the capital of Greece a long long time ago, possibly when it was relocated to Tennessee so Elvis Presley didn't have to leave the country to get home at night. Let's make Milton Keynes the new rock'n'roll capital.

GOODBYE CLEVELAND!

We turned up to soundcheck at The Grog Shop in Cleveland and found the place full of the drunkest people I'd seen since that bonkers festival in Finland. These people were scary drunk, shouting to themselves, threatening and pushing each other about while shooting pool - the barman advised us against soundchecking till the bar was empty because he said if we antagonized the regulars they might shoot us instead.

Later on that evening when the drunks had gone home to beat their wives up and kick the dog, we played to the three who were too pissed to find the door and another six or seven people who'd turned up to see the support act Thin Lizard Dawn. It was the emptiest gig of the tour and possibly our lives and I broke my cardinal pre-show rule by not changing my clothes before I went onstage, staying in jeans and a T-shirt like I was Bryan Adams, just doin' my job. In spite of all this it was the best gig we'd ever played. No, not really. It was rubbish. Rock'n'roll capital of the world my arse.

It's all getting a bit miserable isn't it?
Let's go to the pictures.

We had a night off on the outskirts of Chicago; half of the Carter party went clubbing in the city and the rest of us took a cab to a shopping mall to see John Travolta swap faces with Nicholas Cage. When we left the cinema the mall was shut and completely deserted; it was in the middle of nowhere and I'm still there now.

I never made it to the Chicago Double Door for the best and fullest gig of the tour and I didn't make it across the border into Canada for the three shows there either. Which meant I missed the massive Barrymore's Music Hall venue we were booked to play in Ottawa with its three bars each on a different level of the building. I didn't get to see what such a big venue would look like with such a tiny crowd, or how the audience was so small that they each had their own bar person. I couldn't enjoy the endless free drinks from the incredibly friendly people behind each of the three bars while I was engaged in a long and drunken yet meaningful conversation with Ben and an equally charming young man from Ottawa who threw up all over me, apologizing frantically and blaming it all on his heroin addiction. And last but not least I wasn't around to play our really enjoyable penultimate tour date at a club in Montreal called Foufounes

Electriques which I've been given two different translations for - either The Electric Arse or The Electric Pussy. I'd like to thank our tour manager Nimar, soundman Mark Creepy Crawley and guitar technician Paul Sawyer for continuing to work without being paid despite my absence.

THE END

I once saw a documentary about *The Memphis Mafia*, the bodyguards, drivers, fixers and confidants who hung around with Elvis. They abandoned their wives and families and any hope of a normal life to stick by him, dealing with all his insecurities, addictions and his crazy paranoia about The Beatles. In the documentary my favourite member of Elvis' mob kept saying these insane and yet curiously poetic things, like: 'I didn't know whether to piss or go to a movie.' and ' It was like I had a rattlesnake up my ass and he was looking for his library tickets in a KFC restaurant!'

Actually these aren't quotes but they're very much in the style of the wonderful nonsense he was talking that made him seem to me like the greatest philosopher since Friedrich Nietzsche or Socrates. I'm a real big fan of the colourful way some people have of saying black and white things. Tom Waits does it as well, talking about his songs being his children that he's had to let out into the world and stuff like that. I've never been that good with the psychedelic spoken word or - and here's the biggest pun in the whole book - the quote of many colours, but I try to make up for it with off-the-wall statistics, good hard made-up facts and line graphs.

If you chart the trajectory of Carter's success over our ten years as a band on a line graph using the recognised 'Top 10 richest UK rockers - to years Carter were together' scale you don't get the rollercoaster ride you might expect. It is a bit like the old water chute at Battersea Fun Fair though, or a 1980s sporty hatchback such as the Peugeot 205 GTI or the VW Golf. Here's the graph...

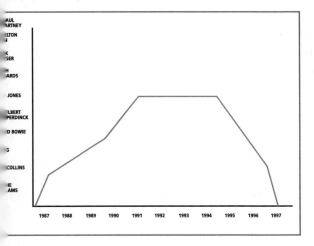

...And here are the statistics...

BOOK 'EM DANNO

I've estimated that between the Augusts of 1987 and 1997 - counting every person that came through the doors as one person, regardless of whether they came to more than one gig - Carter played live to about 900,000 people. Numerically speaking we could have just played one big gig on one of the many beautiful beaches of Hawaii to almost the entire Hawaiian population and got the whole thing over and done with in a day. Or we could have played just one week's worth of gigs to the combined populations of the Maldives, Monaco, St Kitts, San Marino, Belize, Barbados, St. Vincent and the Grenadines, with a couple of weeks' intensive rehearsals at the start of the tour in the Maldives. It wouldn't have been the same.

Either option would have made for a great holiday and the scuba diving and the surf would have been good but we would have missed out on so much. All the car games, the sleeping in fields, the bus wars, Adrian's Magic Pants, the near-death experiences that made us glad to be alive, meeting our heroes, the fights, the riots, the Freddie Mercury nights, the culture, the endless cheese ploughman's sandwiches, novelty crisps and over 38,240 bottles of beer, the hundreds of bands we got to play with, the long fringe, the crazy shorts, the highways, byways, autobahns and mountain roads, locking the door of a service station toilet after a long night on the bus, all the high jinx and low points and everything in between on the ten-year journey around the globe and back again.

And there's so much I didn't tell you about like how we turned up for a gig at The Patti Pavilion in Swansea to find them frantically laying carpets, re-wiring the electrics and building a bar. An episode of the TV programme *Challenge Aneka* had been filmed there and Aneka Rice was challenged to do the place up but she ran out of time and left the job unfinished. Or how me and Fruitbat were checking in our luggage of two silver-flightcased guitars at Chicago O'Hare Airport and the man behind the desk asked us if we had any other guns with us apart from the two in the flightcases. Bill Clinton had just passed through the airport and it was presumed that we were secret service agents accompanying the future President across America. And closer to home we once got lost driving around Newport, Wales looking for a hotel that had been booked for us in Newport, England. Great days, great days.

And finally all the people. The extended Carter family, all eight billion of them who chose to work with us, such a big part of the story even if they aren't mentioned, like Nick Jevons, Kristian King, Pyro,

Richard Beard, the last lookalike in the book Steve Brown (Henry VII) and so many others. The audiences we watched change in shape and size... the old punks and fat blokes who turned up to the first gigs, the teenage girls who joined them when we were in the charts and the old punks and fat blokes who were still there in 1997 when the teenage girls had gone. There was something special about a Carter gig that had the power to make you feel good about yourself for a while, like clicking shut a felt pen or an old fob watch or purse. We played, the audience reacted, we reacted to the audience, the audience reacted to us reacting to them and so on and so on, a cycle of warmth generating around the gig like a non-destructive and good-natured El Niño. My only regret is that I never got to see the band myself.

If you watch one of those television programmes about how we all remember the 1990s it's fairly likely that there'll be no mention of Carter as though we never really existed at all, like we were just the product of an over-active imagination, exactly...exactly. I'd like this last bit to be read by Morgan Freeman or Kevin Spacey and directed by Steven Spielberg.

On Saturday the second of August nineteen ninety seven,

almost exactly ten years to the day that they first stepped onto a stage, Carter The Unstoppable Sex Machine played their final gig at Guildford Festival. They were as angry, abusive and unreasonable as they'd always been. Two days later, on Billy Bob Thornton's 42nd birthday, Carter's guitarist Fruitbat left his home in Brixton to catch a 159 bus to Streatham Common where he was meeting the group's singer Jim Bob for a coffee and a *Kit Kat*. And a *Cornetto*. Just one.

THE PERFECT FADE

The perfect fade requires a steady hand.
On the average recording studio mixing desk
you've maybe got a total of six inches of volume to
slowly bring down to nothing. I love a good long
fade, some people don't. They want to hear the
song end properly, as it would at a gig. Whether
it's a sudden stop, a Beatles-style open seventh
chord or a good old self-indulgent rock ending.
But I love a really long fade, one that just as you
think it's finally over, offers up a fantastic guitar
note or squeal of feedback. Something you have
to turn up the volume of your stereo to hear
properly. I love a long fade, there's an art to it.
There should be an award category
at the Brits for it.
Best fade in a pop single
or something like that.

Onstage with James EMF on guitar
Photographer
Ginny Keith

Mole & Mad Dog, the T-shirt stall, Arezzo Wave, Italy
Photographer:
Ginny Keith

Great Xpectations Finsbury Park
Photographer:
Ginny Keith

Sally From
Bleach & Carter
YTS roadie
Marlon Brown
(Background)
Adrian Boss & Loz
Kingmaker
(foreground)
Photographer:
Ginny Keith

Me & Loz Kingmaker
disagree over a bottle
of JD, Phoenix Arizona.
Photographer: Ginny Keith

Day off on a cigarette boat in LA
Photographer: Ginny Keith

CARTER
THE UNSTOPPABLE SEX MACHINE

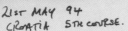
21st MAY 94
CROATIA 5TH COURSE.

Clockwise from top left: Big Al wins the go-kart Krown, Wez, Jim, the 5th course Croatia May 94
Photographer:
Jim Bob

Left: Fruitbat, Wez & Jim at the fanzine Scalextric competition, Chrysalis Records
Photographer:
Ginny Keith

CARTER
THE UNSTOPPABLE SEX MACHINE

the levellers

blur

oasis

suede

carter usm '94

atlanta georgia usa

CARTER
THE UNSTOPPABLE SEX MACHINE

Carter producer & nutter
Simon Painter, Holland
Photographer: Jim Bob

Above: Salv, tourbus USA 97
Photographer: Jim Bob

Opposite: Stevie B in Canada 97
Photographer: Jim Bob

THE UNSTOPPABLE SEX MACHINE

CARTER
THE UNSTOPPABLE SEX MACHINE

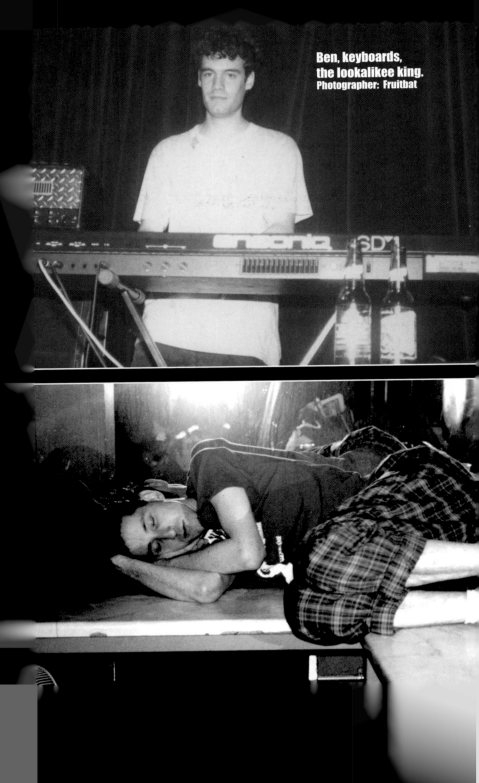

Ben, keyboards,
the lookalikee king.
Photographer: Fruitbat

APPLAUSE

ENCORE

THE GIGS

I got all this information from the pages of my little diaries - spelling mistakes included - and most of the dates we played should be here. There will be a few missing, probably including some that are mentioned earlier in the book. Have a look at the list and if you were at one or more of these gigs, close your eyes, breathe in and lose yourself in the atmosphere. If you're feeling brave, climb up on someone's shoulders or take your first crowd-surf or stage-dive, go on, let yourself go. On the other hand, if you find yourself transported back to one of the shit ones, go and demand your money back and see if you can get the security to throw you out again.

1987

6 AUG	ASTORIA LONDON
13 AUG	CLARENDON HAMMERSMITH
30 SEPT	SIR GEORGE ROBEY LONDON
11 NOV	CRICKETERS KENNINGTON OVAL
26 NOV	CLARENDON HAMMERSMITH
21 DEC	HEAVEN LONDON

1988

1 FEB	CRICKETERS KENNINGTON OVAL
18 FEB	MANCHESTER UNI HALLS OF RESIDENCE
27 FEB	CLARENDON HAMMERSMITH
30 MARCH	HACKNEY EMPIRE
7 APRIL	ALBERT HOFFMAN'S BIKE AT SIR WALTER SCOTT LONDON
23 APRIL	CLARENDON HAMMER-SMITH
25 APRIL	CRICKETERS OVAL
1 MAY	FALCON
31 MAY	CRICKETERS OVAL
2 JUNE	HYPE CLUB AT THE BULL & GATE LONDON
14 JUNE	CRICKETERS OVAL (With Captain Sensible)
28 JUNE	CRICKETERS OVAL
3 AUG	CRICKETERS OVAL
16 AUG	GEORGE ROBEY LONDON
18 AUG	LUTON SWITCH CLUB
12 SEPT	NEWCASTLE CITY HALL (With Siouxsie & The Banshees)
1 OCT	BIRMINGHAM UNI CELLAR BAR
8 OCT	FALCON CAMDEN
14 OCT	EALING COLLEGE
15 OCT	AFRICA CENTRE COVENT GARDEN

26 OCT	CRICKETERS OVAL
27 OCT	LUTON SWITCH
15 NOV	LIMELIGHT CLUB LONDON

1989

27 JAN	HYPE CLUB AT THE BULL & GATE
31 JAN	STOCKTON-ON-TEES DOVECOT ARTS CENTRE
1 FEB	HULL NEW ADELPHI
2 FEB	NOTTINGHAM THE GARAGE
14 FEB	CANTERBURY UNI KENT
18 MARCH	WILLIAM MORRIS CLUB LONDON
22 MARCH	PEGASUS LONDON
7 APRIL	OXFORD JERICHO TAVERN
15 APRIL	HYPE AT THE BULL & GATE
24 APRIL	LINCOLN
27 APRIL	MARQUEE LONDON
4 MAY	T&C 2 THE TWANG CLUB LONDON
6 MAY	NEWCASTLE BROKEN DOLL
11 MAY	HULL ADELPHI
19 MAY	STAFFORD POLY (With Pauline Murray)
27 MAY	STOCKTON-ON-TEES DOVECOT ARTS CENTRE
29 MAY	PLYMOUTH
31 MAY	GLASGOW FURY MURRAYS (With Pauline Murray)
1 JUNE	EDINBURGH THE VENUE (With Pauline Murray)
2 JUNE	LIVERPOOL PLANET X
3 JUNE	LIVERPOOL ST HELEN'S ARTS CENTRE
4 JUNE	BIRMINGHAM THE COD CLUB
6 JUNE	T & C 2 LONDON (With Easterhouse)
9 JUNE	HARLOW SQUARE
14 JUNE	SHEFFIELD TAKE TWO
22 JUNE	POWERHAUS LONDON
6 JULY	SOUTHAMPTON JOINERS ARMS
7 JULY	OXFORD JERICHO TAVERN
8 JULY	HARLOW SQUARE
19 JULY	DINGWALLS LONDON
21 JULY	BRADFORD ONE IN TWELVE
28 JULY	CORNWALL TREEWORGEY TREE FAIRE FESTIVAL
8 AUG	CHELTENHAM PUMP ROOMS
11 AUG	CANTERBURY BROOKSIDE GARDEN FESTIVAL
2 SEPT	OXFORD FARBANK (IN A FIELD)
8 SEPT	IPSWICH (With Mega City 4)

9 SEPT	SOUTHAMPTON JOINERS
19 SEPT	HULL ADELPHI
20 SEPT	SHEFFIELD TAKE TWO
28 SEPT	LUTON SWITCH
1 OCT	KENTON THE PLOUGH
4 OCT	KENT UNI CANTERBURY
6 OCT	SHERBOURNE DORSET ELECTRIC BROOM CUPBOARD (W Ride)
7 OCT	OXFORD CO OP HALL (With Ride)
12 OCT	CHELMSFORD Y CLUB
18 OCT	DERBY DIAL
20 OCT	GLOUCESTER BANANA CLUB
21 OCT	HARLOW SQUARE
27 OCT	COMMUNION AT BULL & GATE (As 'Sheriff Fatmen' - secret gig)
3 NOV	BRADFORD 1 IN 12
4 NOV	BOLTON COLLEGE OF FURTHER EDUCATION
5 NOV	GUILDFORD SURREY UNI (With New FADs)
10 NOV	BIRMINGHAM VARSITY TAVERN
14 NOV	MARQUEE LONDON
15 NOV	BRIGHTON POLY
16 NOV	WINCHESTER ART COLLEGE
17 NOV	LAMPETER ST DAVID'S UNI
18 NOV	LIVERPOOL PLANET X
19 NOV	SHEFFIELD TAKE TWO
22 NOV	QUEEN MARY COLLEGE LONDON (With MC4)
24 NOV	MANCHESTER BOARDWALK
25 NOV	CUBE CLUB AT THE GREYHOUND FULHAM
26 NOV	HULL ADELPHI
28 NOV	BRISTOL TROPIC CLUB
6 DEC	HASTINGS THE CRYPT
7 DEC	BEDLAM AT POWERHAUS LONDON
8 DEC	BIRMINGHAM POLY
9 DEC	SOUTHAMPTON POLY
15 DEC	OXFORD JERICHO TAVERN

1990

JAN 12	BOURNEMOUTH ACADEMY
JAN 13	IPSWICH THE HANGAR CLUB AT THE DOVE
JAN 15	PLYMOUTH THE ACADEMY
JAN 18	SOUTHAMPTON JOINERS
JAN 19	COLEFORD COMMUNITY CENTRE

JAN 20	LEICESTER PRINCESS CHARLOTTE
JAN 25	SALISBURY ARTS CENTRE
JAN 26	OXFORD JERICHO
JAN 27	ROUGH TRADE SHOP COVENT GARDEN
JAN 27	HARLOW SQUARE
JAN 31	WINDSOR OLD TROUT
FEB 2	PETERBOROUGH SHAMROCK CLUB
FEB 3	BOLTON INSTITUTE
FEB 8	COVENTRY POLY
FEB 9	CHELTENHAM SHAFTESBURY HALL
FEB 10	LONDON CUBE CLUB
FEB 11	HULL ADELPHI
FEB 12	NOTTINGHAM TRENT POLY
FEB 13	SHEFFIELD TAKE TWO
FEB 14	WOLVERHAMPTON POLY
FEB 15	MANCHESTER BOARDWALK
FEB 16	NORTH STAFFS POLY
FEB 17	COVENTRY POLY
FEB 18	LONDON STEPNEY (with Band of Holy Joy)
FEB 22	AMSTERDAM PARADISO
FEB 23	NIJMEGEN
FEB 24	ROTTERDAM
FEB 25	NORWICH JACQUARD

FEB 26 TO MARCH 8: PAGES MISSING FROM DIARIES

MAR 9	ESSEX COLLEGE OF FURTHER EDUCATION
MAR 12	LONDON SUBTERANIA NME PARTY
MAR 10	TEESIDE POLY
MAR 16	WORCESTER ARTS CENTRE
MAR 17	BLETCHLEY COUNTERPOINT
MAR 19	LINCOLN
MAR 20	BIRMINGHAM UNI
MAR 21	HATFIELD POLY
MAR 22	CITY OF LONDON POLY
MAR 23	KING'S LYNNE
MAR 24	CAMBRIDGE JUNCTION
MAR 29	SOUTHAMPTON JOINERS
MAR 30	BASINGSTOKE CARIBBEAN CLUB
MAR 31	BRIXTON ACADEMY (With Birdland)
APR 1	TAMWORTH

APR 3	CAMDEN PALACE LONDON
APR 4	NOTTINGHAM KOOL KAT
APR 5	CHELMSFORD Y CLUB
APR 1	STUTTGART ZELLA
APR 17	ARHUS DENMARK MUSIK CATEEN
APR 19	HALLE
APR 20	W BERLIN THE KOB
APR 23	E BERLIN KANAAK KLUB
APR 24	MAGDEBURG KELLER THEATRE
APR 25	LEIPZIG HAUS AUENSEE
APR 27	E BERLIN YO YO
APR 28	DRESDEN RADEBEUL JUGENKLUBHAUS
APR 29	DRESDEN DRESCHEN
APR 30	PRAGUE LUCERNA BAR
MAY 1	PRAGUE COLLEGE FESTIVAL
MAY 2	PRAGUE ROCK CAFE ART GALLERY
MAY 3	PRAGUE JUGEN CLUBHAUS
MAY 5	JUGENDHAUS AM ?
MAY 8	BEZAU VAKUNZ
MAY 9	SOMEWHERE IN SWITZERLAND ?
MAY 11	LEGWARDEN NL 4U
MAY 13	PARIS NEW MORNING CLUB
MAY 24	T&C 2 Q102 GIG
MAY 29	BULL & GATE LAUNCH OF RUBBISH GIG
JUN 2	BRADFORD ICKLEY COMMUNITY COLLEGE
JUN 3	NEWCASTLE RIVERSIDE
JUN 5	LIVERPOOL POLY
JUN 6	GLOUCESTER BANANA CLUB
JUN 7	BIRMINGHAM BARREL ORGAN
JUN 8	OXFORD CO OP HALL
JUN 9	ALDERSHOT WEST END CENTRE
JUN 10	NORWICH JACQUARD
JUN 13	WINDSOR OLD TROUT
JUN 14	SALISBURY ARTS CENTRE
JUN 15	MANCHESTER INTERNATIONAL 1
JUN 16	WORKSOP ARTS CENTRE
JUN 17	HULL NEW ADELPHI
JUN 19	BRIGHTON ZAP
JUN 20	BRISTOL FLEECE AND FIRKIN
JUN 26	YORK UNI
JUN 27	WARWICK UNI

JUN 28	COVENTRY POLY
JUN 29	HARLOW SQUARE
JUN 30	READING AFTER DARK
JUL 5	ABERDEEN CAESAR'S PALACE
JUL 6	GREENOCK
JUL 7	STOCKTON DOVECOT ARTS CENTRE
JUL 9	EDINBURGH THE VENUE
JUL 10	GLASGOW KING TUTS
JUL 11	LEEDS SAN MIGUELS
JUL 13	LONDON ASTORIA
JUL 28	GLOUCESTER PARK
AUG 22	NIJMEGEN DIOGENES
AUG 23	AMSTERDAM MELKVEG
AUG 24	VENRAY DINGENS
AUG 25	DORDRECHT ZOMERMANISE STATIE
SEP 30	BRUNEL UNI
OCT 3	KIDDERMINSTER MARKET TAVERN
OCT 4	OXFORD POLY
OCT 5	NORTHAMPTON IRISH CENTRE
OCT 6	ESSEX UNI
OCT 8	BRISTOL POLY
OCT 9	BIRMINGHAM BURBERRIES
OCT 10	WOLVERHAMPTON POLY
OCT 11	MANCHESTER UMIST
OCT 12	WALES POLY TREEFOREST
OCT 13	SOUTHAMPTON EASTPOINT CENTRE
OCT 17	BLACKPOOL JENKS
OCT 18	GLASGOW KING TUTS
OCT 19	LEEDS UNI
OCT 20	HARTLEPOOL BOROUGH HALL
OCT 21	HUDDERSFIELD POLY
OCT 22	LIVERPOOL UNI
OCT 24	BRIXTON FRIDGE
OCT 26	LEICESTER POLY
OCT 27	KENT UNI
NOV 24	BRIGHTON STEYNNING SCHOOL
NOV 30	ADE HOWELL'S BIRTHDAY PARTY MONMOUTH
DEC 1	GLOUCESTER BANANA CLUB
DEC 6	WATFORD COLLEGE
DEC 7	BIRMINGHAM UNI
DEC 8	BOLTON INSTITUTE

DEC 9	HULL ADELPHI
DEC 10	CAMBRIDGE JUNCTION
DEC 11	SWANSEA MARINA
DEC 12	OXFORD COOP HALL
DEC 14	LONDON T & C CLUB
DEC 18	CUBE CLUB SECRET GIG LONDON
DEC 20	WINDSOR OLD TROUT
DEC 22	HARLOW SQUARE

1991

JAN 17	HMV RECORD SHOP OXFORD ST LONDON
JAN 19	WEMBLEY ARENA BRIT MUSIC WEEKEND
FEB 5	NEW CROSS VENUE
FEB 6	KIDDERMINSTER MARKET TAVERN
FEB 7	EXETER UNI
FEB 8	TAUNTON BISHOP FOXES HALL
FEB 9	SUSSEX UNI BRIGHTON
FEB 10	PORTSMOUTH SOUTH PARADE PIER
FEB 13	BRISTOL BIERKELLER
FEB 14	ULU LONDON
FEB 15	NORWICH WATERFRONT
FEB 16	IPSWICH CARIBBEAN CLUB
FEB 18	BIRMINGHAM GOLDWYNS
FEB 19	TEESIDE POLY
FEB 20	DUNDEE BAR CHEVROLET
FEB 21	GLASGOW THE TECH
FEB 22	LANCASTER UNI
FEB 23	BOLTON INSTITUTE
FEB 24	HUDDERSFIELD POLY
FEB 26	NEWCASTLE
FEB 27	KEELE UNI
FEB 28	BRADFORD QUEEN'S HALL
MAR 1	SHEFFIELD UNI
MAR 3	NOTTINGHAM UNI
MAR 5	HULL TOWER
MAR 6	MANCHESTER UMIST
MAR 7	LEICESTER POLY
MAR 8	LIVERPOOL INSTITUTE FOR HIGHER EDUCATION
MAR 9	READING UNI
MAR 11	CHELTENHAM SHAFTESBURY HALL
MAR 12	CAMBRIDGE JUNCTION

MAR 13	SLOUGH COLLEGE
MAR 14	COVENTRY TIC TOC
MAR 31	DUSSELDORF PHILIPSHALLE
APR 2	NIJMEGAN O42
APR 3	GRONIGEN SIMPLON
APR 4	DEN HAAG PAARD
APR 5	HAARLEM PATRONAAT
APR 6	APELDOORN GIGANT
APR 7	AMSTERDAM MELKVEG
APR 8	HANOVER MAD
APR 9	HAMBURG MARKTHALLE
APR 11	COPENHAGEN BARBUE
APR 12	FULDA KREUZ-KULTUR
APR 13	ENGER FORUM
APR 14	BERLIN LOFT
APR 15	FRANKFURT COOKYS
APR 17	MUNICH BABALU
APR 18	LINZ POSTHOF
APR 19	WIEN SZENE
APR 20	GRAZ TEATRO
APR 21	ZAGREB
APR 22	MARIBOR MKC
APR 26	GENEVA LUISINE
APR 27	FRIBOURG FR-SON
APR 28	LAUSANNE DOLCE VITA
MAY 3	PARIS ESPACE ORNANO
MAY 5	HEILIGENHAUS DER CLUB
MAY 6	BREMEN MODERNES
MAY 7	KOLN ROSE CLUB
MAY 8	MARBURG KFZ
MAY 9	DORDRECHT BIBELOT
MAY 10	HEIST-OP-DEN BERG MONTY
MAY 11	UTRECHT VRIJE VLOER
MAY 12	VENRAY DINGUS
JUN 15	NEW CROSS VENUE
JUN 22	BRIXTON ACADEMY
JUL 11	CHICAGO RIVERIA THEATRE (With EMF)
JUL 12	DETROIT ST ANDREW'S (With EMF)
JUL 13	LAKEWOOD OH PHANTASY THEATRE (With EMF)
JUL 15	NEW YORK RITZ (With EMF)
JUL 16	NEW HAVEN TOAD'S PLACE (With EMF)

JUL 18	BOSTON CITI (with EMF)
JUL 25	NAGOYA QUATTRO
JUL 26	OSAKA QUATTRO
JUL 28	TOKYO QUATTRO
AUG 20	MEAN FIDDLER LONDON
AUG 24	READING FESTIVAL
AUG 27	STUTTGART UNI
AUG 28	MUNICH THEATRE FABRIK
AUG 29	BERLIN LOFT
AUG 30	HAMBURG GROSSE FREIHEIT
SEP 1	ROTTERDAM FESTIVAL
SEP 2	GEAT DEMOCRAZY
SEP 3	FUTURAMA FESTIVAL
	(SOMEWHERE BEGINNING WITH P)
SEP 5	TOLOUSE LE BIKINI
SEP 6	BARCELONA OTTO ZUTZ
SEP 9	BORDEAUX LE JIMMY
SEP 10	RENNES
OCT 10	DUBLIN McGONAGLES
OCT 11	BELFAST CONOR HALL
OCT 14	FOLKESTONE LEAS CLIFF HALL
OCT 16	BRIGHTON THE EVENT
OCT 17	EXETER UNI
OCT 18	CARDIFF UNI
OCT 19	SOUTHAMPTON UNI
OCT 21	HEMEL HEMPSTEAD PAVILION
OCT 22	BRISTOL STUDIO
OCT 24	GUILDFORD CIVIC HALL
OCT 25	CAMBRIDGE CORN EXCHANGE
OCT 26	NORWICH UEA
OCT 28	NOTTINGHAM ROCK CITY
OCT 29	LEEDS UNI
OCT 30	MANCHESTER ACADEMY
OCT 31	SHEFFIELD OCTAGON
NOV 1	LIVERPOOL UNI
NOV 2	GLASGOW BARROWLANDS
NOV 3	NEWCASTLE MAYFAIR
NOV 4	HUDDERSFIELD POLY
NOV 5	LEICESTER DE MONTFORD HALL
NOV 6	BIRMINGHAM HUMMINGBIRD
NOV 7	KILBURN NATIONAL LONDON

NOV 9	BRIXTON ACADEMY
NOV 15	CHICAGO ARAGON BALLROOM (With EMF)
NOV 16	ANN ARBOR HILL AUDITORIUM (With EMF)
NOV 18	PITTSBURGH CARNEGIE (With EMF)
NOV 19	MORGANTOWN W.VIRGINIA UNI (With EMF)
NOV 20	SYRACUSE UNI (With EMF)
NOV 22	MASSA CHUSETTS UNI (With EMF)
NOV 23	NEWARK UNI OF DELAWARE (With EMF)
NOV 24	WAYNE PATTERSON COLLEGE NEW JERSEY (With EMF)
NOV 26	NEW YORK ROSELAND BALLROOM (With EMF)
NOV 27	PHILADELPHIA TOWER THEATRE (With EMF)
NOV 30	SACRAMENTO FREEBORN HALL (With EMF)
DEC 1	SAN JOSE EVENTS CENTRE (With EMF)
DEC 3	SAN DIEGO PRINCE CENTRE BALLROOM (With EMF)
DEC 4	LA UNIVERSAL AMPHITHEATRE (With EMF)
DEC 20	ATHENS RODON
DEC 21	ATHENS RODON

1992

APR 9	BARCELONA FESTIVAL
APR 15	OBAN CORAN HALL
APR 16	TAIN DUTHAC CENTRE
APR 17	DUNFERMLINE GLEN PAVILION
APR 21	UNDERWORLD (With EMF)
APR 23	NEW CROSS VENUE
APR 26	NORWICH WATERFRONT RADIO ONE SOUND CITY
APR 29	GLOUCESTER LEISURE CENTRE
APR 30	READING RIVERMEAD
MAY 1	TONBRIDGE ANGEL CENTRE
MAY 3	PORTSMOUTH GUILDHALL
MAY 5	CAMBRIDGE CORN EXCHANGE
MAY 6	LIVERPOOL ROYAL COURT
MAY 7	HULL CITY HALL
MAY 8	GLASGOW BARROWLANDS
MAY 9	GLASGOW BARROWLANDS
MAY 10	CARLISLE SANDS CENTRE
MAY 11	BRADFORD UNI
MAY 13	PRESTON GUILDHALL
MAY 14	BIRMINGHAM HUMMINGBIRD
MAY 15	BIRMINGHAM HUMMINGBIRD
MAY 16	PLYMOUTH PAVILIONS

MAY 17	NEWPORT CENTRE
MAY 19	DERBY ASSEMBLY ROOMS
MAY 22	BRIXTON ACADEMY
MAY 23	BRIXTON ACADEMY
JUN 4	PARIS ESPACE ORNANO
JUN 5	BERN STUSENBAU
JUN 9	MILAN SHOCKING CLUB
JUN 26	GLASTONBURY FESTIVAL
JUN 27	BIZARRE FESTIVAL ALSDORF
JUN 28	ROSKILDE FESTIVAL
JUN 29	HAMBURG MARKTHALLE
JUL 4	MUNICH MACTWERK
JUL 5	BERLIN NEUEWELT
JUL 6	STUTTGART LONGHORN
JUL 7	VIENNA SZENE
JUL 8	BRATISLAVIA WATER TOWER
JUL 10	FESTIVAL
JUL 11	CALAIS ABANDONED FESTIVAL DISASTER
JUL 25	FINLAND ILOSAARIROCK FESTIVAL
JUL 31	FEILE FESTIVAL IRELAND
SEP 9	BARCELONA ZELESTE
SEP 10	MADRID AQUALUNG
SEP 12	LISBON VIZ DEOPESIARO
SEP 22	MONTREAL LA BRIQUE
SEP 23	TORONTO THE PHOENIX
SEP 24	DETROIT ST ANDREW'S HALL
SEP 25	CHICAGO CABARET METRO
SEP 26	NEW YORK PALLADIUM
SEP 28	PROVIDENCE PALLADIUM
SEP 29	BOSTON AVALON
OCT 1	VANCOUVER 86TH ST MUSIC HALL
OCT 2	PORTLAND ROCKANDY PDX
OCT 3	SEATTLE ROCKANDY
OCT 5	PALO ALTO THE EDGE
OCT 6	SAN FRANCISCO
OCT 8	SAN DIEGO SOUND FX
OCT 9	PHOENIX Q.FEST
OCT 10	LA THE PALACE
OCT 13	DALLAS DEEP ELLUM
OCT 14	AUSTIN BACK ROOM
OCT 15	HOUSTON THE VATICAN

OCT 17	ATLANTA CENTER STAGE
OCT 20	CLEVELAND SHOOTERS
OCT 22	BUFFALO ICON
OCT 23	ASBURY PARK FAST LANE
OCT 24	WASHINGTON DC 9.30 CLUB
OCT 25	NEW HAVEN TOAD'S PLACE
OCT 27	BOSTON THE PARADISE
OCT 29	NEW YORK ACADEMY
NOV 11	AMSTERDAM PARADISO
NOV 12	UTRECHT TIVOLI
NOV 13	NURNBERG MACH 1
NOV 16	DORTMUND MUSIKZIRCUS
NOV 17	HANOVER WELTSPIELE
NOV 19	BREMEN SCHLACTHOF
NOV 20	BIELEFELD PC69
NOV 21	KOLN LIVE MUSIC HALL
NOV 22	BRUSSELS VK
DEC 2	BLACKBURN KING GEORGES HALL
DEC 3	GATESHEAD LEISURE CENTRE
DEC 4	YORK BARBICAN
DEC 6	LIVINGSTON FORUM
DEC 7	ABERDEEN MUSIC HALL
DEC 9	OLDHAM QUEEN'S HALL
DEC 10	LIVERPOOL ROYAL COURT
DEC 11	LEICESTER GRANBY HALL
DEC 12	BIRMINGHAM ASTON VILLA CENTRE
DEC 13	NEWPORT CENTRE
DEC 15	WOLVERHAMPTON CIVIC
DEC 16	CAMBRIDGE CORN EXCHANGE
DEC 17	BOURNEMOUTH BIC
DEC 18	HEREFORD LEISURE CENTRE
DEC 19	ST AUSTELL COLISEUM
DEC 21	BRIXTON ACADEMY
DEC 22	BRIXTON ACADEMY

1993

JAN 24	MELBOURNE BIG DAY OUT
JAN 25	SYDNEY THE VENUE
JAN 26	SYDNEY BIG DAY OUT
JAN 28	SYDNEY EAST LEAGUES
JAN 30	PERTH BIG DAY OUT

FEB 1	ADELAIDE BIG DAY OUT
FEB 3	MELBOURNE PRINCE OF WALES
FEB 5	GOLD COAST PLAYROOM
FEB 6	BRISBANE METROPOLIS
FEB 9	OSAKA QUATTRO
FEB 10	NAGOYA QUATTRO
FEB 12	TOKYO CITTA
FEB 13	TOKYO QUATTRO
FEB 14	TOKYO QUATTRO
FEB 23	BELFAST ULSTER HALL
FEB 24	DUBLIN SFX
MAR 13	T&C SECRET GIG (With Sensless Things)
JUN 8	CAMDEN PALACE
JUN 13	XFM FINSBURY PARK
JUN 26	AREZZO WAVE FESTIVAL ITALY
AUG 12	HULTSFRED FESTIVAL SWEDEN
AUG 13	COPENHAGEN FESTIVAL
AUG 14	GRASPOP FESTIVAL BELGIUM
AUG 20	KOLN MUSIC HALL
AUG 22	FRANKFURT MEGA DOG FESTIVAL
AUG 25	RADIO ONE ROADSHOW SWANSEA
SEP 29	CORK DE LACY HOUSE
SEP 30	BELFAST MANDELA HALL
OCT 1	DUBLIN TIVOLI
OCT 2	BANGOR UNI
OCT 4	CAMBRIDGE CORN EXCHANGE
OCT 5	MIDDLESBROUGH TOWN HALL
OCT 6	GUILDHALL ??????
OCT 7	SHEFFIELD OCTAGON
OCT 8	HULL CITY HALL
OCT 9	GLASGOW BARROWLANDS
OCT 11	ASTON VILLA CENTRE
OCT 12	WOLVERHAMPTON CIVIC HALL
OCT 13	MANCHESTER ACADEMY
OCT 14	READING RIVERMEAD
OCT 15	LEICESTER GRANBY HALL
OCT 17	NEWPORT CENTRE
OCT 18	EXETER UNI
OCT 19	PORTSMOUTH GUILDHALL
OCT 21	TONBRIDGE ANGEL CENTRE
OCT 22	BRIXTON ACADEMY

OCT 23	BRIXTON ACADEMY
OCT 26	BRUSSELS VK
OCT 27	ST NICLAAS PMRC
OCT 28	EINDHOVEN EFFENAAR
OCT 29	AMSTERDAM PARADISO
OCT 30	UTRECHT TIVOLI
NOV 1	DORTMUND MUSIKZIRCUS
NOV 2	BREMEN MODERNES
NOV 3	HAMBURG MARKTHALLE
NOV 4	BERLIN NEUEWELT
NOV 5	HANOVER WELTSPIELE
NOV 7	BIELEFELD PC69
NOV 8	KOLN MUSIC HALL
NOV 10	FRANKFURT MUSIC HALL
NOV 11	STUTTGART LONGHORN
NOV 12	MUNICH CHARTEHALLE
NOV 13	ERLANGEN E.WERK
NOV 15	HALLE
NOV 17	VIENNA ARENA
NOV 18	SALZBURG ROCK HOUSE
NOV 19	FRIBOURG FRISON
DEC 3	SAN FRANCISCO LIVE 105 SHOW
DEC 18	MANCHESTER G-MEX (With Madness)
DEC 19	CARDIFF INTERNATIONAL ARENA (With Madness)
DEC 20	N.E.C. BIRMINGHAM (With Madness)
DEC 21	BRIGHTON CENTRE (With Madness)
DEC 22	WEMBLEY ARENA (With Madness)
DEC 23	WEMBLEY ARENA (With Madness)

1994

FEB 19	FORUM LONDON (Secret Support to Sultans Of Ping)
MAR 16	LA THE ROXY
MAR 17	SAN FRANCISCO SLIMS
MAR 19	SEATTLE OFF RAMP
MAR 20	VANCOUVER TOWN PUMP
MAR 22	SALT LAKE CITY ZEPHYR CLUB
MAR 23	BOULDER FOX THETRE
MAR 25	CHICAGO CABARET METRO
MAR 26	ST LOUIS EVOLUTION
MAR 27	DETROIT ST ANDREW'S HALL
MAR 29	TORONTO OPERA HOUSE

MAR 30	BUFFALO ICON
MAR 31	BOSTON PARADISE
APR 1	PROVIDENCE WBRU BIRTHDAY PARTY GIG
APR 2	NEW YORK IRVING PLAZA
APR 4	PHILADELPHIA THEATRE OF LIVING ARTS
APR 5	WASHINGTON 9.30 CLUB
APR 6	HAMPTON VIRGINIA
APR 7	AUGUSTA NEW POST OFFICE
APR 8	ATLANTA MASQUERADE
APR 9	PHOENIX EDGEFEST
APR 15	TOKYO ON AIR SHIBUYA
APR 16	TOKYO ON AIR SHIBUYA
MAY 11	MALMO SWEDEN
MAY 12	GOTTEBURG SWEDEN
MAY 13	STOCKHOLM
MAY 14	COPENHAGEN
MAY 15	HAMBURG
MAY 20	ZAGREB DOMA SPORTOVA
MAY 28	LITHUANIA
JUL 8	CLAPHAM GRAND LONDON
JUL 15	PHOENIX FESTIVAL
JUL 26	EDINGBURGH RADIO ONE ROADSHOW
SEP 2	BLACKPOOL CENTRAL BEACH R1 ROADSHOW
SEP 11	WINTERTHUR MUSIC FESTIVAL SWITZERLAND
OCT 28	BIRMINGHAM R1 ROADSHOW
NOV 19	KATOWICE POLAND
NOV 24	CORK GRAND PARADE
NOV 25	DUBLIN FURNACE
NOV 26	BELFAST QUEEN'S UNIVERSITY
NOV 27	LIMERICK
NOV 29	KENT UNI
NOV 30	SOUTHAMPTON UNI
DEC 1	READING UNI
DEC 2	BRIGHTON UNI
DEC 3	ESSEX UNI
DEC 4	NORWICH UNI
DEC 6	KEELE UNI
DEC 7	HULL UNI
DEC 8	NORTHUMBRIA UNI
DEC 9	EDINBURGH QUEEN'S HALL
DEC 11	METROPOLITAN LEEDS UNI

DEC 12	PRESTON UNI
DEC 13	DERBY UNI
DEC 14	COVENTRY POLY
DEC 15	BANGOR UNI
DEC 16	CARDIFF UNI
DEC 17	BRISTOL UNI

1995

FEB 6	VIRGIN MEGASTORE LONDON
FEB 24	ATHENS
FEB 25	ATHENS
MAR 4	ABINGDON OLD GAOL
MAR 5	PORTSMOUTH PYRAMIDS
MAR 6	CAMBRIDGE CORN EXCHANGE
MAR 7	BIRMINGHAM QUE CLUB
MAR 8	MANCHESTER ACADEMY
MAR 9	GLASGOW BARROWLANDS
MAR 11	SHEFFIELD OCTAGON
MAR 12	NEWPORT CENTRE
MAR 13	EXETER UNI
MAR 15	LEICESTER DE MONTFORT HALL
MAR 16	FORUM LONDON
MAR 17	FORUM LONDON
MAR 22	AMSTERDAM MILKY WAY
MAR 23	KOLN LUXOR
MAR 24	DORTMUND LIVE STATION
MAR 25	HAMBURG GROSSE FRIEHEIT
MAR 26	BERLIN LOFT
MAR 28	MALMO KB
MAR 29	VAXJO KRISTINA?
MAR 30	STOCKHOLM GINO
APR 1	BIELEFELD HECHELEI
APR 3	FRANKFURT BACHKAPP
APR 4	MUNICH STROM
APR 5	VIENNA SZENE
APR 6	STUTTGART ROHR
APR 8	BRUSSELS VK
APR 18	PARIS ARAPAHO
APR 19	VEVEY ROCKING CHAIR
MAY 10	PORTUGAL FESTIVAL
MAY 18	AIX EN PROVENCE

MAY 19	LAUSANNE FESTIVAL
MAY 27	BRIGHTON FESTIVAL
JUL 8	FRANKFURT FESTIVAL
JUL 9	BELGIUM DOUR FESTIVAL
JUL 28	AUSTRIA FESTIVAL
JUL 29	PRAGUE
JUL 30	BUDAPEST
AUG 5	BENICASSIM FESTIVAL INTERNACCIONAL SPAIN
AUG 13	CARDIFF FREE FESTIVAL
AUG 23	GARAGE LONDON
AUG 27	READING FESTIVAL
SEP 30	BRADFORD UNI
OCT 4	SHEFFIELD UNI THE FOUNDRY
OCT 5	WORCESTER NORTHWICK THEATRE
OCT 6	TRENT UNI NOTTINGHAM
OCT 7	COVENTRY UNI
OCT 8	NORTHAMPTON ROADMENDERS
OCT 10	LIVERPOOL KRAZY HOUSE
OCT 11	NEWCASTLE UNI
OCT 12	LANCASTER SUGAR HOUSE
OCT 13	LEICESTER UNI
OCT 14	ESSEX UNI
OCT 15	NORWICH UEA
OCT 17	HATFIELD FORUM
OCT 19	SWANSEA PATTI PAVILION
OCT 20	BRISTOL UNI ANSON ROOMS
OCT 21	PLYMOUTH UNI
OCT 22	PORTSMOUTH PYRAMIDS
OCT 23	BRIGHTON SUSSEX UNI
NOV 3	AMSTERDAM MILKY WAY
NOV 4	BRUSSELS VK
NOV 5	FRANKFURT BATHSCKAPP
NOV 6	HALLE EASY SCHORRE
NOV 7	BERLIN LOFT
NOV 8	HAMBURG MARKTHALLE
NOV 11	STUTTGART

1996

FEB 28	ABERDEEN LEMON TREE
FEB 29	GLASGOW THE GARAGE
MAR 2	SHEPHERD'S BUSH EMPIRE

MAR 6	LINZ POSTHOF
MAR 7	VIENNA SZENE
MAR 9	DORDRECHT BIBELOT
MAR 10	SITTARD FENIX
APR 19	STOKE ON TRENT BLACK TIE BALL
MAY 10	ABERYSTWYTH UNI BLACK TIE BALL
MAY 25	PASSAU FESTIVAL
JUN 28	CHELTENHAM RACE COURSE BLACK T** BALL
JUL 6	INNS OF COURT BALL
SEP 7	SHEFFIELD LEADMILL
SEP 20	ASTORIA LONDON
SEP 27	SOUTHAMPTON UNI
OCT 1	KINGSTON POLY
OCT 3	UP THE CREEK GREENWICH (Liverpool dockers' benefit)
OCT 4	BIRMINGHAM UNI
OCT 29	NOTTINGHAM ROCK CITY
DEC 10	CAMDEN PALACE FEET FIRST
DEC 14	HARLOW SQUARE
DEC 15	PORTSMOUTH WEDGWOOD ROOMS
DEC 17	HULL ADELPHI
DEC 18	EDINBURGH THE VENUE
DEC 19	OXFORD ZODIAC

1997

MARCH 27	VIRGIN MEGASTORE
APRIL 9	EGHAM ROYAL HOLLOWAY COLLEGE
APRIL 17	RALEIGH PINK TOOTHBRUSH
APRIL 18	LEICESTER PRINCESS CHARLOTTE
APRIL 19	LEEDS DUCHESS OF YORK
APRIL 21	PLYMOUTH COOPERAGE
APRIL 22	EXETER CAVERN
APRIL 23	BRISTOL BEERKELLAR
APRIL 24	WOLVERHAMPTON VARSITY TAVERN
APRIL 25	BRIGHTON PAVILIONS
APRIL 26	FARNHAM MALTINGS
APRIL 27	COLCHESTER ARTS CENTRE
APRIL 29	LIVERPOO KRAZY HOUSE
APRIL 30	BUCKLEY TIVOLI
MAY 1	STOKE STAGE
MAY 2	STAFFORDSHIRE UNIVERSITY
MAY 3	GLASGOW CATHOUSE

MAY 4	ABERDEEN LEMON TREE
MAY 5	EDINBURGH VENUE
MAY 6	NEWCASTLE RIVERSIDE
MAY 7	DERBY GARRICK
MAY 8	MANCHESTER BOARDWALK
MAY 9	GLOUCESTER GUILDHALL
MAY 10	NOTTINGHAM ROCK CITY
MAY 11	SHEFFIELD LEADMILL
MAY 13	NORTHAMPTON ROADMENDERS
MAY 14	READING ALLEYCAT
MAY 15	KIDDERMINSTER MARKET TAVERN
MAY 17	SALISBURY ARTS CENTRE
MAY 20	BOURNEMOUTH THE GARDENING CLUB
MAY 21	DUDLEY JBS
MAY 22	COVENTRY UNIVERSITY
MAY 23	MIDDLESBOROUGH ARENA
MAY 24	SWINDON COLLEGE
MAY 25	HULL ADELPHI
MAY 26	YORK FIBBERS
MAY 27	MAIDSTONE UNION BAR
MAY 28	OXFORD ZODIAC
MAY 29	CAMBRIDGE JUNCTION
MAY 30	LONDON ASTORIA
JUNE 1	BRIXTON GEORGE 4TH (An Evening With Dave)
JUNE 6	BELFAST EMPIRE
JUNE 7	DUBLIN MEAN FIDDLER
JUNE 22	CROYDON FAIRFIELD HALLS
JULY 12	PULLY FESTIVAL SWITZERLAND
JULY 16	BOSTON AXIS
JULY 17	NEW YORK MERCURY LOUNGE
JULY 18	PHILADELPHIA UPSTAIRS AT NICK'S
JULY 19	BALTIMORE FLETCHER'S
JULY 20	CLEVELAND GROG SHOP
JULY 22	CHICAGO DOUBLE DOOR
JULY 23	PONTIAC 7TH HOUSE
JULY 24	TORONTO LEE'S PALACE
JULY 25	OTTAWA BARRYMORE'S
JULY 26	MONTREAL FOUFOUNE'S ELECTRIQUES
JULY 28	NEW YORK MERCURY LOUNGE

AND...

| AUGUST 2 | GUILDFORD '97 FESTIVAL |

AND
THE SONGS

A Sheltered Life
Is This The Only Way To Get Through To You?
Granny Farming In The UK
The Road To Domestos - We didn't play this live, mainly because it was just a recording of a hymn that we nicked. But when my sister Becca got married for the first time, she coincidentally and unwittingly chose the hymn to be played as she waked down the aisle of the church. I nearly wet myself trying not to laugh.

Everytime A Chruchbell Rings - The first song Carter ever played live, at The Astoria on 6th August 1987.

24 Minutes From Tulse Hill - In the early days of bad monitors and toy PA systems we could hardly ever hear our tapes and this song used to get so fast and confusing that we (me and Les) and the rest of the band (the tape) didn't always finish at the same time.

An All American National Sport
Sheriff Fatman - There's a sketch on the TV show *Big Train* where the folk singer Ralph McTell is on stage in a small club and he's just finished playing his one and only hit *Streets Of London*. As he starts his next song the audience keep shouting for *Streets Of London!* until he has to eventually give in and play it again.

The Taking Of Peckham 123
Crimestoppers A' Go Go
Good Grief Charlie Brown
Midnight On The Murder Mile
A Perfect Day To Drop The Bomb - We used to love playing this at the end of gigs. When it goes into the noise and endless samples free for all bit people who hadn't seen Carter before used to look at us thinking, *'what the hell are they doing??'*

GI Blues - We always played this as an encore, it helped to calm the crowd down before they left the venue and may have stopped inner city rioting all over the world, hooray. At the end of the song when I reached the line, 'I'm a GI...and I'm blue' we used to have all the lights turn blue. We once challenged lighting man Pip to make the lights go through the colours as I sang, 'I'm a GI...and I'm, red and yellow and pink and green, orange and purple and ...blue' he did it and it was like winning The World Cup.

Surfin' USM - This recording features the audience. Sampled at the start with the infamous 'You Fat Bastard!' chant. I think it's the Kent University audience.

My Second To Last Will And Testament
Anytime Anyplace Anywhere - I remember vomiting onstage whilst singing this song on more than one occasion. You might not want to read this next bit but I swallowed the puke before it left my mouth. All this goes to prove, you should never mix your drinks. Not even lyrically.

A Prince In A Pauper's Grave
Shoppers' Paradise - We gave the re-titled *Christmas Shoppers Paradise* away as the A-side of the *Christmas As Fuck* 7-inch free single at The Forum Kentish Town on 14th December 1991. It was another one of our ill-conceived 'doing it for the kids' things. There was such a bundle for the freebie records when we attempted to hand them out at the end of the gig that some people got three copies and others got none.

Billy's Smart Circus
Bloodsport For All
Sealed With A Glasgow Kiss - There were two songs we had to play in Glasgow, this was one and the other was performed by the audience. They used to sing *Flower Of Scotland* completely unprovoked by us and it was incredibly moving. I think I knew we knew we were in trouble and our time at the top was passing when we played Glasgow Barrowlands and they didn't sing it

Say It With Flowers
Falling On A Bruise
The Final Comedown
1993
Is Wrestling Fixed? - Just choreographed.
The Only Living Boy In New Cross - Before we played this at an Aids benefit gig in New York I said a few words about the cause which provoked someone in the audience to call me a faggot. I told him that yes I was and if he came up on to the stage I'd suck his cock. He spent the whole song trying to do just that although I think the fellatio was out of the question as he merely wanted to kick my teeth in. Fortunately for me and or him this was the gig with the over-zealous security and he didn't get anywhere near me.

Suppose You Gave A Funeral And Nobody Came

England - I used to do this live as one of my walking around without a guitar, taunting the crowd songs. I'd do crazy things like climb up on top of the PA and then realize I was scared of heights and have to gingerly climb back down or wait for the fire brigade to arrive with a telescopic ladder.

Do Re Me, So Far So Good - We were in Madridejos, Spain filming the video for the single *The Impossible Dream* (the vid is a tribute to the films *Man Of La Mancha, Lawrence of Arabia* and *Carry On Up The Khyber*). At the end of a long day's filming and horse riding in the hot Spanish sun we were sat in the restaurant of the small hotel where we were staying and the video's guest star Ian Dury told me how he'd once half written a song called *Do Re Me So Far So Good* and how when he heard that we'd released a single with the same title he'd considered sending the boys round to 'break my fucking legs'.

Look Mum, No Hands!
While You Were Out
Skywest And Crooked
The Impossible Dream
2 Million Years BC
The Music That Nobody Likes
Mid Day Crisis
Cheer Up, It Might Never Happen
Stuff The Jubilee!
A Bachelor For Baden Powell
Spoilsports Personality Of The Year

Suicide Isn't Painless - Supposedly written after a heated row between me and Loz from Kingmaker in a dressing room in Phoenix, Arizona. The argument was included in an interview with Carter in *Select* magazine and prompted Loz into writing to the magazine to put his side of the story. I then replied to his letter the following month. We were sort of pen pals.

Being Here
Evil
Commercial Fucking Suicide Part 1
Sing Fat Lady Sing
Travis
Lean On Me I Won't Fall Over

Lenny And Terence
Under The Thumb And Over The Moon
Cheap 'n' Cheesy
Airplane Food / Airplane Fast Food
The Young Offender's Mum
Gas (man) - Fruitbat asked his brother Bam Bam to shout out some chords, Fruitbat played them and named the song after his brother who was a gas man). Songwritng...money for old rope.

The Life And Soul Of The Party Dies
My Defeatist Attitude - Our press officer Anton was good friends with Kurt Cobain and because he was so devastated about his death we left the line *'pretending I'm like Kurt Cobain'* - which I'd written before he shot himself - blank on the recorded version of this song.

Worry Bomb - The title track of the album we recorded at The Manor Studios in Shipton-on-Cherwell, near Oxford. It was a great studio in the grounds of an old manor house, where we stayed, spending almost two months playing snooker and tennis and swimming in the outdoor heated pool - unfortunately the go-kart track was temporarily closed. The studio had a long history of famous clients and albums and should have been kept open as a monument to British rock history. So when *EMI* took over the studio they shut it down, stripping all the fixtures and fittings so that nobody else could use them. It's now a French restaurant called *Le Manoir.*

Senile Delinquent - Swearing is wicked.
Me And Mr. Jones

Let's Get Tattoos - At Brighton University we got the barechested dancers from this single's promo video to dance onstage. The same dancers appeared with us on *Top Of The Pops* and the girls in the audience were so excited by them that they wouldn't stop screaming. We were asked to leave the studio during the rest of the show's filming as everyone was looking at our dancers and ignoring Jimmy Nail who they were supposed to be watching perform his new single. Fruitbat recently met an Australian woman whose only exposure to Carter had been the *Let's Get Tattoos* video where the dancers perform as the band. Until the day she met Fruitbat she had thought that Carter were a four-piece boy band.

Going Straight
God, Saint Peter And The Guardian Angel
The Only Looney Left In Town
Ceasefire
Broken Down In Broken Town
A World Without Dave
Before The War
Nowhere Fast
Johnny Cash
And God Created Brixton
Stand Up And Be Counted
Negative Equity
Road Rage
The Wrong Place At The Wrong Time

We didn't get to play any of the following songs from the *I Blame The Government* album live apart from *Growing Old Disgracefully, Girls Can Keep A Secret* and *Psycho Bill*.
23:59 End Of The World . Sunshine . The Undertaker And The Hippy Protest Singer. Sweetheart Sugar Baby . Growing Old Disgracefully The Man Who Bought The World. Winning The War. I Blame The Government. Citizen's Band Radio. Psycho Bill. Closedown. Girls Can Keep A Secret

THE NON ALBUM TRACKS
R.S.P.C.E.
Twin Tub With Guitar
Rubbish - John Peel was never really a big Carter fan but when he interviewed us at Reading Festival in '91 he told us that he liked us a lot more after we sampled him saying 'what do you think of the programme so far?' on this single. A similar tactic worked to our advantage on the single *Glam Rock Cops* as the producer of *Top Of The Pops* liked the way we name-checked the programme on the song, it's so much easier than relying on chart placings and stuff like that. Our next planned single if we hadn't split up was entitled *Later With Jools Holland* - it was to be a double A-side with the power ballad *CD:UK*.

Alternative Alf Garnett
2001: A Clockwork Orange
Re-Educating Rita
Randy Sarf Git

After The Watershed (Early Learning The Hard Way)
The 90's Revival
A Nation Of Shoplifters
Watching The Big Apple Turn Over
Turn On, Tune In And Switch Off
When Thesauruses Ruled The Earth
Bring On The Girls - The Family Cat came onstage dressed as women to surprise us when we were playing this live once.

Always The Bridesmaid, Never The Bride - We didn't play this live but I was told that Evan Dando from The Lemonheads used to do a version and that he thought the song was beautiful.
Lenny And Terence
Her Song
Stuff The Jubilee (1977)

Glam Rock Cops - When we released this as a single we had a great poster with the slogan 'not all coppers are bastards' across the top. When the fly posters stuck them up in London they folded the top offending part of the poster over. I suppose they were breaking the law already and they didn't want to upset the police anymore, even though it's actually a sort of compliment to the police.

Turbulence! - Written after my nightmare flight home from Zagreb. Before we'd left London I'd watched a TV documentary about the safety - or lack of - of Aeroflot aircraft (why is there always a documentary about the dangers of flying every time I have to fly somewhere?). So I was tense already as Croatian Airlines got their planes from Aeroflot and on the journey home I was overcome with fear and was convinced I was about to die. The majority of other passengers were Christians who'd been in the Former Yugoslavia doing charitable deeds for the Lord and as we taxied down the runway the plane shook violently, the hand-luggage doors kept opening - every time the stewardess shut an overhead storage door another one would open, it was like Laurel and Hardy - and the Christians began to sing. They knew that if they were going to die, that was fine because they were going to a better place. At best, my final destination would be Hell, Purgatory or more likely just spread about the Croatian countryside. I hate flying.

King For A Day
Especially 4 U
This One's For Me
Born On The 5th Of November
Tomorrow When You Die
The Aftertaste Of Paradise
D.I.V.O.R.C.E.F.G.
Elvis Lives & Carterbreakamerica
Junkmale

UNRELEASED
Hounded
Everything You Ever Wanted To Know About Everything

ABOUT THE AUTHOR

Jim Bob lives in South London with his soulmates Jacqueline and Holly. Since the split of Carter he has released two albums and three singles with his disco-pop-punk group Jim's Super Stereoworld, three solo albums as Jim Bob and played various live shows both with his band and on his tod. In 2001 Jim Bob and Fruitbat joined each other onstage once again as part of supergroup Who's The Daddy Now?

These days you'll probably catch him sat on a stool in a club somewhere playing Jim Bob songs both old and new on his acoustic guitar like some modern-day Robert Zimmerman, buy him a drink.

For more information on the man who once had the spaghetti hair, visit his website www.jim-bob.co.uk

Also available from
CHERRY RED BOOKS

Rockdetector
A-Z of BLACK METAL
Garry Sharpe-Young
Paper covers, 416 pages, £14.99 in UK
ISBN 1-901447-30-8

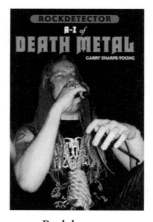

Rockdetector
A-Z of DEATH METAL
Garry Sharpe-Young
Paper covers, 416 pages, £14.99 in UK
ISBN 1-901447-35-9

Rockdetector
A-Z of POWER METAL
Garry Sharpe-Young
Paper covers, 512 pages £14.99 in UK
ISBN 1-901447-13-8

Rockdetector
A-Z of THRASH METAL
Garry Sharpe-Young
Paper covers, 460 pages £14.99 in UK
ISBN 1–901447–09–X

www.cherryred.co.uk

Also available from

Rockdetector
A-Z of DOOM, GOTHIC
& STONER METAL
Garry Sharpe-Young
Paper covers, 455 pages £14.99 in UK
ISBN 1-901447-14-6

Rockdetector
A-Z of '80s ROCK
Garry Sharpe-Young & Dave Reynolds
Paper covers, 752 pages, £17.99 in UK
ISBN 1-901447-21-9

Rockdetector
OZZY OSBOURNE
THE STORY OF THE OZZY OSBOURNE BAND
(AN UNOFFICIAL PUBLICATION)
Garry Sharpe-Young
Paper covers 368 pages £14.99 in UK
ISBN 1-901447-08-1

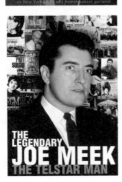

Those Were The Days

Stefan Granados

An Unofficial History of the Beatles' Apple Organization 1967-2002

Paper covers, 300 pages including photographs
£14.99 in UK

The Rolling Stones: Complete Recording Sessions 1962-2002

Martin Elliott

Paper covers, 576 pages plus 16 pages of photographs
£14.99 in UK

Goodnight Jim Bob – On The Road With Carter The Unstoppable Sex Machine

Jim Bob

Paper covers, 228 pages plus 16 pages of photographs
£12.99 in UK

Our Music Is Red - With Purple Flashes: The Story Of The Creation

Sean Egan

Paper covers, 378 pages plus 8 pages of photographs
£14.99 in UK

Bittersweet: The Clifford T Ward Story

David Cartwright

Paper covers, 352 pages plus 8 pages of photographs
£14.99 in UK

The Spirit Of Wimbledon: Footballing Memories Of The Dons 1922-2003

Niall Couper

Paper covers, 288 pages and photographs throughout
£14.99 in UK

CHERRY RED BOOKS

We are always looking for interesting books to publish.
They can be either new manuscripts or re-issues of deleted books.
If you have any good ideas then please
get in touch with us.

CHERRY RED BOOKS
a division of Cherry Red Records Ltd.
Unit 17, Elysium Gate West,
126-128 New King's Road
London SW6 4LZ

E-mail: iain@cherryred.co.uk
Web: www.cherryred.co.uk